Axel Smits
Bart Van den Bussche

REWARD

Attracting and retaining key talent with compelling reward

Lannoo
Campus

Disclaimer

Photo credits:
iStock (pp. 3, 21, 35, 47, 49, 55, 59, 64, 67, 77, 95, 104, 109, 135, 150, 163, 165, 173, 193, 207)

ISBN 9789401438667
D/2024/45/336
NUR 800

First edition, 2024

Responsible editor
LannooCampus Publishers
Vaartkom 41 box 01.02
3000 Leuven
Belgium
www.lannoocampus.com

P.O. Box 23202
1100 DS Amsterdam
Netherlands

Table of contents

Understanding reward

Attractive and compelling reward packages

Special dossiers

Conclusion

Foreword

In my career, I have had the privilege of witnessing the power of clarity when it comes to shaping the success and alignment of organisations. The questions of why we are here, what we do and how we do it are not mere philosophical ponderings; they form the very essence of an organisation's purpose, strategy and culture. Understanding these fundamental aspects is crucial for effective decision making and direction. In this context, an organisation's total reward strategy emerges as a vital pillar supporting every action that it takes.

Reward, as a topic, has always fascinated me. The numbers, facts and data associated with it provide a structured approach that helps organisations make well-informed and data-driven decisions. However, I quickly realised that reward is not just about the quantitative aspects; it carries a significant emotional component as well. People need to feel that the reward they receive is fair, transparent and based on their performance and contributions.

Throughout my career, I have found that some of the most challenging professional conversations I've had are related to reward. It is a sensitive and delicate matter that can impact employee morale, motivation and overall satisfaction. That's why having exceptional reward experts by your side, both within and outside the organisation, is of the utmost importance. I am immensely grateful for the time I spent as a reward specialist and for the ongoing support I receive from these professionals. Their insights and expertise are invaluable in navigating the complexities of reward management.

Furthermore, in the ever-evolving landscape of business, it is crucial to continuously and proactively stay up to date on the dynamic aspects of reward. The world around us is changing rapidly, and reward systems must adapt to keep pace. Factors such as sustainability, pay transparency and flexible work arrangements are gaining prominence, and organisations must ensure that their reward systems and solutions can accommodate these shifts. Staying informed and proactive in understanding these developments is essential for effectively managing rewards in the changing landscape we face.

In conclusion, reward is not a mere transactional exchange of numbers and data; it is about recognising and valuing the contributions of individuals within an organisation. It is a sensitive and delicate matter that requires the expertise of reward specialists. By staying informed and proactive, organisations can effectively manage rewards in a changing landscape, ensuring employee satisfaction and business success.

This book offers a comprehensive review of what modern reward is all about, delving into the various dimensions of reward management to provide valuable insights and perspectives. Whether you are an HR professional seeking to enhance your understanding, a board member responsible for shaping reward strategies or simply someone interested in gaining a deeper insight into this hot topic, this book is highly recommended. I hope you find it as enlightening and thought-provoking as I did, and that it serves as a guide in your journey towards unlocking the true potential of reward management.

Line De Decker
Chief People and Sustainability Officer Aliaxis

A word from the editors

What makes reward interesting now?

Throughout history, reward in its various shapes has played a crucial role in the evolution and progress of mankind. The pursuit of reward in the form of victory, treasure, food, fulfilment, etc. has been omnipresent as a motivator since the beginning of time. Reward is the carrot that keeps us going, driving our behaviour, starting in our childhood and staying with us until the very end.

So, if reward is such a large part of our daily lives, why are we sharing our interest with you now? As we explain in the following pages, we are currently in a period of flux, with societal influences and global disruptions impacting the relationships between organisations and employees that were previously relatively stable. And this has an impact on reward. In no particular order, some of these influences and disruptions are:

- **Wellbeing at work**
  A career is more like a marathon than a sprint, which is why it is important for people to be able to deal with the pressures and challenges of an ever more rapidly changing environment. This requires that the classic principle of a healthy mind in a healthy body is respected more than ever.

  In practice, this means that employers need to understand that they have a responsibility to create a working environment that equips their employees to work under pressure and embrace the changes they face. When faced with today's labour shortage, employers cannot afford to offer an outdated working environment. Employers should enable hybrid working within a well-defined framework and provide an activity-based office space with a warm, welcoming atmosphere so that people want to be there instead of the office being a place where they have to be.

  And it doesn't stop there. Organisations should implement policies that encourage a healthier lifestyle, embedding wellbeing in the working culture by encouraging employees to move more, get enough sleep, eat and drink well, breathe well, relax regularly and, most importantly, have enough fun.

  Lastly, wellbeing also includes diversity and inclusion in the workplace, and this is intrinsically linked to reward as compensation for labour. In order to create a truly great place to work, an employer needs to make sure there is no distinction between its people based on their gender, sexual preference, ethnicity, or any other potentially discriminating characteristic. Even unconscious biases should be identified and excluded wherever possible. And this should, of course, also be reflected in people's reward to ensure equal pay for equal work or work of equal value.

- **To work or not to work**

  Reward for labour is often taxed quite heavily, which triggers some people to question whether it makes sense for them to work when they could live off an allowance from the government. Although being remunerated for working is always more gratifying than receiving an allowance, it is fair to question the benefits of working where the net difference between a salary and an allowance is small. Governments are responsible for ensuring this difference is significant enough, as it touches on the productivity of an entire society where everyone should be encouraged to contribute in line with their capabilities.

  Policy makers have a duty to ensure their citizens are encouraged to seek reward for their labour, which should be both fulfilling and financially beneficial. The government should also focus on the wellbeing of its population, for example, preventing illness rather than curing it and boosting citizens' energy levels so they are up to the tasks ahead. Without governments doing their part, a negative spiral starts where increasing numbers of people either prefer not to work or burn/bore out while doing so. Subsequently, governments need more money to take care of those who do not work, raising taxes even further and making it even less appealing to work (hard).

  Too many governments have created the idea that people can have more for less, encouraging part time work, prolonged leaves and early retirement beyond what makes sense economically. An economy (currently) needs human labour to fuel its growth and the ongoing war for talent illustrates an almost permanent shortage in multiple labour markets. Until human labour is (at least partially) taken over by smart technologies, more people will need to work (harder) than is the case today.

- **Mankind versus machine**

  Artificial intelligence (AI) is currently the focus of a lot of scare stories: will it really turn out to be a giant job killer as some predict? Will an AI, once it is able to become conscient, ask for a reward for its continuous efforts and if so, what type of reward would that be? While the many technological waves we have seen throughout history have changed the labour landscape and the related reward models, they have also increased productivity and mankind's ability to leverage technology to do things which would have been impossible otherwise.

  Although nobody can say what will change or when, it is fair to assume that basic tasks are likely to be taken over by technology. However, technology could be used to upgrade jobs instead of replacing them, making the job content more appealing and probably more demanding. People will need to ensure they remain relevant. The fear of becoming obsolete (FOBO) may motivate employees to reskill or upskill to maintain or improve their career prospects.

  Based on the spread of technology that we have seen so far, we can also assume that technology will be concentrated in a limited number of countries, leaving us to question what this will mean for jobs everywhere else. Countries will need to keep up with the technology race to enable their citizens to earn a decent living. When we reach this point, reward models will change significantly, as labour may not remain the dominant driver of economic growth.

As well as these influences and disruptions, there are other factors driving the changes in reward. For example, labour laws and regulations, which can vary across different countries and jurisdictions, can impact the minimum wage, working conditions and other aspects of the reward for labour. Another example of a driver is the rise in working from anywhere (WFA). While this has increased the size of the potential labour pool, it has also increased the complexity of the organisation's reward system: should the employee's remuneration be aligned with the headquarters, market levels in their location or the cost of living?

Taking into account these influences on, disruptions to and drivers of the traditional working relationship between employers and employees, we believe that there is room for ambitious organisations to use reward to position themselves to attract and retain the talent they need to achieve their goals. However, reward needs to be used effectively in order for the organisation to maximise their return on the investment they have made in their employees. With this book we aim to provide you with the information you need to successfully implement efficient reward systems that work to support your goals, empowering your organisation to realise the full potential of its mission statement and ambitions.

Axel and Bart

Editors

Axel Smits

Since 2016, Axel has been the Chairman and Senior Partner of PwC Belgium, a network firm with about €400 million in revenues and about 2,400 employees. From January 1, 2024, Axel has combined his roles as Chairman of PwC Belgium with that of Managing Partner of PwC Europe. Axel also leads PwC Belgium's People Related Services business and runs the Reward Services team with Bart Van den Bussche as his co-pilot.

Before assuming his current position, Axel was in charge of the firm's Belgian Tax and Legal practice, a position he combined with heading up PwC's EMEA Tax and Legal network. A lawyer by training with additional degrees in taxation, accounting and finance, Axel is a chartered tax consultant with a particular focus on international tax planning. He serves clients across the globe and is very active as both a speaker and a writer of articles and books in his area of expertise, including topics like intellectual property as well as substance in international tax planning.

Bart Van den Bussche

Bart is an experienced Director within the Reward Services team at PwC Belgium. With nearly two decades of expertise, Bart specialises in advising clients on various aspects of reward, ranging from design to implementation. As a chartered tax consultant, Bart possesses extensive knowledge of individual income tax, particulary in relation to executive remuneration and employment structures in an international context. He also brings valuable experience in the field of remuneration advice, with a specific focus on partnership compensation structures.

In addition to his core areas of expertise, Bart actively contributed to the roll-out of employee preference studies in Belgium. These studies provide valuable insights into how financial and non-financial rewards impact employee motivation and retention, enabling organisations to optimise their reward strategies. With his extensive knowledge and expertise, Bart is often requested to be a guest speaker and he publishes on a regular basis.

Contributors

Alyssia Salaris

Alyssia assists national and international clients on various reward topics, and has relevant experience in executive remuneration, international employment tax and partnership compensation.

Antoine Awad

Antoine advises national and international clients on matters related to reward and personal income tax. He supports clients with a diverse range of topics such as structuring employee benefits, remuneration packages and partnership compensation. Antoine also assists organisations in navigating tax incentives, in particular related to wage withholding tax exemption.

Aurore Zadeling

Aurore is committed to supporting her national and international clients with inquiries related to income tax and rewards. Her expertise lies in optimising remuneration packages to align with relevant regulations, best practices and stakeholders' expectations. This includes improving remuneration design and disclosure, integrating sustainable objectives into pay structures, conducting pay audits and helping clients to transition towards greater pay transparency.

Britt Verhelst

Britt assists national and international clients on various reward matters and she has experience in executive remuneration and transactional rewards.

Delphine Kempeneers

Delphine gives advice on rewards and personal income tax to multinationals and Belgian-based clients. She has expertise in national and international employment tax, executive remuneration and employee benefits.

Dominique Vanhove

Dominique is an expert on a diverse range of HR topics with a focus on employee benefits and share-based compensation. He has provided advice with respect to share-based compensation and long-term benefits to quoted and unquoted organisations and counselled the private equity industry regarding transactions and on-going business. Furthermore, he advises executives on their (inter)national tax affairs.

Els Kegels

Els has 30 years' of experience as a tax consultant and has a comprehensive understanding of how national and international tax rules largely determine a reward package. As member of PwC Law Firm Services Team, her focus is on partnerships and she is involved on almost a daily basis in partnership structures and their compliance obligations.

Emmanuel Saporito

Emmanuel is a Director in PwC's Reward Services practice, where he is an expert on a diverse range of tax topics and has specifically developed high-end experience in executive remuneration, international taxation, equity incentive plans (design, tax and legal structuring) and compensation and benefits for quoted and unquoted organisations and the private equity industry.

Eva Fernandez Teixeira

Eva advises national and international clients on reward matters, with a focus on analysing, structuring and optimising employee benefits and remuneration packages to meet all Belgian legal, tax and social security requirements. Eva also helps executives and international law firms with their legal and reporting obligations. Additionally, she is active in the PwC sustainability team as a project manager.

Florian Paternoster

Florian assists organisations with their queries related to remuneration package optimisation and other HR topics with a focus on pensions, excel and Alteryx.

Isabelle Meuleman

Isabelle has over 15 years of broad HR experience focused on using total reward and recognition to attract and retain the right talent. Her expertise covers reward modelling, job classification, performance management and benchmarking on both the client and the consultancy side.

Joyce Kahe Mbang

Joyce is an expert in the field of remuneration strategies. She has experience working with compensation and benefits, including reward architecture, benchmarking and job classification.

Kato Van Heucke

By doing reward scans, Kato assists organisations to create attractive, sustainable and future-proof remuneration packages. This involves performing legal analysis and preparing estimates to simulate the cost net ratios for the employer's cost and net income.

Leyla Keskin

Leyla assists Belgian residents and non-residents with reward queries and income tax formalities. She also focuses on partnership compensation.

Lisa Davister

Lisa assists Belgian residents and non-residents with reward queries and income tax formalities. She focuses on payroll consulting and payroll design.

Luc Legon

Luc is an expert on a diverse range of HR topics with comprehensive experience in the design, tax and legal structuring of reward policies with a strong focus on equity incentive plans for quoted and unquoted organisations and the private equity industry. He assists quoted and unquoted organisations to design, implement and administer their long-term incentive plans (LTIPs). He also helps Belgian and international private equity houses to implement their management incentive plans (MIPs), ensuring that the MIP is perfectly balanced from an incentive, tax and legal perspective in both Belgian and foreign jurisdictions. Additionally, Luc provides high-end individual tax consulting to private clients in relation to their executive responsiblities or private tax affairs.

Lynn Michiels

Lynn gained her specific payroll experience by performing payroll and benefits administration for very large organisations. At PwC she assists clients with all their payroll-related questions and projects. She is passionate about working with clients to ensure their payroll systems add real value to their business.

Matthias Vandamme

Matthias supports clients with their personal income tax compliance, correct application of R&D incentives on a workforce-level and mobility questions (car policies, mobility budget, alternative remuneration, etc.). He is also passionate about optimising (internal) processes with the help of new technologies, tools and Responsible (Gen) AI.

Maxime Duymelinck

Maxime has over 10 years of expertise in guiding clients through various aspects of rewards. Her role involves providing strategic guidance and overseeing the design and implementation of reward systems, both nationally and internationally. She has developed a specialised skill set in executive remuneration and incentive scheme design, with a strong emphasis on optimisation and alignment with tax and governance considerations.

Maxime Franzen

Maxime is specialised in a diverse range of tax topics and has high-end experience in international taxation, equity incentive plans (design, tax and legal structuring) and partnership compensation.

Melissa Balcaen

Melissa focuses on job architecture, performance management, reward modelling and benchmarking. She supports clients with their non-financial rewards.

Michaël Gozzo

Michaël is an experienced personal income tax consultant with a focus on the fields of executive remuneration, international tax and alternative and flexible remuneration. He assists national and international organisations with tax-related issues concerning their employees and executives or the structuring of their reward packages. Michaël also assists organisations to obtain tax incentives related to withholding tax and advises private individuals regarding their tax reporting obligations and other relevant tax-related matters.

Michelle Koopmans

Michelle supports national and international clients with inquiries related to income tax and reward. As part of the Central R&D team, Michelle has extensive expertise and experience with R&D tax incentives. She also focuses on implementing new technologies and tools to automate different processes.

Natacha Vandendries

Natacha delves into job architecture, benchmarking and organisational talent management. Her role involves supporting clients to fine-tune their talent strategies and design beneficial remuneration structures.

Pieter Gillemon

Pieter is a Director in PwC's Reward Services practice, where he specialises in employee benefits such as retirement plans, life insurance, disability insurance and medical insurance. He has a strong focus on pension strategy and execution. With 25 years of practical experience and a deep technical knowledge of pensions, Pieter's extensive expertise in this field is widely recognised. His broad practical experience and deep technical knowledge allow him to effectively address a wide range of financial, legal, tax and HR inquiries related to pensions.

Pieter Nobels

Pieter is a Director in PwC's Reward Services practice. With his broad HR experience, he is passionate about helping organisations to design and deliver an impactful employee experience. In his daily work, he combines his tax experience, comprehensive knowledge of technology and data, user experience understanding and change management expertise. Over the past 20 years, Pieter has served clients in both the public and private sector in various industries. He has pioneered new HR programmes for flexible rewards, data-driven reward harmonisation, HR analytics, sustainable mobility policies and AI-driven workforce cost optimisation.

Sandra De Weerd

Sandra is knowledgeable about a diverse range of reward topics. With over 25 years of experience designing and structuring reward policies within the tax and legal framework, Sandra's expertise lies in financial wellbeing, driven by her passion for analysing remuneration packages and identifying optimisation opportunities. She has comprehensive expertise in crafting flexible reward schemes that encompass both financial and non-financial elements. These reward schemes are supported by the results of her work helping clients to conduct preference studies.

How to use this book

To simplify navigation of this book, we have divided it into three parts.

The first part gives the background to reward, explaining how it is linked to motivation, how it works to attract and retain talent and how it has been impacted by some of the megatrends facing today's world.

The second part, the main section, introduces and explains our five pillar approach to building effective reward systems that help organisations stand out in the talent market. The pillars include the scope of the reward system, job architecture and benchmarking, the mix of reward components, what is driving the change in the reward system and the impact of the organisation's structure on the reward system. Each chapter can be read on its own to give insights on one aspect of a reward system, or all together for organisations interested in their complete reward strategy.

The last part is a series of special dossiers that either encompass multiple pillars or give extra detail on a specific situation or topic. These chapters highlight the changing impact of reward and how we are in a position to ensure this impact becomes increasingly positive for employees, organisations and society.

Understanding reward

1.
Reward
and motivation

Key takeaways

1. Understanding the connection between motivation and reward is crucial for effectively motivating employees and efficiently allocating the reward budget.

2. There are two main types of motivation: intrinsic (driven by personal satisfaction and a sense of accomplishment) and extrinsic (driven by tangible reward or recognition).

3. Traditional monetary reward may not always be the most effective approach.

4. Motivational theories dating back to the 1940s are relevant when developing and implementing a reward system today.

5. Tailoring approaches and incentives to different generational groups can boost motivation and engagement in the workplace.

Given the substantial investment that organisations make in remuneration, it's natural for them to diligently monitor the budget allocated to employee reward to determine how effectively remuneration programmes contribute to organisational effectiveness and growth.

A primary concern when designing a solid reward system is how well it motivates employees, which is why it is important to consider motivation in relation to reward. This chapter tackles this connection, explaining motivation, illustrating how relevant theories have evolved over time and exploring the latest trends.

1. What is motivation?

Our take on a well-known fable shows that it is not always easy to recognise what motivates individuals:

In a lush, green forest, the animals decided to hold a grand race to settle a long-standing debate: who was the fastest, the boastful hare or the steady tortoise? The wise owl, seeing an opportunity for a lesson, announced a tempting reward for the winner – a feast of the forest's finest foods. The hare, confident in its natural speed, saw the feast as an easy win, while the tortoise, slower yet determined, viewed the race as a chance to prove its perseverance.

As the race began, the hare sprinted ahead, leaving the tortoise far behind. Confident of its inevitable victory and driven by the promise of the reward, the hare decided to rest, thinking a short nap wouldn't cost it the race. Meanwhile, the tortoise, understanding its limitations and motivated not just by the reward but by the challenge itself, continued at a steady pace. The tortoise passed the sleeping hare, crossing the finish line first to the astonishment of the forest's inhabitants. The hare awoke to find that its over-reliance on the external reward of the feast, and underestimation of the tortoise's steady motivation, had cost it the race.

The hare was even more surprised when the tortoise offered to share the prize, as the victory of winning the race itself had already given him the best prize imaginable.

1.1. Defining motivation

So, what is motivation? The word motivation derives from the Latin 'movere', meaning 'to move'. As such, a motive refers to a reason or driving force behind a person's actions, choices or behaviour. It is the underlying purpose or motivation that moves someone to do something or nothing. Motives can be influenced by various factors such as personal beliefs, desires, emotions, needs and external circumstances. Due to the insights it provides into human behaviour and decision-making processes, understanding motives is crucial in fields such as HR and reward management.

1.2. Types of motivation

There are two main types of motivation: intrinsic and extrinsic.

Intrinsic motivation comes from within an individual when they engage in an activity that they find inherently rewarding, enjoyable or fulfilling. Employees driven by intrinsic motivation are motivated by internal factors such as personal satisfaction, curiosity, autonomy in the job or a sense of accomplishment or proudness. As these factors are concerned with the quality of working life and not imposed from outside, they are likely to have a deeper and longer lasting effect[1].

Intrinsic motivation is also a factor for managing employees, as an employee carrying out a job that they are highly interested in or passionate about will be easier to motivate and manage. Rather than trying to mould each employee into someone who loves their position, the organisation should create a workplace that is dedicated to finding out what its employees need and then providing it[2].

Extrinsic motivation, on the other hand, comes from external factors. It involves engaging in an activity to earn a reward or avoid punishment. For employees, extrinsic motivators can include tangible reward (like money) or intangible reward (such as praise or recognition). While these factors can have an immediate and powerful effect, they run the risk of being a short-term motivator[3].

Figure 1: The concept of total reward.

	COMMON EXAMPLES	REWARD ELEMENTS	DEFINITION
INTRINSIC Internal value	• Leadership • Values • Employer's reputation	Psychological alignment	TOTAL REWARD
	• Work-life effectiveness • Workability • Recognition • Job content • Building for the future • Work atmosphere • Quality of work • Job security • Talent and performance management	Engagement factors	TOTAL REWARD
EXTRINSIC Everything we can assign a monetary value to	• Tangibles • Cars • Clubs • Discounts	Active benefits	TOTAL REWARD, TOTAL REMUNERATION
	• Retirement • Health and wellbeing • Holidays	Passive benefits	TOTAL REWARD, TOTAL REMUNERATION
	• Share plans • Long-term incentives	Long-term variable pay incentives	TOTAL REWARD, TOTAL REMUNERATION, TOTAL DIRECT COMPENSATION
	• Annual incentive compensation • Bonus	Short-term variable pay incentives	TOTAL REWARD, TOTAL REMUNERATION, TOTAL DIRECT COMPENSATION, TOTAL CASH
	• Base salary	Base cash based upon job description	TOTAL REWARD, TOTAL REMUNERATION, TOTAL DIRECT COMPENSATION, TOTAL CASH

It should be noted that extrinsic reward, such as pay or tangible incentives, is sometimes seen as undermining intrinsic motivation, because when people are rewarded for completing a task, they may come to see the reward as the primary or sole reason for doing the task, rather than finding inherent satisfaction in the activity itself[4].

However, research does not back up this claim. In fact, reward has been shown to increase motivation and performance on low interest tasks. While on high interest tasks, positive effects are obtained when participants are verbally praised for their work and tangible reward is explicitly tied to performance standards and successes[5]. The same research suggests that the negative effects of reward can be easily prevented while attaining human happiness and freedom through the effective use of reward. This highlights the relevance of a solid and well-built reward strategy.

1.3. Non-monetary motivation

Despite the negative reputation that reward may have, organisations have traditionally used monetary reward to attract and retain employees, as well as to drive performance and increase motivation. This includes a whole gamut of incentive plans that reward performance (bonus schemes). However, research delving more deeply into the subject reveals more nuanced results.

First, the effect of incentive pay schemes appears to be temporary, as performance eventually revolves back to its baseline level. And secondly, it appears to influence the quantity rather than the quality of the output produced[6].

A 2023 PwC study shows that young people attach high value to personal recognition and appreciation[7]. As a result, it is important for organisations to look beyond bonuses and variable (target driven) pay when it comes to designing a remuneration policy. In fact, performance-related pay is sinking further down the preference lists year after year. These days, young talents attach higher value on personal recognition and having an approachable manager.

With the rise of hybrid working, employers should be aware that working from home may make young people feel less recognised and their achievements less noticed. However, recognition can come in the form of a salary increase and a permanent contract to help mitigate this. Young people like to be rewarded systematically for their work and look for job security.

It is also clear that young people consider the people they work with to be important. Organisations, therefore, need to look closely at whether people within their teams are complementary to each other and whether they can handle the calibre of the work. As a result of the tight labour market, unsustainable workloads are growing to unhealthy proportions, resulting in increasing drop-out rates and turnover. Organisations that are better able to retain their talents will suffer less.

Considering the labour market shortage, the same PwC study looked into the willingness of young employees to work more. The idea was that this could help alleviate the labour market shortage. However, the study shows that young people would rather work fewer hours than more, making the labour market shortage larger rather than smaller, especially when combined with the challenges related to part-time work, retirement age and labour migration. Organisations are finding that robust time off and vacation policies and other non-monetary reward can help them compete for talent in this tight labour market[8].

2. Foundational motivation theories

The first theories linking motivation with reward emerged in the early days of industrialism. Early theories, including Thorndike's law of effect and Skinner's law of reinforcement[9], focused on the reinforcement and reiteration of desired behaviour. Neglecting all internal elements of behaviour, these theories only paid attention to how the behaviour is externalised and its consequences. In other words, they linked positive consequences to certain desired behaviours.

In the context of labour, Frederick Taylor stated that *"whenever the workman succeeds in doing his task right, and within the time limit specified, he receives an addition of from 30 per cent to 100 per cent to his ordinary wages."* He believed that employees need to be 'induced' to maximise their productivity[10].

These early theories sprouted from a mechanistic view of people, whereby the employee operated within a strict framework, like a small cogwheel in a bigger machine, driven by money in the same way that machines are driven by steam. They believed that employees were primarily motivated by money and that management needed to control the work process to ensure efficiency.

Although few employers still regard their employees in this way, it is nevertheless interesting to note that the performance-based pay system that Taylor describes still remains a widely spread principle in the majority of modern-day reward systems.

As human sciences further evolved in the 1920s and 30s, experts realised that the mechanistic, pure one-dimensional view on motivation ignored the broader perspective of human relations and psychological aspects that influence the employees' state of mind and, thus, productivity.

For example, the Hawthorne studies, conducted at the Western Electric Company's Hawthorne plant in the 1920s and 1930s[11], illustrated the positive effect of *"merely feeling observed and valued"*[12] on employee productivity. It highlighted the impact of psychological and social factors, shifting the focus of motivation theories from mere economic and environmental factors to include the role of human relations and employee attention in the workplace. With this newly discovered spectrum of different motivational drivers, new theories started to investigate how all these factors related to each other.

In the period of economic reconstruction after World War II, there was a significant interest in the question of how to motivate employees as this was seen as being essential to stimulate production and economic growth. In the post-war period, three major motivation theories were formulated: Maslow's Hierarchy of Needs, Herzberg's two-factor model and McGregor's Theory X and Theory Y. While none of these theories is considered to offer the complete solution, they each contain elements that are frequently referenced by modern managers when discussing motivation.

Interestingly, these post-war theories attempted to answer two questions around motivation. Firstly, what are the foundations of motivation for people? And secondly, what causes people to be motivated?

Figure 2: Timeline depicting the different theories of motivation.

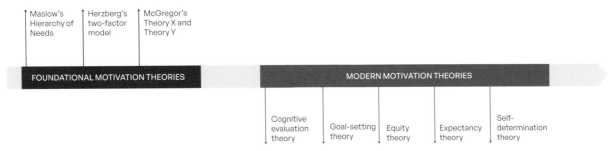

2.1. Maslow's Hierarchy of Needs

Figure 3: Maslow's pyramid of needs.

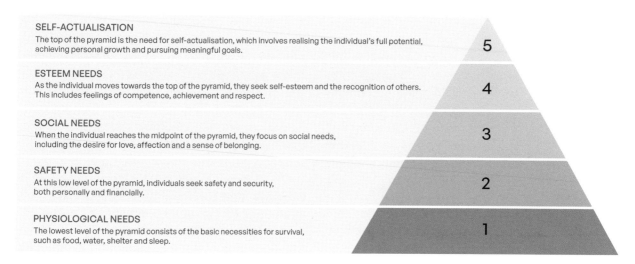

SELF-ACTUALISATION
The top of the pyramid is the need for self-actualisation, which involves realising the individual's full potential, achieving personal growth and pursuing meaningful goals.

ESTEEM NEEDS
As the individual moves towards the top of the pyramid, they seek self-esteem and the recognition of others. This includes feelings of competence, achievement and respect.

SOCIAL NEEDS
When the individual reaches the midpoint of the pyramid, they focus on social needs, including the desire for love, affection and a sense of belonging.

SAFETY NEEDS
At this low level of the pyramid, individuals seek safety and security, both personally and financially.

PHYSIOLOGICAL NEEDS
The lowest level of the pyramid consists of the basic necessities for survival, such as food, water, shelter and sleep.

In his 1943 paper 'A Theory of Human Motivation', Abraham Maslow identifies the impetus for all our actions and attitudes as our ultimate desire to satisfy our needs[13]. Maslow, who is considered to be the founding father of motivational theories, proposed that humans are motivated by five universal levels of needs which he ranks in a hierarchy of needs, forming Maslow's pyramid of needs (see figure 3).

Maslow claims that individuals move through these five levels sequentially, and that only when a lower need is satisfied, can the next highest need level become predominant. For example, someone who is hungry or thirsty will not care much about their social status or personal growth until they satisfy their physiological needs. The hierarchy is often represented as a pyramid, with the most basic needs at the bottom and the most advanced ones at the top.

According to Maslow's theory, only an unsatisfied need can motivate behaviour as the individual's attention is always turned to satisfying the next higher need. Moreover, this implies that to motivate someone, their current level of needs should first be determined before triggering their next level of needs. Although Maslow's theory focused more on developmental psychology, the principles were later applied to the workplace.

In the context of employment, Maslow's theory suggests that while monetary reward is important, it only addresses the basic level of needs. For deeper motivation and engagement, employers need to address higher-level needs such as belonging, esteem and opportunities for personal growth and self-actualisation. Figure 4 shows Maslow's pyramid presented in terms of reward and recognition.

Figure 4: Using Maslow's pyramid to look at reward and recognition.

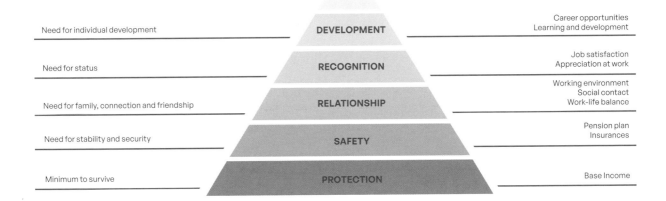

Need for individual development	DEVELOPMENT — Career opportunities / Learning and development
Need for status	RECOGNITION — Job satisfaction / Appreciation at work
Need for family, connection and friendship	RELATIONSHIP — Working environment / Social contact / Work-life balance
Need for stability and security	SAFETY — Pension plan / Insurances
Minimum to survive	PROTECTION — Base Income

Today, many recognition programmes are based on Maslow's theory. For example, attempts to satisfy needs related to social interaction and self-esteem are commonly part of a reward system. This is because lacking recognition will result in employees getting stuck in the lower levels of Maslow's pyramid preventing personal growth and self-fulfilment.

However, it must be said that Maslow never substantiated his theory with objective or empirical research. As such, his theory has little or no scientific basis. Moreover, stating that all need structures are arranged according to the dimensions Maslow suggests seems rather simplistic and rigid as individual experiences, age, life stage and cultural factors may also influence the prioritisation of needs. Maslow's hierarchical set-up is therefore not always in line with the individual choices that people make in life (see box 'Maslow and reward systems'). Besides these critical points, Maslow's central themes of respect for individual autonomy and the promotion of personal development form the core of many of today's psychological treatments.

Maslow's theory was later further refined by Alderfer, who introduced the ERG-model. His theory suggests that there are three groups of core needs: existence (E), relatedness (R) and growth (G), hence the acronym ERG. The existence group combines Maslow's first two levels of physiological and safety needs, while relatedness covers the social needs

and growth encompasses the esteem and self-actualisation needs. Alderfer also stated that some people can be triggered more strongly by different elements than others and that the same event can impact the different E-R-G levels at the same time. For example, an artist may pursue self-actualisation through their art at the expense of their physical health by spending their money on paint instead of food[14].

Moreover, Alderfer introduced the hypothesis of frustration-regression. If a 'higher' need is not fulfilled, the individual will work more strongly towards actualising a lower-level need.

Maslow and reward systems
If we look at Maslow's pyramid in a hierarchical way, we see things that don't always play out in practice. For example, some organisations give out spot awards, a reward that has a genuinely low financial value, but are granted for a specific action or realisation beyond what is normally expected. According to Maslow's pyramid, these spot awards would only work if the recipient had already realised their previous levels. In reality, this is not always the case. A spot award lets an employee know that someone has noticed their noteworthy contribution, which is highly valued, irrespective of whether or not the previous levels are all fully satisfied.

2.2. Herzberg's two-factor model

Figure 5: An overview of Herzberg's two-factor model.

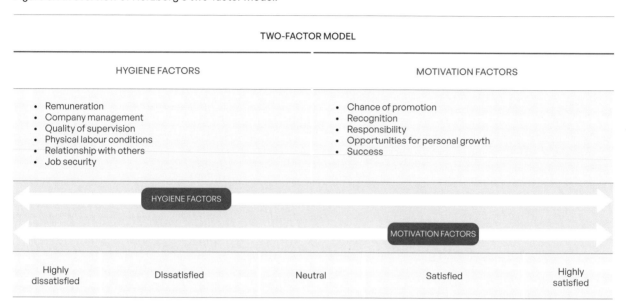

After Maslow, Herzberg's two-factor model was next to emerge. Both Maslow and Herzberg believe that people are motivated by their needs, which are translated into goals for them to achieve. According to Maslow, there are five levels of needs whereby the needs at a higher level only emerge when a lower level is satisfied. Herzberg simplifies Maslow's theory and assesses two groups of factors that affect job satisfaction and motivation (see figure 5).

Frederick Herzberg conducted a qualitative study into sources of job satisfaction and dissatisfaction for accountants and engineers in the 1950s[15]. He identified two sets of factors (or needs): needs related to hygiene that cause dissatisfaction and needs related to motivation that encourage satisfaction.

Also known as maintenance factors or dissatisfiers, hygiene factors are associated with job dissatisfaction if they are absent or do not meet the employee's expectations. However, job satisfaction does not necessarily increase when they are present. Examples include salary, working conditions, organisational policies, interpersonal relationships and job security.

Motivation factors or motivators are factors that, when present, lead to job satisfaction and motivation. Examples include achievement, recognition, the work itself, responsibility, advancement and personal growth; in other words, intrinsic motivators. Improving these factors can enhance job satisfaction and motivation.

Herzberg's theory suggests that job satisfaction and dissatisfaction are not on a single continuum but rather two separate and independent dimensions. In other words, the opposite of satisfaction is not dissatisfaction, nor vice versa. The factors that promote satisfaction are therefore not the same factors whose absence leads to dissatisfaction. They should be seen as two sliders that can be moved from side to side, influencing only their specific channel[16].

According to Herzberg's theory, employers who try to increase employee motivation by increasing salaries end up disappointed. Once employees are accustomed to a new level of income, they are more likely to view it as a hygiene factor. As soon as the increase in payments becomes a regular part of the salary, it ceases to affect the growth of motivation. People tend to be more motivated when they really want something than when they already have it.

Herzberg's theory has been widely criticised for being unsupported by quantitative data, as well as the methodology he used to qualify his research findings. However, its strength comes from its role in job design where it maximises the opportunities to obtain intrinsic satisfaction from work and thus improve the quality of working life. As Herzberg famously remarked: *"if you want people to do a good job, give them a good job to do"*.

Herzberg is right but, at the same time, it should be emphasised that, besides the motivators and demotivators, equal work for equal pay is also key. The notion of equal pay is explained in more detail in chapter 10.

Herzberg and reward systems
Applying Herzberg's theory to reward systems involves creating a balance between addressing hygiene factors to prevent dissatisfaction (e.g., ensuring that the basic needs and expectations of employees are met regarding fair remuneration) and incorporating motivators to enhance job satisfaction and motivation (e.g., offering opportunities for skill development and career advancement). It is important to recognise the dynamic nature of both factors and adapt reward systems accordingly.

2.3. McGregor's Theory X and Theory Y

Douglas McGregor was a social psychologist who introduced two contrasting sets of assumptions about human behaviour in the workplace: Theory X and Theory Y[17].

Theory X takes a negative view of employees, assuming that they inherently dislike work and will avoid it if they can. Because of this, employees need to be closely supervised, directed and coerced to achieve organisational goals. Decision making is top-down, with employees expected to follow instructions.

Theory Y is more positive, assuming that employees are internally motivated, enjoy their job and work to better themselves without a direct reward in return.

Employees are ambitious and creative with a strong work ethic if the work is fulfilling and aligned with their values. The decentralised decision-making process uses an engagement model to involve employees.

McGregor's theories were ground-breaking because they challenged the traditional views that employees were inherently lazy and needed to be closely supervised. Instead, he suggested that how managers perceive their employees influences their managerial style and, consequently, employee behaviour.

For McGregor, Theory X and Theory Y are not opposite ends of the same continuum, but rather two different continua in themselves. In order to achieve the most efficient production, a combination of both theories may be appropriate.

McGregor and reward systems
In McGregor's Theory X, managers believe that employees are primarily motivated by external reward, so the reward system focuses on tangible reward, such as monetary incentives, bonuses and promotions. Extrinsic motivation is used to drive performance and achieve organisational goals.

In Theory Y, managers believe that employees are internally motivated by factors such as personal growth, autonomy and a sense of purpose. So, the reward system focuses on intrinsic reward and creating a work environment that fosters employee engagement and satisfaction.

By considering both Theory X and Theory Y, organisations can design a balanced reward system that caters to the diverse needs and motivations of their employees. This may involve a combination of extrinsic and intrinsic reward, depending on the nature of the work and employee preferences.

3. Modern motivation theories

3.1. Cognitive evaluation theory

The cognitive evaluation process refers to the way individuals interpret and assess the impact of external events on their intrinsic motivation. Cognitive evaluation theory predicts and interprets the effects of external events on intrinsic motivation and other closely related internal variables by providing an analysis of the relative salience of the informational versus controlling aspect of the external events.

According to this theory, the use of extrinsic reward may destroy intrinsic motivation[18]. If external factors support the individuals' sense of autonomy, competence and relatedness, their intrinsic motivation is likely to be enhanced. However, conversely, if these factors are perceived as controlling or manipulative, intrinsic motivation may decrease. The cognitive evaluation theory thus focuses on the need to increase the intrinsic motivating factor.

Deci and Ryan asserted that external events such as reward and communications can have two functional aspects: an informational aspect and a controlling aspect. The informational aspect conveys meaningful feedback in the context of self-determination. This means that the individual is either told that they are competent at the target activity or how to become more competent at it. The controlling aspect of reward and communications pressures people towards specified outcomes. For example, a reward is considered to be controlling if it is experienced as making people do something i.e., the activity must be done in a particular way, at a particular time or in a particular place, to receive the reward.

Just as research has shown that informational reward or communications tend to enhance intrinsic motivation, an even larger body of data has confirmed that controlling reward and communications undermine intrinsic motivation[19].

Cognitive evaluation theory and reward systems
The cognitive evaluation theory suggests that the use of extrinsic reward in a reward system should be carefully considered to avoid undermining intrinsic motivation. For example, instead of solely relying on monetary reward, organisations can provide employees with meaningful feedback and recognition that enhances their sense of autonomy, competence and relatedness. This can be achieved through performance evaluations that focus on individual growth and development, providing employees with opportunities to learn new skills or acknowledging their achievements publicly.

3.2. Goal-setting theory

Goal-setting theory was developed inductively within industrial and organisational psychology over a 25-year period, based on around 400 laboratory and field studies. These studies showed that specific, high (hard) goals lead to a higher level of task performance than easy, vague or abstract goals such as the exhortation 'to do one's best'. As long as the individual is committed to the goal, has the requisite ability to attain it and does not have conflicting goals, there is a positive, linear relationship between goal difficulty and task performance. Because goals refer to future valued outcomes, the setting of goals is first and foremost a discrepancy creating process. It implies the individual is not content with their present condition and their desire to attain an object or outcome[20].

Goals are related to effort, as goals set the primary standard for self-satisfaction with the individual's performance. High or hard goals are motivating because they require the individual to attain more in order to be satisfied compared to what they need to do to achieve low or easy goals. Feelings of success in the workplace occur to the extent that people see that they are able to grow and meet job challenges by pursuing and attaining goals that are important and meaningful[21].

Motivation increases if people have clear goals and SMART (specific, measurable, achievable, relevant and time-bound) objectives. The goal-setting theory emphasises the importance of clear, challenging goals and individual attitudes toward achievement in shaping behaviour and outcomes. While this theory is often applied in sports, it is also appropriate for the workplace where it requires the implementation of a solid performance management system and feedback culture. Participation in goal setting is important and feedback is vital in maintaining motivation, particularly towards the achievement of higher goals[22].

Goal-setting theory and reward systems
The goal-setting theory emphasises the importance of clear, challenging goals and individual attitudes towards achievement for shaping behaviour and outcomes. In the context of a reward system, organisations can align reward with goal attainment. For example, employees who achieve their goals can be rewarded with bonuses, promotions or other forms of recognition. Additionally, providing feedback and supporting employees as they work towards their goals can help maintain motivation and increase the likelihood of goal achievement.

3.3. Equity theory

Equity theory suggests that employees compare their own inputs and outputs (e.g., effort and reward) to those of others, and when there is a perceived imbalance, they will act to restore equity. It states that employees are motivated to balance their own perceived fairness levels with those around them. In other words, if they feel they are being treated unfairly, they will be less motivated to work hard[23].

In equity theory, motivation increases if people are treated equitably and equally in comparison with a comparable group of people. Equity is achieved when the ratio of an individual's outcomes (such as reward, benefits or recognition) to inputs (such as effort, time or skills) is perceived as equal to the ratio of a relevant comparison (e.g., a co-worker). Inequity occurs when there is a perceived imbalance in the ratio, either in favour of the individual (underpayment inequity) or in favour of the comparison to others (overpayment inequity). This theory assumes that employees compare the input of their work (effort, experience, competence) with the returns (salary level, recognition) of others[24].

The theory is the basis of the intriguing prediction that individuals who are overcompensated in a payment scheme in which greater output leads to greater reward (such as occurs in a piece-rate system of remuneration), will seek to restore equity by restricting the quantity and increasing the quality of their output. In addition, undercompensated individuals in a contingent pay scheme will seek to restore equity by increasing the quantity and restricting the quality of their output[25].

Equity theory and reward systems
Equity theory states that employees compare their performance and reward to those of others, acting to restore equity when they perceive an imbalance. In the context of a reward system, organisations can ensure fairness and equity by providing reward that is equal to employees' efforts and contributions. This can be achieved through transparent and consistent reward architectures (see chapter 6), regular salary reviews and opportunities for career advancement based on merit and performance.

3.4. Expectancy theory

Expectancy theory provides a framework for understanding how individuals make decisions about their effort and motivation based on their expectations about the outcomes of their actions. It suggests that individuals are motivated to perform if they know that their extra performance will be recognised and rewarded. The theory highlights the importance of perceived links between effort, performance and outcome in shaping behaviour and motivation[26].

When individuals are deciding which activity to pursue, they evaluate the expectancy, instrumentality and valence of the possible activities. The combination of these three assessments is thought to represent the overall motivational force for a goal. The goal with the highest motivational force is then adopted for pursuit. The first cognitive process (expectancy) is about the question of whether a given effort will lead to adequate performance: if I exert myself and do my best, will I also perform well? The second cognitive process (instrumentality) addresses the question of whether the performance will be rewarded: if I perform well, will I receive a reward for it? The third cognitive process (valence) deals with the question of whether the performance and its reward have personal value: is performing well important to me? And is the reward I will receive for it of any value to me? Together these cognitive variables explain differences in motivational strength. Therefore, people will choose to exert themselves in activities that they consider achievable and important and yield something they appreciate[27].

Expectancy theory and reward systems
Expectancy theory suggests that individuals are motivated to perform if they believe that their efforts will lead to desired outcomes. In the context of reward systems, organisations can enhance motivation by clearly linking performance to reward. For example, employees who consistently demonstrate high performance can be rewarded with bonuses, incentives or other forms of recognition. Providing employees with a clear understanding of the performance-reward relationship can increase their motivation to exert effort and achieve desired outcomes.

3.5. Self-determination theory

The self-determination theory changes the lens of motivation. Deci and Ryan used experiments to illustrate that an individual's motivation is not just the sum of internal and external motivation. Instead, the relationship between the two variables is much more complex as external reward can have a negative effect on internal motivation[28].

The authors started from the hypothesis that every individual has three basic psychological, internal needs: the need for autonomy, relatedness (or belonging) and competency[29]. While the extent to which an individual seeks to fulfil these needs is dependent on their interactions with the environment, these three needs are universal to everyone.

This contextualisation allows the authors to look at a much broader and differentiated spectrum of motivation types. They determined that certain elements can impact the three basic needs in such a way that the individual is motivated to do something just because they like it. In other words, some extrinsic motivation can act in a similar way to intrinsic motivation.

Deci and Ryan refer to these types of motivation as autonomous motivation, compared to controlled motivation which is very much 'stick and carrot' driven.

Autonomous motivation finds its origin in the individual's values and interests, and research has proven it to be a strong driver for better performance and engagement[30]. The wrong use of control-type motivation reduces the positive effect of autonomous motivation, as the reward can downgrade the activity from fulfilling (one of) the intrinsic psychological needs, to a mere pay-for-performance activity.

The self-determination theory focuses on broader, non-monetary and contextual forms of reward, such as belonging to a group or aligning personal values. As such, it not only highlights the importance of a more holistic view on reward, but it also demonstrates the complexity of getting extrinsic reward right.

Self-determination theory and reward systems
Self-determination theory emphasises the importance of fulfilling individuals' basic psychological needs for autonomy, relatedness and competence. In the context of reward systems, organisations can promote autonomous motivation by aligning reward with employees' values and interests. For example, offering opportunities for personal and professional growth, allowing employees to have a say in goal-setting and decision-making processes and fostering a supportive and inclusive work environment to enhance intrinsic motivation and engagement.

4. A generational perspective to reward

In this section we looked at reward and motivation theories.

The foundation of the motivational theory was laid by Maslow's Hierarchy of Needs, which was later fine-tuned by Herzberg and Alderfer. More recently, other theories were developed, each with their own focus and own accents. Each theory has believers and non-believers, supporters and critics. Most likely, the truth lies out there and combines elements from each of these theories.

Every theory provides a number of guidelines, and there is nothing wrong with applying a combination of variety of theories. Some aspects may work with some employees while they have no impact on the behaviour of others.

Moreover, when considering how to motivate employees, organisations should also be aware of the fact that generational differences in the workplace must be considered. Different generations, such as Baby Boomers, Generation X, Millennials and Generation Z, often have distinct values and expectations that influence how they approach work and what motivates them to thrive. Each of these generations has been shaped by different historical events, cultural influences and technological advancements, which have contributed to their unique preferences. Figure 6 gives a brief overview of some key characteristics associated with each generation and how this impacts their drivers and motivators for performance.

Understanding and respecting generational differences can help organisations create inclusive and engaging work environments that motivate and engage employees across different age groups.

Combine these generational differences with other factors, such as gender and civil status, and it is clear that there is no one-size-fits-all approach, making the application of motivation theories to reward systems a complex and nuanced process.

When designing a reward system, it is not necessary for employers to become experts in motivational theories. However, reflecting on best practices and considering the principles outlined in these theories can be beneficial.

Ultimately, the goal of applying motivational theories to reward systems is to encourage employees to consistently give their best effort. By understanding and incorporating elements from various theories, organisations can create a more effective and personalised approach to motivating their workforce. Remember, there are hares and tortoises. An ideal reward system should motivate both to join the team, run a marathon and cross the finish line together.

Figure 6: Key characteristics of different generations and their impact on motivation.

	BABY BOOMERS	GENERATION X	GENERATION Y OR MILLENNIALS	GENERATION Z
Who?	Individuals born in the post-World War II period, up to the mid-1960s.	Individuals born between the mid-1960s and the 1980s.	Individuals born between the early 1980s and mid-1990s.	Individuals born between mid-1990's and the early 2000s.
Age in 2024	Close to retirement age.	45 – 60	30 – 45	20 – 30
What are they typically **looking for**?	Job security.	Work-life balance.	Work-life integration.	Mix work and life. True digital nomads who are connected at all times for private and professional purposes.
What does their **career journey** typically look like?	Loyalty to their employer (in return for job security) means they often stay with a single organisation.	Open for career advancement.	Regularly changing their professional environment enables them to gain a broader expertise.	Full of challenges and a constant search for growth opportunities.
What do they typically **value**?	Traditional work structures. They value a strong work ethic.	Independence and autonomy. They tend to be self-reliant.	Work that aligns with their passions and purpose.	Diversity, inclusivity and social responsibility.
What typically **drives and motivates** them?	Opportunties for promotions and financial recognition.	Opportunities for personal growth and development.	Opportunities for collaboration, feedback and work that has a positive impact.	Opportunities for creativity, flexibility and continuous learning.

2.
Functions of reward systems

Key takeaways

1. The primary function of a reward system is to compensate employees for their work.

2. As well as shaping the employer-employee relationship, reward systems have three secondary functions: attracting and retaining skilled employees, driving employee competence development and promoting social cohesion.

3. It is important to strike a balance between designing an effective reward system, with a clear framework and purpose, and addressing the complexities that may arise.

4. Potential pitfalls when developing and implementing a new reward system include unclear communication, a lack of equity and an overemphasis on monetary reward.

The previous chapter focused on people and, more specifically, their behaviour and motivation. The organisation's strategic business goals determine the desired functions of the reward system, which are then translated into an HR and reward strategy. These strategic goals form the foundation of the creation of correct employee behaviour[31]. This chapter elaborates further on how reward can contribute positively to people-related challenges from an organisational perspective.

Reward is one of the defining characteristics in an employment relationship. In return for the employee's efforts, they are remunerated by their employer. However, well-structured remuneration systems are much more than this simple transaction, especially in a challenging global economic climate that puts pressure on the current reward systems.

The primary function of a reward system is to compensate the employee for the work that they undertake on behalf of an organisation. It also has secondary functions, such as shaping the relationship employees have with their employer and the way employees interact with each other. The right reward system is critical for attracting and retaining human capital, as well as driving competence development in employees, motivating employees to perform to their maximum potential or become a catalyst of social cohesion within an organisation.

This chapter focuses on these secondary functions of reward systems. We start by looking at how a reward system can help an organisation to attract and retain talent. This is followed by how to apply reward systems to leverage employee knowledge, growth and competency development and how reward systems can act as a driver of social cohesion within an organisation. Finally, we look at how to avoid potential pitfalls when developing well-structured reward systems.

1. The dynamics of talent demand and supply

The ability to attract and retain talented human capital in the information age has been recognised as one of the main sources of competitive advantage for global economies[32]. Because of this, one of the most important secondary functions of reward systems today is attracting and retaining skilled employees during periods where the supply of available talent with specific skills is limited.

Market dynamics during periods with a limited supply of labour make it difficult for organisations to recruit enough of the right people, as well as influencing how willing most employees are to stay at an organisation for extended periods of time.

As an employer, such a period is tricky to navigate. Today, estimates state that the worldwide talent shortage will reach 85 million unfilled jobs by 2030[33]. If all other factors remain constant, this estimate implies that today's shortage of talent is here to stay. This is reinforced by the fact that some countries or regions are already facing so-called full employment (i.e., an employment rate of over 80% and an unemployment rate of under 5%). In other words, everyone who wants to work has a job and employers may be unable to find additional employees to fill open positions in a certain region or country[34]. However, in reality not all other factors will remain constant, suggesting that the shortage of talent could evolve differently. Some indicators that could trigger an alternative evolution include:

- Gen AI and automation: The emergence of Generative AI and increasing automation can transform or even replace traditional jobs, reducing the need for human labour. This could decrease the pressure on the shortage of talent in certain industries, while simultaneously increasing the demand for new skills and expertise. See the technical disruption section in chapter 3 for more information.
- Sourcing to low-cost countries: organisations may choose to out- or near-source certain functions or tasks to low-cost countries, competing on cost efficiency and locally available skilled

talent. In combination with remote working, this is likely to result in a trend towards hybrid teams, both in terms of cost and talent, collaborating closely together as a single team instead of a remote delivery centre.

Figure 7 shows that in 2022, 11 EU countries had employment rates above 78%, including 5 with rates above 81%. The same year saw an average of 75% of the EU's 20-64-year-olds were employed, the highest share recorded since the start of the time series in 2009 according to Eurostat[35]. The situation is not restricted to the EU as figures from the US Bureau of Labor Statistics show that there is a similar situation in the US, with an unemployment rate of just 3.6% in 2022[36].

While a 70% employment rate suggests a relatively high level of workforce participation, it is essential to consider why this might be insufficient. Structural challenges, such as the rigidity of the labour market, long-term illness and periods of inactivity due to health-related reasons, can further complicate the employment landscape, contributing to challenges in achieving sufficient employment. See chapter 7 for more information on employee wellbeing.

1.1. Attract

During periods with limited supplies of talent, the dynamics of the recruitment process differ from what is considered normal. Instead of having to compete against other talented people with a similar profile, skilled individuals now have a variety of potential employers to choose from. As a result, employers need to find ways to distinguish themselves from their competitors in order to attract the talented individuals the organisation needs.

Not being able to attract sufficient skilled employees is something that concerns CEOs worldwide. PwC research shows that over 50% of CEOs worldwide worry about labour and/or skill shortages impacting their profitability 'to a large extent' or 'to a very large extent'[37]. Figure 8 shows that, according to CEOs questioned for PwC's 26th Annual Global CEO Survey, labour or skills shortages are the third most important threat to profitability in their industry over the next 10 years. Therefore, it is crucial for employers to remain one step ahead of their competitors by presenting themselves in a way that is attractive to potential new hires. But what does it mean to be an attractive employer?

Figure 7: Employment rates across Europe in 2022, shown as a percentage of the total population aged 20-64.

Figure 8: Challenges to profitability according to CEOs.

QUESTION : To what extent do you believe the following will impact (i.e., either increase or decrease) profitabilty in your industry over the next 10 years? (Showing only 'to a large extent' and 'to a very large extent' responses)

1.1.1. Base salary

When talking about ways to stand out as an employer, the most obvious reaction is for employers to provide a higher salary than their competitors. It seems obvious that when comparing job opportunities, individuals attach a lot of importance to the salaries related to each offer and, therefore, are more likely to simply choose the best paying job.

Employee remuneration accounts for a large proportion of employer costs for organisations all over the world. Organisations know that failing to offer an attractive reward package may impact their ability to recruit skilled people, which in its turn has an adverse effect on employee turnover, which can generate major costs[38].

The fact that the reward system is internally fair does not mean that it's also externally competitive. Offering a non-competitive salary may complicate an organisation's ability to recruit new employees or even lead to its current workforce leaving for other firms. In this case, it can be beneficial to perform an external market comparison against salaries offered by other organisations. Benchmarking external and internal equity is explained in more detail in chapter 6 on reward architecture.

Offering larger, similar or smaller base salaries than those offered by competitors is an important decision as this impacts the organisation's expenses, as well as its ability to attract and retain employees. Determining factors for this decision are, for example, the level of competition in the relevant labour market, the financial health of the organisation or organisational factors such as its strategy, relevant industry or its size[39].

1.1.2. Other benefits

While an attractive salary is important for remaining competitive in today's labour market, studies also show that simply increasing salaries might not be enough, or even the right route to take. This is because most employees take a more holistic approach when scouting a new job opportunity, taking into account other monetary and non-monetary benefits such as flexible work schedules or locations, employer subsidised insurances and/or pension schemes, an appealing organisational culture and the way the professional goals of an employer line up with their own morals.

Millennials and Generation Z seem to perceive their jobs to be more than just a way to earn money. For these generations, finding meaning in what they do is increasingly important and they care more about intangible reward such as career advancement, skill training, social connections and organisational purpose than older generations did[40].

Many organisations view employee benefits as a necessary evil, something they have to provide because their competitors do and their employees expect it. As a consequence, a lot of employers fail to see the potential of a well-structured benefit package. However, employee benefits can have a substantial impact on employee retention, attraction and performance and, therefore, they should be viewed strategically, with a focus on how these benefits can help organisations achieve their strategic goals and create a sustainable competitive advantage[41].

It is important to note that there's no one-size-fits-all solution. Every organisation has different goals that it wants to achieve and a different workforce composition to help it achieve those goals. On top of this, every employee is different, with a unique background, goals and values. Getting to know and responding to these differences is key for organisations to utilise their reward systems to their full potential. More on this topic can be found in the employee preferences section in chapter 7 on reward mix.

1.1.3. Employer branding

As well as an appealing reward strategy that includes a competitive salary and other attractive benefits, employer branding can also play an important role in making an organisation more appealing to potential employees in the labour market.

Employer branding is the result of applying marketing principles to human resource management (HRM)[42]. Instead of targeting a specific group of potential buyers to sell their products to, employers define the type of employee they want to sell their organisation to and create an employer brand tailored to attracting them.

Research shows that employees actually prefer organisations with a strong employer brand over organisations with a weak or a negative image. Furthermore, an employer branding strategy tailored to the employees that the organisation wants to attract is important, as the beliefs a job seeker holds about a potential employer can create or destroy value for an organisation. This is because these beliefs determine how a potential employee pursues and processes information about an organisation, whether they would accept a job offer from the organisation and what they expect from the organisation as their new employer[43].

A strong employer brand helps organisations shorten the time they need to fill vacancies, attracting new hires that fit the organisational culture. This is vital because winning when there is a shortage of talent is not just about attracting any employee to the organisation, it's about attracting the right ones[44].

When designing an employer branding strategy, it is important to note that different components of employer attractiveness have different levels of perceived importance which may vary depending on the individual employee. While research has clearly demonstrated this for gender, it hasn't found any significant effects due to age or current employment status[45].

An organisation's corporate brand must be aligned with its intended target audience[46]. It is important that the employer's brand is appealing and innovative, but at the same time there must be a balance between the real brand and the promised brand[47].

A PwC study showed that young job seekers want to gain a deeper understanding of a workplace before applying, with 95% of job seekers researching a potential employer via informal channels and social media platforms. Young people are conscious and possess all the right tools to look behind the scenes and clearly see the brand[48].

In order to create an employer brand that is able to attract enough of the right employees, it is important for organisations to first look inwards. What are the values of the organisation and employer? What are the organisation's goals? And what sets the organisation apart from its competitors? Only then can an employer define an employer branding strategy that will help to attract the people the organisation needs.

1.2. Retain

As well as difficulties in attracting and recruiting skilled employees, a second important symptom of the shortage of talent is employers having difficulties in retaining talented employees within their organisation. When there is a shortage of talent, employees are less loyal to an organisation, resulting in shorter stays with each employer.

Employee retention is influenced by several factors within organisations, such as remuneration and reward, career progression, working environment, organisational culture, training, safety and hygiene at work, exchange of opinions and communication. Therefore, the organisation's reward system has a vital role to play when it comes to retaining employees, just as it does for attracting employees.

In fact, a reward system can be specifically composed to target employee retention with increased pay, learning and development opportunities, job advancement opportunities, retention bonuses and more. Long term incentives (LTIs) such as executive share option schemes, organisation share option plans, share incentive plans, save-as-you-earn schemes, executive deferred annual cash-based bonuses and executive restricted/performance share plans can also be effective. On top of this, flexible work schedules and locations increase employee retention[49]. More on the different components found in reward systems can be found in chapter 7 on reward mix.

2. Learn and develop

The increasing acceleration of the speed of change has resulted in new jobs that require new skills in order for organisations to be future fit. Combined with the shortage of talent, an organisation's flexible strategy could include tapping into the profiles of employees that do not yet have the required skill set for the new jobs.

Organisations could therefore offer to reskill or upskill their staff. The difference between these two concepts is that upskilling focuses on teaching staff additional skills to optimise their performance and create more specialised individuals. The goal of reskilling, on the other hand, is to train employees to be employable in a different position within the organisation, making them more versatile. In fact, the motivational theories covered in chapter 1 can also be used to show how reward can support a culture of learning and continuous improvement.

A reward system needs to be competitive in comparison to other organisations as well as internally equitable, which implies a fair relationship between an individual's salary and the salary of the other employees within the organisation. An internally fair reward system can be obtained via two methods: a function-based method and a person-based method. The function-based method grants a certain value to a specific function, which is translated into a reward system as we will see in chapter 6 on reward architecture.

To obtain a reward system that supports a learning mindset, the organisation needs to start from a more person-based method which focuses on skills and competences[50], where skills are the qualities that an employee requires for their current or future position and can be acquired through training, and competences are the general qualities which are required for the performance of certain tasks[51]. Therefore, competences can also support the desire to obtain new knowledge and efficient working methods[52]. This person-based approach also fits perfectly within an organisation's human capital management (as part of the HRM strategy) as it centralises the individual and their skills and competences[53].

By implementing skill-based pay (or knowledge-based pay), employees are compensated for their demonstrated knowledge, skills and ability, which motivates them to acquire new skills, formal certification and demonstrate a more proactive behaviour with innovation, adaptability and technical expertise[54]. Therefore, the organisation can keep a competitive advantage, create effective employee performance and support long-term organisational goals (instead of short-term thinking)[55]. Scientific research has already shown that skill-based pay increases the motivation for skill development[56] and that employees often react positively when there is a strong link between skills and salary[57] and the reward system is perceived as equitable[58]. In fact, perceived fairness in reward has a strong effect on the way employees show desired behaviours[59].

Some pay elements, including pay progression, bonuses and non-financial reward, can support a skill-based reward system. The conditions that need to be fulfilled to receive a pay progression or bonus need to include an evaluation of the acquired, demonstrated and relevant skills for the job or function. Skills developed via training are easily recognised by both employees and employers, but organisations need to be aware of the difference between the objective cost of skills on the employer-side and the subjective cost of skills on the employee-side. Employees also have a subjective view on their skills in comparison to their colleagues, which can create a perception of unfairness towards a skill-based pay progression. Therefore, the determination of salary and progression needs to be rigorous and transparent[60].

As total reward is gaining in popularity, non-financial reward can also support a skill-based approach by creating a work environment that emphasises the importance of continuous improvement. This includes acknowledging, appreciating and recognising employees that show the motivation to enhance their competences and skills and giving employees the opportunities to grow when they invest in their skills[61].

Although there are a lot of upsides to skill-based reward systems, there are some issues that organisations need to be aware of. Favouritism might influence who does or does not go on training and, while someone is in training, an increase in work pressure can occur for their colleagues. The cost and effectiveness of the training is another question: should the organisation pay for skills that the employee does not use when performing their work? And how can the organisation measure the effectiveness of the training? Lastly, the organisation should also look at the total cost. In addition to increased remuneration for the employee, the organisation may also need to increase their training budget. This needs to be measured against the cost of losing people and trying to attract and on-board new people together with the opportunity cost in terms of economic added value if certain vacancies are not filled[62].

In general, the continuous improvement of employees' skills and knowledge is vital for organisations to adapt to a constantly changing environment and stay ahead of the competition. Therefore, integrating a reward system that supports this continuous improvement helps organisations to achieve their long-term strategic goals.

3. Social cohesion

The importance of social relations and teamwork on the workfloor is increasingly acknowledged by employers thanks to teamwork creating alignment in production, supporting mutual learning[63]. Organisations are trying to create a workplace that facilitates social interaction by organising formal and informal team activities[64], for instance, team building events and Christmas and New Year parties. Scientific research also shows an increase in job satisfaction and organisational commitment in organisations with high social cohesion as well as decreasing employee turnover and absenteeism[65].

Reward systems can also be a driver towards more social cohesion within an organisation, but only when the team concept is embedded into the organisation's culture[66]. Social cohesion through reward can be accomplished by implementing a collective reward system which can either be a team-based pay system or a profit-based pay system[67].

In order for teams to be effective, a supportive reward system that recognises the desired behaviour and skills (e.g., cooperation and knowledge sharing), needs to be in place[68]. Therefore, team-based pay can motivate employees to increase their cooperation and align their actions. Good teamwork increases efficiency, productivity and profitability[69].

In a team-based pay system, the chosen reward elements need to align with the characteristics of the team's and the organisation's context[70], and the team division and goals need to be clear for all employees[71].

Special awards can also be distributed to teams that achieved an outstanding performance. Organisations can increase the effectiveness of team-based pay by implementing clear and explicit objectives and metrics in order to determine successful team performance and linking reward to the team performance by providing good feedback[72]. Competition between teams or rewarding individual team members is counterproductive as it leads to a decrease in information sharing and social relations[73].

Unfortunately, there are also some downsides to team incentive plans. The size of the group reduces the visibility of the individual's contribution to the team results, which in turn can reduce the motivational effect[74]. The group results can also be influenced by things outside the team's control[75]. Employees sometimes perceive team incentive as not equitable or they compare themselves with others within the team and overvalue their own contribution to the group results, leading to feelings of unfair treatment when receiving an equal amount as their peers[76]. Team incentives can also trigger free-riding, although this has already been refuted as better social relations between team members limits the presence of free-riders[77]. These downsides can be reduced by also implementing individual pay elements to satisfy the individual recognition[78].

On the other hand, profit-based pay systems are not related to the performance of specific teams but reward the success of the organisation as a whole[79]. Profit-based pay increases the commitment of employees to the organisational goals, which may result in higher performance and social cohesion.

However, employee trust in the organisation's management is of utmost importance for the effectiveness of profit-based reward[80].

With profit-based pay, employees share in the organisations' success via profit sharing plans, gain sharing plans, success-sharing plans and stock ownership plans (see chapter 7 on reward mix). This system, however, has some downsides as employees are not always able to attribute their own performance to the organisation's results and the return is uncertain. Lastly, the delayed consumption of stock options plans can be seen as a loss by the employee and a high enough stock market return is required to compensate for the loss[81].

In some countries, including Belgium, employers also have the possibility to offer their employees various social advantages which can help to increase social cohesion between employees and employer[82]. As non-taxable income, these social advantages are beneficial for employees.

Generally, group and organisational plans are the most efficient ways to establish social cohesion and teamwork, both of which empower employees to benefit from the positive financial results due to increased performance.

4. Avoiding potential pitfalls

Reward systems play a crucial role in attracting and retaining human capital when faced with a shortage of talent. They are also powerful drivers of competence development in employees and can motivate employees to perform to their maximum potential. Additionally reward systems can also be a catalyst of social cohesion within an organisation.

It is important to strike a balance between designing an effective reward system and navigating the complexities that can arise. Some of the potential pitfalls to avoid are discussed below.

4.1. Unclear communication

The objective of a solid remuneration strategy is to attract and retain talent by promoting the organisation as a modern and innovative employer who recognises and values employee input. Reward systems are a sensitive matter, so communication plays a crucial role.

Successful communication about changes in the reward system follows an 8-step approach:

1. Understand the needs of the target audience.
2. Conceptualise, determine and plan communication.
3. Identify the right key messages and manage communication effectively.
4. Utilise appropriate communication tools and channels.
5. Make communication interactive.
6. Develop a network of influencers.
7. Collect feedback and capture ideas.
8. Measure success.

Clarify communication
Any changes to a reward system need to be communicated. If the key messages about the change are unclear, inconsistent or contradictory, employees may struggle to grasp the intended purpose and impact of the change, leading to confusion, resistance and a lack of buy-in.

4.2. Too complex

Albert Einstein said *"If you can't explain it simply, you don't understand it well enough"*, and this also applies to reward systems. If employees do not comprehend their remuneration and/or do not receive adequate support from their employer to gain clarity, they may lose trust in their organisation. HR professionals should be capable of explaining their organisation's reward system and its legal implications in an understandable and straightforward manner. If not, the introduction of complex bonus schemes or another reward system may have a negative impact and become a detractor, even if the intentions are initially good.

Furthermore, by making the reward system too complicated (or not explaining it clearly enough), the organisation runs the risk that certain employees who understand the system well will game the system. Such behaviour should be avoided as it stimulates competition instead of collaboration.

Simplify reward
Every component of the reward system has an appropriate personal income tax and social security treatment. In countries with a high tax burden on labour income (e.g., Belgium, France and Germany)[83], it is challenging to keep the reward system simple while employers search for alternative employee benefits. These benefits often have a divergent parafiscal treatment in comparison to a regular cash payment, potentially leading to confusion from employees. Paying for benefits that employees do not understand - or even worse, are unaware that they are receiving - is never a good idea. Therefore, complexity should be avoided, keeping it manageable for the HR department and understandable for employees.

4.3. Not equitable

The reward system should be designed in such a way that it is internally fair. Individuals compare their own efforts and pay-offs with those of others and negative reactions may occur when expectations are violated. If the system is not sufficiently generous to some employees (especially when compared to others), the first group may become convinced that they are seen as underperformers and might lose motivation.

Besides internal fairness, the reward programme should be market conforming (external fairness), which is discussed in the benchmarking section of chapter 6 on reward architecture.

Equitable for all
A clear illustration of the consequences of an inequitable reward system is a series of experiments conducted by Frans de Waal and his colleagues, which involved capuchin monkeys and unequal reward distribution[84]. In this experiment, two capuchin monkeys are placed in separate cages next to each other and trained to perform a simple task, such as handing a small stone to a researcher. In exchange for completing the task, the monkeys receive a reward. Initially, both monkeys receive cucumber slices as a reward for their task, and they happily participate. However, the experiment takes an interesting turn when one of the monkeys starts receiving a more desirable reward (i.e., grapes) instead of cucumbers for the same task while the other monkey continues to receive cucumbers. When this happens, the monkey receiving cucumbers becomes visibly upset and rejects the cucumber slices by throwing them back at the researcher and, in some cases, even refuses to perform the task. This behaviour is interpreted as a response to inequity. The monkey that sees its counterpart receiving a more valuable reward for the same task reacts negatively to the perceived unfairness of the situation.

4.4. Only cash-driven reward

Making it all about money creates an environment where employees are only driven by extrinsic motivation (see chapter 1).

A variety of reward
Top athletes or renowned artists may quit their profession when they are no longer financially compensated for their performance. However, their dedication does not stem solely from monetary incentives. A significant portion of their satisfaction comes from applause or achieving milestones like an Olympic medal or selling out a world tour. The same principle applies to employees: they work for financial remuneration, but they go the extra mile for appreciation and self-fulfilment.

5. Well-structured reward systems

As we have seen, a well-structured reward system can help businesses to overcome their people-related challenges from an organisational perspective.

With today's shortage of talent, reward systems have a crucial role to play in attracting, recruiting and retaining a talented workforce. Organisations should pay attention to the base salary, as well as to the benefits that attract the employees that employers want to recruit. A strong employer brand can also help the organisation to attract and retain the right people.

The reward system can also drive the development of competences in employees, motivating them to perform to their maximum potential. This is crucial for organisations that want to be future fit when facing the speed of change. An important driver here can be a skill-based pay system that consists of pay progression, bonuses and/or non-financial reward.

A third function is the use of a reward system as a driving force for social cohesion within an organisation. This is an important function as research shows that there are multiple benefits to teamwork between employees, such as increased job satisfaction and organisational commitment, mutual learning and decreased absenteeism. Reward systems can be a catalyst for social cohesion by implementing a team-based pay system consisting of, for example, merit pay systems or bonuses, preferably accompanied by clear and explicit objectives and metrics to determine successful team performance.

3.
The impact of today's world on reward

Key takeaways

1. The immediate and long-term consequences of climate change include the unbalancing of the labour market as climate refugees move to safe harbour regions, which impacts governments, organisations and employees.

2. Driven by revolutionary technologies, technical disruption has both positive and negative implications for organisations and the workforce.

3. Migration influences salary growth by affecting the size and composition of the available labour. It also forces organisations to adapt in order to manage their changing workforce.

4. The fracturing world is marked by increased competition among nation states, reducing international cooperation and creating challenges for organisations.

5. Together these megatrends result in social instability with wealth concentration, polarisation and declining trust in institutions. Addressing these social issues requires redistributive tax systems, as well as inclusive reward systems.

We started by focusing on the people's side of reward, more specifically on how reward can motivate employees in their work. Following this, we shifted the focus to the organisation's side of reward where we analysed how the employer can have a positive impact on people-related challenges with their reward system. Following these insights, the first part of this book concludes with a broader outlook by looking at some large global shifts that are currently reshaping our world and their impact on reward systems.

1. PwC megatrends

Megatrends are profound, global phenomena that have enduring impact, reaching every corner of the world as they shape our collective future for years to come. According to PwC, there are currently five broad megatrends defining the business environment: climate change, technological disruption, demographic shifts, a fracturing world and social instability[85]. While none of these megatrends is new, their magnitude, impact and interdependence are increasing.

1.1. Climate change

Climate change, driven primarily by human activities such as burning fossil fuels and deforestation, is altering the Earth's climate at an unprecedented rate. Understanding the possible concrete consequences for economies and human wellbeing, both in the short-term and long-term, is crucial for determining how this might affect the reward packages of the future.

Figure 9: The five PwC megatrends impacting society and today's business environment.

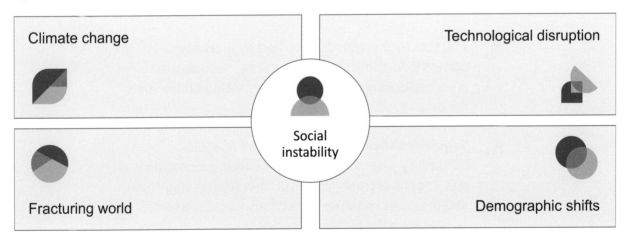

1.1.1. Short-term consequences

We are already being confronted with the first consequences of climate change. Certain regions in the world are facing heatwaves, storms and heavy rainfall with increasing frequency and intensity, leading to the loss of human lives and affecting human health in general, as well as damaging property and infrastructure. For example, heat-related illnesses and deaths during heatwaves, floods and mudslides, and the spread of diseases like malaria and dengue fever as warmer temperatures expand the habitats of disease-carrying organisms.

The agricultural industry is one of the industries already affected, with decreasing returns, lower quality crops and the loss of livestock. Gradually, over time, some regions may no longer be fit for agricultural activities.

1.1.2. Long-term consequences

In the longer term, climate change will threaten low-lying islands and coastal cities due to the rise of the sea level. As saltwater intrudes more and more into freshwater sources, it will affect the competition to secure water, both for drinking and agriculture. With water an important cornerstone for life on earth, the loss of keystone species might cascade through the food webs, potentially leading to the collapse of entire ecosystems.

As a result, mass migrations of climate refugees fleeing from uninhabitable regions due to extreme weather events, rising sea levels and food shortages will affect the labour law market and trigger imbalances in terms of talent demand and supply. This may result in shortages in the workforce in regions under climate distress, which could further affect the viability of the economy and the financial health of governments confronted with falling revenues due to declining tax collection from the remaining workforce. This fall in revenues and economic activity will be particularly damaging when accompanied by an increase in climate related expenses, such as repairing infrastructure and increased healthcare costs.

Regions that qualify as a safe climate harbour might be flooded by climate refugees putting available accommodation and health care systems under pressure. Such a wave of immigration may lead to tension in terms of inclusion and social unrest and increased competition for available jobs due to an oversupply in terms of available workforce.

1.1.3. Moving forward: the role of reward

Starting from these consequences, it is clear that it will be ambiguous how climate change is likely to impact employees' wallets and the type of jobs available to them. In climate distressed regions, both governments and organisations that cannot delocalise might be in a weaker position to attract and retain people. From a reward perspective, this could result in employees needing to be lured with extra premiums (climate premium, hardship allowance, etc.), perks and tax incentives in order to work in less attractive climate regions, further fuelling the climate inflation spiral.

In climate safe harbour regions, employees might be more vulnerable when it comes to their purchasing power. As climate change disrupts resources like food, water and energy, their scarcity can also lead to increased production costs. This often translates to higher prices for goods and services, reducing the purchasing power of employees' salaries. Furthermore, due to the surplus of available people that are willing to work, most of the workforce might be faced with downward pressure in terms of salary and perks compared to the happy few with skills that are still rare to find (e.g., in emerging new jobs and industries focused on sustainability, renewable energy or resource-efficient technologies).

This means that organisations will need to fundamentally rethink how they manage their business, including how they reward people. Again, this impacts the short term. According to a recent PwC survey which polled 4,410 CEOs in 105 countries and territories, inflation is already one of the key threats for the next 12 months[86].

While governments will be affected in terms of the consequences of climate change, they still have a key role to play in mitigating climate change. In this respect, they can use their steering role via tax systems to encourage actions that mitigate the consequences of climate change on society and ecosystems, for example, facilitating the energy transition or implementing works to mitigate flooding.

1.2. Technological disruption

Revolutionary technologies are fuelling disruption, with ongoing technological advancements unfolding at an astonishing pace. Technologies such as (generative) AI, robotics, energy storage, DNA sequencing, blockchain technology and quantum computing will reach their tipping points over the next 5 to 10 years. The implications of this rapid technological change can be positive as well as negative for organisations and the workforce.

Figure 10: The time it took different products and technologies to reach 50 million users[87].

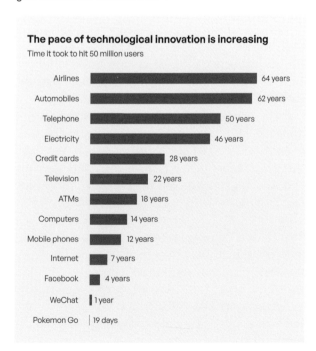

1.2.1. Impact on organisations

Some organisations will not be able to digitally transform and accelerate their execution, leading to failure as they become less relevant to stakeholders and lose customers. However, organisations will be able to differentiate from their competition by using the full power of technology to redefine the value they create for their customers and society at large.

Smaller organisations will find it more difficult to afford the technical investment required to compete in the digital world. In addition to the high initial investment, smaller organisations will also be unable to benefit from the economies of scale that come from an extensive network. In this respect, Belgium is changing its investment deductions, providing an additional tax deduction for investments made in new technologies for small- and medium-sized organisations.

1.2.2. Impact on the workforce

Technological changes will also impact the workforce. On one hand, technology can increase productivity, increasing the employee's added value, but on the other hand, it can partially or completely replace the same employee. While recent developments in Gen AI seem to be very focused on back office activities, the same developments can be used for tasks currently done by more highly-educated people, especially those active in the professional services or financial industry.

In the longer-term this could heavily impact the role of learning and development programmes, as organisations could restart hiring school leavers without a diploma and with limited training needs as long as they could execute their job and related tasks, assisted by Gen AI, instead of employing highly-educated people with a desire to be trained and grow further.

Post Covid-19, working (partially) remotely has become the new normal thanks to technology. In the short term, the renewed work-life balance seems pleasant and is further encouraged via systems like workation. However, this technology makes it easy for organisations to recruit more cheaply from a worldwide talent pool in the longer term. These developments might put an end to the so-called 'war for talent'.

1.2.3. Moving forward: the role of reward

These consequences mean that the technological wave will have an impact on reward as it acts as a catalyst for shifts in the labour market. While automation, in particular, raises significant concerns by jeopardising numerous jobs and exerting downward pressure on salary growth, it is crucial to recognise that reality is more complex[88].

The ECB has determined that digitalisation influences salary growth through various channels, often leading in divergent directions (figure 11). For example, task-biased technological change (TBTC), Gen AI, machine learning and robotics all contribute to the destruction of existing jobs which pushes salaries down, while relatively new jobs that require specific skills have an upward impact on salaries.

Skill-biased technological changes (SBTC) suggest that technological advancements raise the productivity of highly-skilled employees relative to lower-skilled employees, increasing the need for organisations to look for more highly-skilled employees. Such an increase in demand would contribute positively to a salary premium.

Thanks to technology, employers have access to a global talent pool, enabling them to move tasks or jobs abroad or outside the organisation. Technology (i.e., social media) has enabled people to become more impatient as they expect instant gratification. This effect is now more pronounced in the on-demand economy, with labour becoming more flexible and increasingly offshore, which has a negative impact on salaries and increased competition for the spoiled, onshore employees.

Figure 11: The effects of digitalisation on salaries.

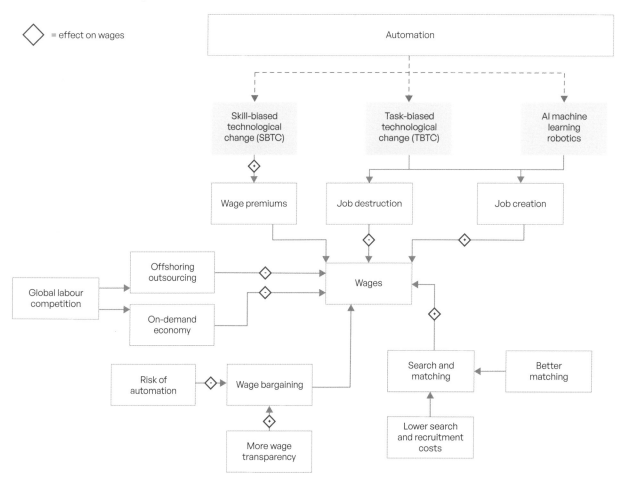

AI and digitalisation lowers search costs and facilitates better matching between employees and employers. CVs are increasingly screened by AI, with ever-improving results thanks to the AI actively learning. If an organisation feels that they have attracted the right talent, they may be willing to pay more from the start, which has a positive impact on salaries.

Finally, there is the effect of increased transparency due to technological enhancements, new regulations, such as the EU's pay transparency directive (PTD), and specific reporting obligations, including S1 from the corporate sustainability reporting directive (CSRD). The PTD aims to close the gap between men and women in terms of equal pay for equal work, putting positive pressure on pay. It also gives employees additional power that might compensate for the risk of automation due to digitalisation which strengthens the employer's position (see chapter 10 for more information on PTD).

There are a lot of factors that influence the impact on salaries. While the overall effect may remain unclear, there will be winners and losers on a micro-level. And, due to the recent evolution in AI, the winners might not be the highly-educated employees.

To end this section on a positive note, AI-driven tools can create personalised learning paths for employees based on their skills, strengths and weaknesses. Such a tailored approach to training and skill development can help employees upskill or re-skill faster, ensuring they are more adaptable to changing job requirements and enhancing their value to employers. It is important to note that motivation and eagerness remain key.

1.3. Demographic shifts

The risk and impact of mass migration of climate refugees was discussed under the climate change megatrend. Today, a lot of EU countries have employment growth thanks to foreign citizens (see figure 12)[89].

Migration has played an important role for labour market development[90], which has influenced salary growth in different ways. For example, migration increases the overall size of the labour force, which may impact salary levels. It can also shift the composition of the workforce, with the differences in skills, ages and generations between migrants and non-migrants affecting salary dynamics. When faced with

Figure 12: Contribution of employees to employment growth by citizenship between the second quarter of 2013 and the first quarter of 2019.

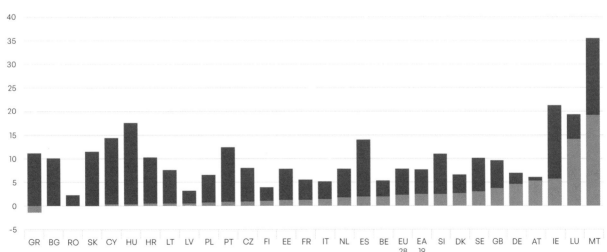

■ Employment growth since Q2 2013 due to foreign citizens ■ Employment growth since Q2 2013 due to citizens of the reporting country

an ageing population or shifts in the generational makeup, organisations need to adapt their strategies to attract, retain and effectively manage their changing workforce. Additionally, an organisation with a low level of diversity or inclusivity risks losing out on the benefits of varied perspectives and experiences, as well as potentially facing legal and reputational consequences.

As well as migration, the ageing population is also a significant demographic shift that poses both challenges and opportunities for organisations worldwide. As life expectancy increases and birth rates decline, the proportion of older adults in the population is steadily rising. This shift has profound implications for various aspects of society, including the labour market where it presents challenges, particularly in terms of workforce supply and productivity. For example, with a larger share of the population reaching retirement age, there is a potential decline in the overall size of the labour force which can lead to labour shortages in certain industries and

sectors, impacting economic growth and productivity levels. Moreover, the ageing workforce brings about changes in the composition of the labour force as older workers often possess valuable skills, knowledge and experience accumulated over their careers. However, they may also face age-related health issues or technological skill gaps that require adaptation and support from employers.

1.3.1. Moving forward: the role of reward

A flexible reward approach may help to meet the differing needs of a multi-generational and diverse workforce. In this respect, different packages can be put together by grouping employees with similar preferences (see figure 13 for an example).

One potential issue for organisations with multi-generational workforces is salary levels. In general, older employees tend to earn higher salaries even though their salary increases tend to slow as they progress through their career. Organisations can significantly change their overall salary costs

Figure 13: An example of grouping employee packages that can be offered to employees with similar preferences for different types of reward.

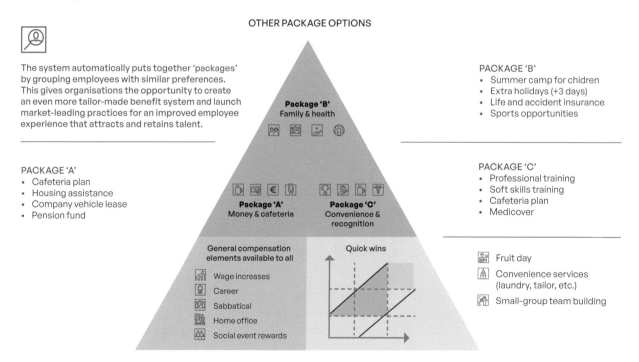

by changing the age makeup of the workforce. For instance, the average hourly salary of an employee aged 60 or above can be over 50% higher than that of an employee aged less than 30[91], so this demographic shift has contributed to the overall growth in average salaries. However, a recent study on the changing composition of the workforce states that the increase in older employees is not a significant factor in explaining why salary growth has been relatively restrained in the eurozone in recent years[92]. This means that this demographic shift requires careful consideration and strategic planning. Organisations must adapt their practices to effectively manage an ageing workforce, leveraging the skills and experience of older employees.

Employee age also impacts reward. As older workers are typically more comfortable when it comes to cash flow (e.g., their mortgages are paid off and their children support themselves), their salary is less of a focus for them. However, older people may value age-friendly policies. By providing flexible work arrangements, specific training opportunities, health and wellbeing programmes and medical checks, employers can tap into the valuable expertise of older employees while addressing their specific needs.

In addition to age-friendly schedules, pension arrangements become extremely valuable in the context of an ageing workforce (see chapter 11 for more information on occupational pension schemes). Pension schemes provide financial security during retirement to allow older employees to maintain their standard of living, support retirement planning which enables older employees to have a sense of control and confidence in their financial future, aid in employee retention as employees approaching pensionable age become more aware of the importance of having a pension plan in place and demonstrate social responsibility by showing that an organisation cares about the financial security and wellbeing of its employees, particularly as they age. By offering a comprehensive pension plan, organisations can effectively address the specific needs of older employees and create a supportive work environment that encourages employees to stay in the labour market.

Indeed, in this context, questions about the impact of early retirement, combined with other safety nets and trends towards shortening the working week, also become relevant. This is because these trends deteriorate the variety of the labour market in terms of the available workforce and create an imbalance between those unwilling to work and those that actually work and contribute to the social safety nets.

1.4. Fracturing world

The world is facing more geostrategic fractures as more nation states compete for influence based on increased selfishness and protectionism. A fracturing world is typically characterised by the rise of populism, nationalism and protectionism. These trends reduce international cooperation, causing countries to fall back on their self-interest with some focusing on their national resilience and local supplies while others build internal capacity and friend-shoring, further shifting power structures.

Doing business in a world of conflicting rules and regulations puts a significant burden on organisations, leading to multiple effects on the labour market such as more organisations facing a downturn due to a decrease in international trade.

The fracturing world may also affect global mobility and talent movement across borders. Increased regulation, such as work permits and taxation that focuses on local first, may hamper future international employment or the migration required to help reduce the mismatch between available and required skills.

On the one hand, there is a trend that people, especially younger generations, are majorly influenced by their location as well as by a borderless, global community supported by disruptive technologies and social media. This virtual space leads to global patterns, rather than local ones. A recent PwC study shows that 58% of the respondents are willing to move abroad for their work or career[93].

However, in terms of overall relative importance, young people are still more interested in career opportunities in organisations in their home country rather than career opportunities abroad. This may help organisations as they transition to embracing alternative delivery models via remote employees in different jurisdictions acting as one team with one purpose. Again one size does not fit all in this context. For example in Türkiye, the same study suggests the opposite is true there as young people are more interested in international opportunities.

1.4.1. Moving forward: the role of reward

In a fracturing world, where economic, social and political systems are becoming increasingly fragmented, organisations face unique challenges in attracting and retaining talent. The role of reward becomes crucial in addressing these challenges and adapting to the changing dynamics of the global landscape. Traditional financial rewards may be less effective, and organisations may need to consider non-financial rewards to motivate and engage employees. There may be a shift towards individual rewards and recognition, rather than collective or team-based reward, so that organisations need to align their reward models with a more individualistic mindset. Reward models may also need to incorporate purpose and values, recognising employees for contributing to a larger mission.

Balancing fairness and equity is crucial in a fracturing world as perceptions of fairness and equity may vary across different groups or individuals. Organisations will need to carefully consider how they design and customise their reward models to

Figure 14: Percentage of respondents interested in moving abroad for their work or career based on the region where they currently reside.

QUESTION : Are you interested in moving abroad for your work/career?

Region	Percentage
Eastern Europe (Russia)	53%
Southeast Europe (Türkiye)	76%
South Africa (Republic of South Africa)	69%
Central Europe (Hungary, Slovakia)	58%
Western and Southwest Europe (Austria, Belgium, the Netherlands, Spain)	58%

ensure they are perceived as fair and equitable, taking into account the diverse perspectives, needs and preferences of their employees.

Moreover, although there is a trend of global patterns and virtual communities supported by available technology, working from anywhere (WFA) and digital nomadism is not encouraged in a fractured world as (tax) regulations are not (yet) adapted and tend to use physical presence as a nexus for taxation, limiting the opportunities for international employment.

On the positive side, this increased regulation and focus on local employment may lead to higher wages and better benefits for workers in their home countries. This could be due to reduced competition from international talent and a greater emphasis on retaining and attracting local talent. Organisations may need to offer more attractive compensation packages to entice skilled workers to stay or return to their home countries. On the negative side, increased regulation and focus on local employment may make it more difficult for individuals to move abroad for work or pursue international career zopportunities. This could restrict the pool of talent available to organisations and limit the diversity of skills and perspectives within teams, and at the same time limit career growth for individuals.

1.5. Social instability

Having learned more about the challenges, changes and corresponding uncertainty in relation to climate change, technological disruption, demographic shifts and a more fracturing world, it is not surprising that these trends feed social instability. Social issues are becoming increasingly prevalent across all facets of our world and daily life. They fall into five areas: asymmetry, disruption, age, polarisation and trust.

Asymmetry comes in different forms, such as money, power and education. With salaries stagnating and the cost of homes rising fast, wealth is increasingly concentrating in the hands of fewer and older people[94], contributing to the generational wealth gap and erosion of the middle class. Poverty, including the number of working poor and those in extreme

poverty, will continue to grow. In this respect, the tax systems of countries must play their redistributive role by taxing all forms of income in a similar way, with the broadest shoulders bearing the heaviest burdens. As we saw in the section on equal pay and the PTD, organisations can contribute to improving this asymmetry by applying a right and transparent reward philosophy that ensures equal pay for equal work, so no frustrations arise at this level.

The gap between individuals, organisations and nations that can adapt to the disruption caused by climate change, technology and other significant events, and those that cannot, will continue to widen. This growing gap poses a particular risk for governments already burdened by pandemic debt, sluggish economic growth and inflation, as they may struggle to meet the evolving needs of their citizens. Similarly organisations will experience an increasing disparity between winners and losers. And individuals who start at a disadvantage will face even greater challenges, while resilience will become a highly valued attribute.

Age poses a challenge across many nations, where those with ageing populations struggle to meet the labour and tax demands associated with an older demographic, while younger economies face difficulties in fulfilling the educational and employment requirements of their youth. This leads to a deepening polarisation in society, with citizens perceiving governmental shortcomings and fostering growing distrust and intolerance towards those perceived as different.

Society experiences a deepening polarisation as individuals perceive their governments as failing them. This growing disillusionment leads to increased distrust and intolerance towards those who are different, exacerbating divisions.

Lastly, as trust in institutions, especially governments and social establishments, continues to decline, governance becomes increasingly complex and fragmented. However, it is crucial to recognise that solving global issues necessitates a foundation of trust in these institutions.

Regardless of the cause, social instability often contributes to burn/bore out. To give a few examples of this connection:

- Economic uncertainty: Recessions, job insecurity, income inequality or other forms of economic instability can contribute to burnout as individuals may experience heightened stress, fear and pressure to perform in uncertain economic conditions.

- Work-life imbalance: In times of social unrest or political turmoil, individuals may feel compelled to work longer hours, take on additional responsibilities or constantly stay connected to work to secure their livelihoods. This work-life imbalance can lead to burnout due to chronic stress and lack of time for self-care.

- Social disconnection: Social instability can erode social support systems, disrupt relationships and create feelings of isolation. When individuals lack a strong support network, they may experience increased stress and emotional exhaustion, which are key components of burnout.

- Organisational instability: In times of social unrest, companies may face challenges such as layoffs, restructuring or changes in leadership. These organisational disruptions can create a sense of uncertainty, mistrust and job insecurity among employees, contributing to burnout.

- Mental health impact: Mental health can be significantly impacted by social instability, resulting in increased rates of anxiety, depression and other mental health disorders. Burnout is closely linked to mental health issues, as prolonged stress and emotional strain can lead to exhaustion, cynicism and reduced effectiveness at work.

1.5.1. Moving forward: the role of reward

Social instability often stems from the perception of unfair wealth distribution and income inequality. While reward is unlikely to solve social instability on its own, reward systems can be designed to address part of these concerns by ensuring fair remuneration practices, promoting pay equity and providing opportunities for upward mobility. By addressing income disparities through fair reward structures, organisations can contribute to reducing social tensions and promoting stability.

Social instability can also be fuelled by factors such as job insecurity, lack of work-life balance and inadequate support systems. Reward systems that prioritise employee wellbeing, such as comprehensive healthcare benefits, flexible work arrangements and mental health support, can help alleviate some of these concerns. In this respect, the focus should switch from financial reward to total reward and ultimately to total wellbeing.

The connection between social instability and burnout underscores the importance of total wellbeing. By addressing physical, mental, emotional and social aspects of wellbeing, individuals can better cope with the effects of social instability, reduce burnout and enhance their overall quality of life. Chapter 7 sheds more light on this.

Lastly, social instability often arises from divisions and intolerance within societies. Reward systems that promote diversity and inclusion can help bridge these divides by recognising and valuing individuals from different backgrounds, perspectives and experiences.

2. Aligning reward systems with business strategy

While the impacts and implications of the PwC megatrends discussed should not be underestimated, it is also important to ensure that an organisation's reward system is carefully managed in order for it to be successful and effective.

This means carefully considering the design, implementation and evaluation methods of the reward system and integrating it in the larger business context so it aligns with the business strategy and organisational goals. Reward systems are doomed to fail when they are taken off the shelf and simply implemented rather than developed specifically to meet the needs of the organisation and continuously managed afterwards[95].

3. Flexible reward strategies

As organisations start to realise the consequences of the demographic shifts as explained above, they are forced to find ways to adapt in order to stay in business. This includes adapting the way they attract and retain talent. While we have seen that reward systems are an effective way forward, it doesn't mean that the same reward system will always continue to work for an organisation. It remains crucial for organisations to reassess their total reward system to harmonise with the actual market situation and how it will potentially change. When rethinking reward systems, it is vital to consider several aspects, including ways to implement a tailored and flexible approach, how and when to upskill employees, ways to improve employee satisfaction and how to measure and monitor the organisation's unique situation.

3.1. A tailored and flexible approach

In today's constantly changing world, it is important to have a flexible reward strategy. Introducing a flexible income plan reflects the recognition that a one-size-fits-all approach to remuneration may not meet the diverse needs and preferences of a modern workforce. Offering a flexible income plan can also be a competitive advantage in attracting and retaining top talent.

At the same time, we should remember that some flexible reward practices are implemented solely because they are considered to be the next best practice, an attempt to increase tax efficiency and/or because other firms in the industry offer them. Instead, flexible reward should be embedded in and driven by the firm's external and internal business contexts. This implies that a strategic reward management perspective is needed to guide decision making about flexible reward plans and that flexibility is an important tool from a strategic reward perspective[96].

3.2. To upskill or not to upskill?

The world is constantly changing. The type of workforce required has also evolved rapidly. Many jobs are changing or becoming redundant as automation, data analysis, AI and other emerging technologies increasingly deliver productivity. But technology is only as good as the leaders who identify its opportunities, the technologists who deliver it and the people who work with it every day. That's where some organisations are coming up short: they need the right mix of skilled and adaptable people, aligned to the right culture and with the right mindset and behaviours to help power the business. Employers who make good-faith efforts to upskill their people build trust, which in turn can enhance the organisation's reputation in a world where trust is an increasingly valuable commodity.

3.3. Happy employees serve happy clients

We live in times of uncertainty, disruption and increased stress. The way that people are able to cope with this directly impacts productivity levels and how well people are able to work. This means that wellbeing is of vital importance to the C-suite. Wellbeing policies and behaviours should be factored into every aspect of the employee experience, starting at recruitment and extending to everyday ways of working, collaborating and living.

Happiness is another driver for better performance as happy employees are more likely to be motivated, take ownership and deliver better work. While it is not the role nor the responsibility of the employer to make employees happy, they should create an environment where employees can thrive and excel. This type of environment has the added benefit of protecting and safeguarding mental health.

3.4. Through measurement to knowledge

Being successful is not about offering more than the competition. It's about understanding the organisation, its strategy and, especially, its workforce.

As mentioned above, using a one-size-fits-all approach to work-related preferences is no longer a winning strategy. A winning employee value proposition (EVP) is a tailored proposition that enables organisations to successfully and effectively attract and retain the right talent.

It is therefore key to know and measure what employees want to work for. Better data about workforce preferences will lead to better decisions on cost and value. Nobel Prize winning Dutch physicist Kamerlingh Onnes used the phrase "*through measurement to knowledge*" and this also applies to all workforces.

Listening to employees, e.g., by conducting a preference study or even a short pulse survey, provides organisations with valuable insights into what employees are looking for on the labour market. This type of future-focused and predictive performance data often requires a shift in the type of data organisations collect and how it is used internally, but it pays off with better decisions, lower costs and increased engagement, giving organisations a competitive advantage when attracting and retaining talent. We will come back to this in chapter 7 on reward mix.

4. Transforming our world

Climate change, technical disruption, demographic shifts, fracturing world, and social instability: this chapter has focused on how our world is being transformed by investigating the megatrends that society is currently facing. While none of them are new, their impact and interconnectedness are increasing all the time and have, and will continue to have, a huge impact on our personal and work lives, including the reward systems that organisations offer employees.

However, there is a way forward. Each of these megatrends offers organisations opportunities to achieve their future ambitions by implementing a tailored and flexible reward system that appeals to potential and existing employees as happy employees are more productive and motivated.

An attractive reward system can also be cost efficient, as employees often find flexibility in their reward system to be more important than simply receiving a larger salary although a competitive base salary is a must have in terms of hygiene factor. This is why it is vital for the organisation's reward system to align fully with its business strategy and goals. Disillusioned employees will leave, taking their talent, skills and knowledge with them.

Attractive and compelling reward packages

4.
Creating
a reward system

The five pillar approach

1. **Reward scope**

2. **Reward architecture**

3. **Reward mix**

4. **Reward in transactions**

5. **Reward in different types of organisations**

In the first part of this book, we looked into reward: its importance (chapter 1), function and role in organisations today (chapter 2) and in the future (chapter 3).

Here in the second part, we focus on how to create a reward system that works for both organisation and employees, giving employers a competitive advantage in the market.

Creating a comprehensive reward system involves designing a structured system that recognises and reinforces positive behaviours within the organisation. It needs to motivate individuals while contributing to a productive organisational culture.

Five strategic elements, or pillars, form the foundation of every successful reward system. Each pillar plays a crucial role in shaping a reward system that aligns with the organisation's goals, values and broader external context.

Addressing each pillar thoughtfully ensures that the reward system is well-structured, fair and effective in driving positive behaviours and contributing to a positive organisational culture. This chapter gives a brief overview of these five pillars, with more in-depth information on each pillar in the following chapters.

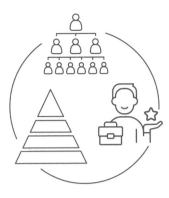

1. Reward scope

The first pillar to consider when implementing a new reward strategy is the scope. Are all employees eligible or is the programme focused on specific levels, for example, top executives or middle managers? Regardless of how broad or narrow the scope is, it is important to pay attention to differentiation and equality. Read more on reward scope in chapter 5.

Figure 15: The scope of beneficiaries for broad and narrow reward packages.

2. Reward architecture

3. Reward mix

Another important pillar when building a reward strategy is its structure. This includes the internal architecture and the external positioning.

Internally, organisations need to investigate their current reward structure and how this structure fits with their job roles. This helps to ensure equal pay for equal work or work of equal value throughout the organisation. And externally, organisations use benchmarking to compare the organisation's situation with their competitors' employees within the same region or industry.

By investigating reward, both internally and externally, organisations can be certain that their reward system is built on a firm foundation, ready for the future. This is explained in more detail in chapter 6.

After deciding who benefits from the reward system and how to structure it, the next pillar to consider is the reward mix to offer employees.

This balance of tangible and intangible, or financial and non-financial, reward makes up the organisation's employee value proposition (EVP), in other words, the unique set of benefits and experiences that employees receive in return for the skills, capabilities and experience they bring to the organisation. It is vital for organisations to reframe their EVP so they stand out from the crowd and attract and retain employees.

Over time, we have seen the EVP move from purely financial reward to total reward, which incorporates both financial and non-financial benefits such as development, training, flexibility and recognition. Just offering total reward is not enough for organisations to stand out in the competitive marketplace for talent. Increasingly, potential employees are demanding more, which highlights the importance of the move from total reward to total wellbeing.

To find out more about how to create a total reward blueprint for a reward system, turn to chapter 7 on reward mix.

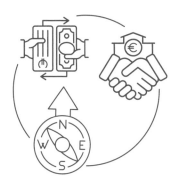

4. Reward in transactions

The fourth pillar looks at the need to do something new: in other words, what is driving this new or adapted reward strategy?

By better understanding the transactional context and clearly identifying the driving forces behind the change, the reward system can be tailored to address specific organisational challenges and objectives, such as motivating and retaining executives during an M&A, corporate spin-off or private equity investment.

Reward in transactions is covered in more detail in chapter 8.

5. Reward in different types of organisations

The last pillar concerns how to structure the reward system and the impact of the organisation's structure on it.

Designing an effective reward system necessitates a thoughtful consideration of the organisational structure, recognising that the chosen model can significantly impact the overall reward strategy.

Chapter 9 discusses the complexity of crafting a tailored approach for partnerships and the distinction between quoted and unquoted entities.

5.
Reward scope

Key takeaways

1. The identification of the reward scope is crucial to create a difference between a broad-based and narrow-based reward programme.

2. A tailored reward approach for executives requires specific diligence.

3. There is a shift from a 'pay for performance' to a 'pay for sustainability' approach.

4. Board members' remuneration should reflect their time commitment and responsibilities.

5. Transparency, including remuneration disclosure, is crucial for building trust among stakeholders.

This chapter focuses on the first of the five pillars for (re-)designing a reward programme: identifying the reward scope. When developing a reward strategy, one of the primary questions to address is the scope. Are all employees eligible for reward (broad based), or is the programme focused on specific levels within the organisation, such as top executives (narrow based)? However, before diving into how to link reward complexity to the scope, we start by looking at important foundations like equal pay for equal work, employee preferences and balancing constraints and considerations.

1. The foundations of reward scope

1.1. Equal pay for equal work

The baseline should always be equal pay for equal work. Arbitrary distinctions between the same level or categories of employees is a justifiable source of frustration and forbidden by anti-discrimination labour laws.

While most leaders are convinced that they compensate their employees fairly, a deeper delve into their HR data may reveal areas for improvement, often triggered by an unconscious bias and unbalanced representation within the organisation.

Being an equal pay for equal work employer is important for the organisation's future, especially as Generation Z and Millennials frequently express concern about this issue. Additionally, creating a sustainable workforce is a key component of the 'social' in environmental, social and governance (ESG), which is currently highly scrutinised by investors and shareholders. For more information on the legislation related to equal pay and pay transparency, see chapter 10.

1.2. Listen to the workforce

As we discussed in chapter 1 on motivational theories, listening to the workforce ensures the developed reward system takes into account the preferences and needs of employees from all generations. While an organisation is unable to please everyone all the time due to budgetary constraints, practical considerations or management decisions, it should develop a reward system that fits its employees, and not vice versa.

1.3. Balance constraints and considerations

Certain groups of employees require a tailored reward approach due to unique constraints and consideration. For example, remuneration for executives in industries like banking and insurance face limitations to curb excessive variable remuneration for identified staff members whose professional activities significantly impact the organisation's risk profile. In these cases, more emphasis is placed on the fixed component of their remuneration (see chapter 12 for more information specific to the banking and insurance industries).

As the section on narrow-based strategies below explains, executive remuneration should align with responsibilities and market competitiveness, and comprise fixed (base salary and benefits) and variable (short-term and long-term incentives) components. Incentives play a crucial role in talent retention, motivating high-profile executives to influence the organisation's strategic direction and achieve certain KPIs. Variable remuneration should connect reward to overall and individual performance, aligning executives' interests with sustainable value creation.

Media scrutiny often questions exorbitant C-level executive payments, sparking a reflection on perceived value in different roles. Consider who holds greater value, the star player of a football club who scores the decisive goal in the Champions League or the CEO of a pharmaceutical organisation that is introducing a life-saving medicine to the market. There is no right or wrong answer here, it is all a matter of perspective.

In addition to the points discussed above, it is crucial to determine the scope of the reward system. Is the organisation considering implementing a broad focused strategy that covers all employees? A narrower strategy for top executives? Or some combination of the two? Deciding on the scope will influence the chosen approach and final solution.

2. Broad-based reward strategies

Broad-based reward strategies apply different remuneration components to a broad range of people within an organisation. Even though these remuneration components are often the same, it is still possible to differentiate in terms of amounts or levels. Furthermore, the actual payout is not static thanks to the evolution of fixed components, such as base salary, as well as the inclusion of profit share schemes and other variable components.

This section starts by investigating base salary and its evolution, before looking at other aspects that influence employee remuneration, including collective bargaining agreements and profit participation. This discussion of broad based reward strategies finishes by reviewing some ways that an organisation can be flexible and differentiate itself from its competition.

2.1. Base salary and its evolution

A fixed base salary is the starting point of almost all reward systems, ensuring that employees can financially meet their fundamental needs in their daily lives. As life gets more expensive, the evolution of base salary plays an important role in protecting the financial wellbeing of employees in terms of their purchasing power. However, the cost of these basic needs is volatile and inflation plays an important role in the current economic landscape. When faced with inflation, it is logical to expect that the base salary would be subject to a positive evolution, possibly with a lagging effect, to protect households' purchasing power.

Countries in north-west Europe follow a similar pattern concerning average salary levels. Within the EU, Greece is an outlier to this pattern, as can be seen in figure 16. This clearly illustrates that the average wage level has increased significantly over an eleven-year period. The wages in Luxembourg show the largest increase of more than 30%, closely followed by Germany at a little under 30%. Belgium completes the top three, with an increase of almost 25%. As a comparison, Greece saw a decrease in average salary levels during the same period, linked to the Greek debt crisis and the corresponding impact on the economic activity of the country.

Figure 16: The evolution of average salary levels in various countries, 2012-2022 based on OECD figures.[97].

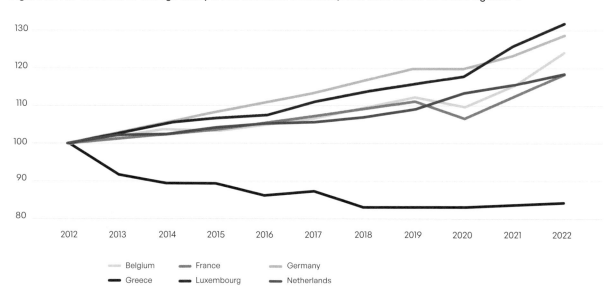

2.1.1. Inflation

Inflation occurs when there is a broad increase in the prices of goods and services, resulting in the same amount of money buying fewer goods or services in the future. In other words, inflation reduces the value of currency over time.

How is inflation measured?

The cost of the average basket of goods and services consumed by the average household annually is calculated as the rate of inflation. This takes into account that every household has different habits and priorities, resulting in a different spending pattern and includes everyday items (food, petrol), durable goods (clothing, electronics) and services (insurance, rent, haircuts). To measure inflation, the cost of the basket is compared to the cost of the basket one year prior.

Consumer price inflation in the euro-zone is measured by the harmonised index of consumer prices (HICP) which was introduced in 1997 to streamline inflation percentages and make data comparable between EU member states. The HICP is also used by the European Central Bank (ECB) for its monetary policy.

The impact of indexation on salary

When it comes to indexation and salaries, the ECB states that "*Formal wage indexation can be defined as the presence of clauses in laws or contracts whereby wages (either public or private) are to a large degree automatically linked to price developments*"[98]. However, the ECB also believes that it is risky to have automatic indexing as it could affect the country's aim of reaching price stability.

In practice, there are three possible approaches to indexing salary to inflation:

1. Retrospective or backward-looking indexation
   This is the most common approach and the easiest to calculate. In this case, salaries are adjusted based on the observed rates of inflation. This means that there is always a lag in maintaining the feeling of a consistent level of income.
2. Forward-looking indexation
   Used in Estonia and Slovenia, this approach adjusts salaries based upon a forecast of future inflation.
3. Combination
   Finland, Ireland, and Italy use a combination of the first two approaches. Indexation is based upon a forecast of future inflation, but it is also corrected for the past level of inflation in case the forecast is too high or low.

In addition to these three approaches to indexing salary to inflation, the euro-zone has four salary indexation methods, ranging from countries where inflation plays no formal role in salary setting to countries that apply automatic salary indexation.

The most extreme influence of indexation on salary setting can be found in countries that automatically apply salary indexation to counteract the effects of inflation and safeguard the purchasing power of their households. Other countries, including Belgium, Cyprus and Luxembourg, have a semi-automatic system. In Cyprus and Luxembourg, indexation is linked to the national index, excluding increases in indirect taxes for Cyprus. The Belgian system is a little different (see box on the next page).

The second option is to take the inflation benchmark into account when automatically indexing salaries to guide salary negotiations. Compared to the first option, this is less widespread across Europe. In Finland and Spain the indexation of salaries is generally included in collective salary agreements. This has resulted in inflation having a less direct and guaranteed impact on salary than the first option. Finland uses the forward-looking indexation method, but allows the possibility of an intervention if there is an unforeseen increase in the national index. While in Spain, the indexation of salaries is foreseen by industry salary agreements, where salaries are retroactively adjusted upwards if the national consumer price index (CPI) exceeds the government reference rate.

The third option is to use automatic salary indexation within a limited scope so it only applies to those who are the most vulnerable for price increases, i.e., the lowest income households. This option is used in France, Malta and Slovenia.

The last option is that inflation has no formal impact on salaries. This method is used in the European countries not mentioned above.

Indexation in Belgium

In Belgium, all employee salaries are indexed based on a four-month floating average of the so-called health index. This is the national index, excluding elements that harm the health of households. In practice this means that products like alcohol, tobacco and car fuels are excluded (see figure 17).

The four-month period was chosen in order to avoid indexing salaries and causing sudden and coincidental shocks of the index. Even though the calculation method is the same, not all employees in Belgium see their salaries indexed

at the same moment in time. Two distinctive methods currently exist.

The first method is used for public servants, as well as around 40% of private industry employees. When the 2% trigger index is exceeded in a given month, salaries are increased by 2% (for civil servants the increase takes place two months after the moment of the exceedance).

The second method indexes salaries at fixed, predetermined moments, either (bi)-monthly, quarterly, half yearly or annually.

Figure 17: Monthly evolution of inflation showing the difference between the Belgian national consumer price index and the health index[99].

Year-on-year growth rates in %, the values in the white area are forecasts

2.1.2. Other factors impacting wage evolution

Inflation is not the only factor that plays a role in the evolution of base salaries. Other factors like competitiveness, productivity and profitability, as well as tax and social security aspects are all important. In this section we will briefly touch upon these factors.

The first factor that can impact wage evolution is the level of salary competitiveness and average increases in neighbouring countries. This is a vital factor to consider during negotiations to determine salary levels in smaller countries such as Belgium, Cyprus, Estonia, Finland, Greece, Ireland, Luxembourg and Norway.

Setting salary norms in Belgium
In Belgium, the salary norm is set by the employer and employee union representatives. To preserve competitiveness, this uses an estimated salary increase in neighbouring countries as an indication of the maximum increase for Belgium. However, it is important to note that the Belgian system has automatic indexation, which is not present in neighbouring countries. If the social partners are unable to find a common ground for the salary increases, the government can intervene and determine the so-called salary norm.

A second factor is productivity and profitability. When examining the impact of productivity and profitability on wage evolution we can distinguish three groups. Firstly, countries that consider productivity in the economy as a whole, such as Cyprus, France and Germany. Secondly, countries that take the industry into account, for example Belgium, Estonia, Germany and the Netherlands. Other countries have a more limited view and pay attention to the employer's own performance when determining whether employees will receive a salary increase. In most cases, the level at which productivity developments are taken into account is consistent with the levels agreed upon in collective agreements.

By looking at the total impact of the above factors on wage evolution, we notice that these elements can't account for the entire impact. According to an ECB white paper, the final factor to consider is the role that policy makers, either intentionally or unintentionally, can play in the wage setting process[100]. For example, changes in taxation and social contributions are often considered to be triggers for salary negotiations.

Changing taxation legislation and income
In Belgium the taxation legislation for copyright income was significantly amended at the end of 2022. The scope of the updated regulations has been dramatically reduced, with a large impact on the beneficiaries of this type of income. As the average tax pressure on these individuals substantially increases, a lot of employees have requested a salary increase in order to maintain the same net income they had prior to the change in legislation.

2.2. Collective bargaining agreements

A collective bargaining agreement (CBA) is typically an agreement negotiated and concluded between one or more trade union organisations and either one or more employers' organisations or one or more employers. They establish individual and collective working rules between employers and employees in an organisation and/or industry. The CBA also aims to regulate the rights and duties of different stakeholders[101].

CBA procedures are used across most of Europe, including Belgium[102], and play an important role with respect to broad-based remuneration. The length of these CBA procedures also has an impact on salary rigidity or flexibility, with longer procedures leading to more rigid wages and differences between European jurisdictions[103].

This type of agreement is all about collective bargaining, collective targets and collective gain sharing between the employer and employees, irrespective of the organisation's profits. This constitutes the main difference between collective bargaining agreements and profit participation, which is the next broad-based reward strategy that we look at.

The collective bargaining agreement 90 (CBA90), a well-known agreement within the Belgian labour and tax landscape, illustrates the importance of CBA on broad-based remuneration in Belgium. Since January 1, 2008, CBA90 introduced a system of non-recurring result-linked benefits, enabling employers to grant bonuses in a tax-friendly manner to their employees based on the achievement of collective objectives during a certain time period.

There are some rules regarding the implementation of the CBA90 bonus. For example, it needs to be granted to all employees within the same category when they achieve a collective (not individual) target which is definable, transparent, measurable and verifiable. Furthermore, the possibilities for the target are broad, but cannot be something that will clearly be achieved when the CBA90 bonus is established to avoid disguising a classic cash bonus as a CBA90 bonus[104]. It is also interesting that the CBA90 bonus does not have to be 'all or nothing', instead it can be partially paid, depending on how much of the initial target is achieved.

The CBA90 bonus scheme is very popular in the Belgian market thanks to the transparency of its targets and the tax optimisation approach. In 2021, 12.7% of employees in Belgium received a CBA90 bonus. This percentage rose to 13.9% in 2022 before falling slightly to 12.9% in 2023[105].

Figure 18 illustrates the financial differences between a classic cash bonus and a CBA90 bonus. The cash bonus is subject to employee social security contributions (13.07% uncapped), employer social security contributions (+/- 27.5% uncapped) and income tax (53.5% which is the 50% taxes plus the estimated 7% local taxes, after the deduction of the employee social security contributions). This gives the employee a gross to net ratio of 40.42%. The CBA90 bonus, because of its tax friendly characteristics, allows a gross to net ratio of 86.93% for employees.

While these figures speak for themselves, the CBA90 bonus is not a magical solution due to the maximum threshold foreseen by the law and the collective agreement required to start the process. However, it is an interesting option when employers are willing to increase the purchasing power of their workforce while minimising the tax burden of the benefit. This example clearly shows how collective bargaining agreements play a role in relation to broad-based remuneration and how they can impact employees' net salary.

Figure 18: Cash bonus versus CBA90 bonus: a comparison of the gross to net ratio.

	Cash bonus	CBA90 bonus**
Total costs employer*	€1,275.00	€1,330.00
Employer social security contributions (estimate)	-€275.00	-
Employer contribution CBA90	-	-€330.00
Gross bonus	€1,000.00	€1,000.00
Less: employee social security contributions (13.07%)	-€130.70	-
Less: solidarity contribution (13.07%)	-	-€130.70
Sub-total: taxable income	€869.30	€869.30
Less: Belgian income taxes (estimated at 53.5%)	-€465.08	-
Net for the employee	€404.22	€869.30
Ratio employer costs/net	31.70%	65.36%
Ratio gross employee/net	40.42%	86.93%
Holiday pay on variable remuneration (15.67%)	Yes	No

* The total cost for the employer is determined in order for the employee to get a gross bonus of €1,000.00

** Limited to a net amount of €3,496.00 (i.e., gross amount of €4,020.00 for income year 2024). Amount indexed every year.

2.3. Profit participation

Profit participation enables the organisation to share part of its profits with its employees during a specific financial year without the employees being a shareholder of the organisation itself.

Profit sharing can be seen as an effective way to motivate and retain employees, as well as helping to attract key new talents. As a tool, it aligns the organisation's and employees' interests, creating a sense of ownership among the workforce to promote employee retention. It is also a successful tool for the organisation's long-term growth.

Obviously, this depends on the conditions associated with the profit sharing process, which should be scrutinised per country. It is also important to note that in order to meet these objectives, the profit sharing scheme must be supported by a beneficial tax rate and/or social security contribution in comparison with the employees' normal salary.

Profit participation is often considered to be an alternative to using standard indexation to reduce the salary gap and increase the purchasing power of employees in an optimised way.

While the theory behind profit participation schemes is positive, there are some practical downsides that are found in almost all organisations that voluntarily apply it. As it is a collective scheme, these downsides include a lack of flexibility as it is not tailored to individual employees or executives, nor is it suitable for some groups of employers. However, as a profit participation scheme, the organisation can only distribute profits if there are any, which aligns employee interests with that of the organisation. If the organisation does not have any distributable profits, there is no profit participation bonus.

This type of bonus benefits both organisations and employees. A profit participation scheme can enable organisations to promote an atmosphere of trust and transparency within the workplace by rewarding their employees in a simple and flexible way through a bonus, which represents either a sum of money or a percentage of either their remuneration or the distributable profit, without granting them voting rights in the organisation. By means of a profit participation scheme, employees feel that their commitment to the organisation is strengthened and they are encouraged to remain invested in the long-term success of the organisation (for at least as long as the organisation continues to be profitable).

However, a profit participation bonus can only be set up for all employees, each of whom receive an equal amount or an equal percentage of their remuneration. Some modulations are possible within the framework of the law, enabling organisations to adapt the amounts for predetermined objective categories of employees.

Profit participation in Belgium, France and Luxembourg
In France and Luxembourg, there are differing approaches to profit participation. In 2021 Luxembourg introduced rules for profit sharing schemes ('prime participative'), where organisations can give a premium to employees, with 50% tax exemption under certain conditions. As the premium is paid at the employer's sole discretion, it is not mandatory[106].

Profit participation in France ('la participation') enables an organisation to distribute part of its profits to its employees in a tax optimised way. The scheme aims to collectively guarantee employees the right to share in the organisation's profit. Unlike in Belgium and Luxembourg, this scheme is compulsory for organisations with more than 50 employees (implemented via a collective bargaining agreement) and optional for smaller organisations.

Belgium's updated profit participation laws from January 1, 2018, aim to improve the purchasing power of employees by enabling organisations to motivate their employees with a bonus that is attractive from a tax and social security perspective. Furthermore, by linking the bonus to profit, the legislation also encourages further business development[107].

Unlike CBA90, profit participation can only happen if the organisation is profitable during the specified financial year and, therefore, is

dependent on the shareholders' decision after the financial year has been closed. However, profit participation is more flexible than CBA90 as it does not require collective bargaining. Belgian organisations can implement both schemes simultaneously, as the targets and objectives are not linked to each other. Even so, profit participation is less popular than the CBA90 bonus, with 1.9% of employees benefiting from profit participation in 2023 compared to 12.9% who received a CBA90 bonus[108].

Profit participation payments are not subject to normal social security contributions, but to an employee solidarity contribution of 13.07% (there is no employer social security contribution due). The residual amount (after deduction of the employee solidarity contribution of 13.07%) is only subject to taxation of 7.00%. As illustrated in figure 19, the classic cash bonus is subject to employee social security contributions (13.07% uncapped), employer social security contributions (+/- 27.5% uncapped) and income tax (53.5% which is the 50% taxes plus the estimated 7% local taxes, after the deduction of the employee social security contributions). This gives the employee a gross to net ratio of 40.42%. The profit participation bonus, thanks to its 7.00% tax rate, allows a gross to net ratio of 80.84% for employees. This makes it a good alternative or a complement to a classic cash bonus even though there are differing conditions for each.

Figure 19: Cash bonus versus profit participation: a comparison of the gross to net ratio.

	Cash bonus	Profit participation**
Total costs employer*	€1,275.00	€1,250.00
Employer social security contributions (estimate)	-€275.00	-
Non deductibility corporate income tax	-	-€250.00
Gross bonus	€1,000.00	€1,000.00
Less: employee social security contributions (13.07%)	-€130.70	-
Less: solidarity contribution (13.07%)	-	-€130.70
Sub-total: taxable income	€869.30	€869.30
Less: Belgian income taxes (estimated at 53.5%)	-€465.08	-
Less: assimilated taxes (7%)	-	-€60.85
Net for the employee	€404.22	€808.45
Ratio employer costs/net	31.70%	64.68%
Ratio gross employee/net	40.42%	80.84%
Holiday pay on variable remuneration (15.67%)	Yes	No

* The total costs for the employer is determined in order for the employee to get a gross bonus of €1,000.00

** The premium is limited to 30% of the total salary mass per person (i.e., the personnel costs included in section 102 'personnel cost' of the social balance sheet).

2.4. Flexibility vs differentiation

While this section has focused on broad based reward strategies, employers often notice that one size fits nobody. As they are pushed to remain an attractive employer, organisations are looking to differentiate themselves from the competition. In this respect it is important to understand the differences between offering flexibility and applying differentiation.

2.4.1. Flexibility in employee reward
This refers to the adaptability of the reward system to accommodate individual preferences and needs even if the reward component that is made flexible is considered a broad based reward component[109].

It acknowledges that employees have diverse motivations, priorities and preferences, and aims to provide a range of options that cater to these variations. A flexible reward system allows employees to choose from a menu of reward components or benefits, such as time-off options, mobility options (e.g., public transport, bicycle or company car) and/or additional insurance coverage. Moreover, flexibility in where and when the work is performed is also regarded as an important benefit or differentiator to attract and retain employees.

The main benefits of flexibility are:

- Personalisation
  Flexibility allows employees to tailor their reward to align with their personal and professional goals, fostering a sense of individuality and personal connection with the organisation. Employers can use personalisation to become more inclusive e.g., allowing employees with different ages or backgrounds to tailor their package to their needs.
- Increased satisfaction
  When employees have the autonomy to select a reward that resonates with their needs, they are more likely to feel valued and satisfied, which contributes positively to their overall job satisfaction. Often employees view the fact that they are offered flexibility as more positive than the actual choice itself.
- Adaptability
  As employee preferences evolve over time, a flexible reward system adapts to changing needs, ensuring that the organisation remains responsive to the dynamic nature of its employees. In the absence of flexibility, a change in a reward package often occurs when changing roles or employer.

2.4.2. Differentiation in employee reward

Differentiation, on the other hand, involves customising reward based on performance, skills or contribution levels. It recognises that not all employees contribute to the organisation in the same way and at the same level. A differentiated reward system tailors reward and recognition to the specific achievements and efforts of each employee, creating a sense of fairness and meritocracy.

The main benefits of differentiation are:

- Motivational impact
  Recognising and rewarding high performers with differentiated reward can serve as a powerful motivator, encouraging employees to excel and contribute their best to the organisation.
- Fairness
  Differentiation ensures that reward is distributed based on merit, promoting a fair and transparent system that fosters a culture of accountability and performance.

- Strategic alignment
  By aligning reward with organisational goals and priorities, differentiation helps reinforce desired behaviours and outcomes, driving the overall success of the organisation.

3. Narrow-based reward strategies

While broad-based reward strategies focus on all employees regardless of level, narrow-based reward strategies are directed at a select group of high-level individuals within the organisation, typically executives, directors and other key people. This type of strategy is usually designed to align the interests of these key decision makers with the overall success of the organisation.

Executives and directors typically bear a higher level of responsibility for the organisation's performance and strategic direction. As a result, their remuneration may include a larger component of variable pay, such as performance-based incentives, stock options and bonuses linked to the organisation's financial and sustainable performance. The structure of the reward system is often competitive to ensure that the organisation can secure and keep individuals with critical leadership skills.

The information below on narrow-based reward strategies has been inspired by the corporate governance principles applicable to quoted organisations, as well as the trends observed in PwC's annual executive remuneration surveys[110]. While executives' remuneration in unquoted organisations is not bound by the same regulations, the remuneration practices observed in quoted organisations can be considered to be benchmarks or best practices for them.

3.1. Executive remuneration

3.1.1. Reviewing remuneration

Responsible remuneration governance practices require the organisation to remunerate board members and executives fairly and responsibly[111]. Following the advice of the Remuneration Committee when required, the remuneration policy adopted by the board should be designed to achieve the following objectives:

- Attract, reward and retain the required talent;
- Promote the achievement of strategic objectives in accordance with the organisation's risk appetite and behavioural norms; and
- Boost sustainable value creation.

In addition, the board should ensure that the remuneration policy is consistent with the organisation's overall reward system. It is also important to note that executive remuneration is subject to increasing scrutiny by various stakeholders. Executive remuneration often gets significant attention from the media, especially when the level of remuneration is perceived as excessive or disconnected from the organisation's performance, as it may aggravate issues of remuneration fairness, negatively influence public sentiment and impact the organisation's reputation.

For quoted organisations[112], the revised EU Shareholders Rights Directive (SRD II) introduced the shareholders' right to vote on the executive remuneration packages offered by the organisation (the so-called Say on Pay). Shareholders have the opportunity to express their approval or disapproval of the proposed executive remuneration through their (binding) votes at least once every four years or every time there is material change to the policy[113]. Concerns about inappropriate or unfair remuneration practices may influence shareholders' views on executive pay. Consequently, shareholders may use their voting rights to express dissent related to media scrutiny, internal remuneration disparities, the CEO pay ratio[114] or the organisation's approach to sustainability matters such as climate change or diversity and inclusion.

3.1.2. Determining remuneration

In quoted organisations, executive remuneration is reviewed annually through consultation between the Remuneration Committee, the Board of Directors and shareholders. The results of the PwC annual survey[115] show an increase in shareholder oversight of remuneration (from 71% in 2021 to 80% in 2022 and 91% in 2023).

An executive's remuneration package should reflect the responsibilities and complexity inherent in the position and be competitive in comparison to other similar positions in the market. Executive pay, for example, is influenced by various factors including the market and competition (100%), expected responsibilities (98%), qualifications (76%), amount of experience (74%), relevance of experience (54%) and profile/reputation (17%)[116].

Large organisations, whether measured by workforce size, market capitalisation or revenue, often indicate increased responsibilities and complexities for the CEO, which is reflected in their remuneration.

Remuneration can also vary significantly across industries. Different industries may have distinct market norms and benchmarks for executive remuneration, for example, bank and insurance undertakings are subject to specific regulations on remuneration for certain categories of workers (see chapter 12 for more information). Industries with higher levels of competition or specialised knowledge, such as the IT industry, may offer higher remuneration to attract and retain top executive talent[117].

It is important to note that while these factors play a role in determining remuneration levels, the overall reward system is also impacted by the organisation's reward philosophy and corporate governance practices. Additionally, external factors such as market conditions, economic trends, investor expectations and shareholder views can also influence CEO remuneration decisions.

Lastly, the type of employment may also influence executive remuneration packages. According to PwC's annual survey[118], most executives in Belgian quoted organisations have self-employed status (89% vs. 11% employee). In Belgium it is common practice for self-employed individuals to perform their services through a management organisation.

3.1.3. Remuneration components

Executive remuneration packages usually include a mixture of fixed and variable remuneration components. The fixed components include the base salary, benefits (e.g., pension plan, health plan) and perquisites (e.g., company car, smartphone, allowances). The variable part comprises bonuses, short-term incentives (STIs) and long-term incentives (LTIs). The latter are meant to support the organisation's sustainability and long-term performance.

Figure 20 provides an overview of the different components that make up the annual package for CEOs of Belgian quoted organisations in all industries[119].

Figure 20: CEO remuneration components (all industries).

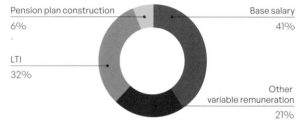

Pension plan construction 6%

Base salary 41%

LTI 32%

Other variable remuneration 21%

It is important to note that these proportions are not valid for organisations operating in the bank and insurance industry as they are subject to additional restrictions that prohibit excessive variable remuneration for their 'identified staff' or 'material risk takers' (i.e., staff whose professional activities have a material impact on the organisation's risk profile). The philosophy behind these restrictions is that the share of the fixed or guaranteed component in the overall remuneration package should be enough to avoid staff being too dependent on the variable component. This aims to avoid rewarding staff for overly risky behaviours which exceed the organisation's risk appetite (see chapter 12).

For all industries, the remuneration policy should enable the organisation to operate an entirely flexible bonus policy, including the option of not paying out a variable component. As these policies result in the proportion of the variable components being lower than in other industries, the proportion of base salary in the CEO package is usually higher.

Variable remuneration

One of the key distinctions between a broad-based reward system for all employees and a narrow-based reward system for executives lies in the composition of their remuneration packages. Executives typically receive a substantial proportion of their remuneration through performance bonuses, stock options, restricted stock units (RSUs) and other long-term incentives. In contrast, employees may have access to stock options or equity, but such incentives are uncommon and insignificant in comparison to the long-term incentives that executives commonly receive.

The reward system should describe the different remuneration components and determine an appropriate balance between fixed and variable components, as well as between cash and deferred remuneration[120].

By deferring a portion of executive pay, organisations align executive interests with the long-term health of the organisation, reducing the temptation for short-term, risky decision-making. Deferred remuneration plans often include vesting periods, encouraging executives to stay with the organisation for an extended period. It is therefore a strategic tool that aligns executive behaviour with the organisation's long-term (sustainable) objectives, retains skilled leadership and enhances accountability.

PwC's survey shows that a quarter of the organisations in the sample defer payment of at least 50% of the variable portion of executive remuneration, including between 25% and 100% of deferred bonuses[121]. For more information on short and long-term bonuses and instruments, including stock or share related long-term incentive plans (LTIPs), see chapter 7 on reward mix, and details of corporate governance rules on remuneration for quoted organisations can be found in chapter 9.

Benefits

Figure 21: Type of pension plan offered to executives.

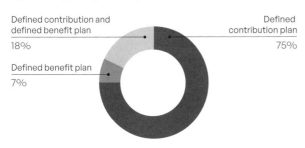

Defined contribution and
defined benefit plan
18%

Defined benefit plan
7%

Defined
contribution plan
75%

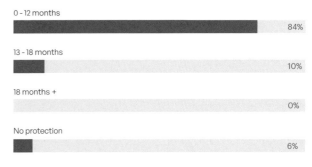

0 - 12 months
84%

13 - 18 months
10%

18 months +
0%

No protection
6%

Alongside base salary and variable remuneration, employer contributions into a pension plan form a crucial part of the overall remuneration structure. The inclusion of pension or group insurance benefits enhances the attractiveness of the executive package, providing a greater sense of long-term financial security and wellbeing.

In the population that benefits from a pension plan, 75% of executives have a defined contribution plan, 7% have a defined benefit plan, while 16% have a combination of both. None of the executives in the PwC survey had been offered a cash balance. Additionally, while 41% of executives have life insurance and 40% have a disability plan, half of all executives have neither[122].

Termination protection
In countries such as Belgium, all arrangements for executives, including notice period and termination terms and payments, should be disclosed in the remuneration policy and are subject to restrictions for directors of quoted organisations[123].

The PwC survey indicates that most executives (84%) have up to 12 months of severance pay, while a minority may receive over 12 months worth of severance remuneration (10%). Only 6% of executives are not granted any protection upon termination[124].

3.1.4. Sustainable performance

The shift from a 'pay for performance' to a 'pay for sustainability' philosophy reflects a growing emphasis on responsible corporate behaviour and the integration of ESG goals into executive remuneration. Stakeholders, including shareholders, investors and the public, are increasingly valuing sustainability alongside traditional performance metrics. And the integration of sustainability into executive remuneration aligns with increasing regulatory and stakeholder demands for transparency and responsibility. Consequently, variable remuneration should be structured to link reward to overall corporate and individual performance, so the interests of executives are aligned with the organisation's sustainable long-term value creation.

Shareholders are increasingly urging organisations to adopt this approach, with several large organisations already taking steps in this direction[125]. Nevertheless, linking remuneration to ESG performance can be motivated by value creation for all stakeholders, which goes beyond value creation for shareholders. This is for three main reasons: ESG goals can align organisations with societal expectations not directly linked to stock prices, shareholders' preferences may extend beyond financial value creation and/or ESG can form a crucial element of the organisation's purpose[126].

Investors, in particular, are keen on the explicit connection between ESG goals and executive remuneration. This involves linking incentive plan metrics to the organisation's ESG strategy, which encourages the achievement of those goals and signals their significance.

Quoted organisations are obligated to disclose financial and non-financial KPIs, including in executive remuneration plans, where specific ESG metrics and targets necessitate the transparent reporting of achievements. Such a disclosure should also provide investors with the information they need to evaluate whether these indicators are connected to material sustainability risks and opportunities[127].

In this context, remuneration should be seen as a tool to motivate desirable behaviours while avoiding incentives for unethical or misconduct, thereby holding executives accountable for delivering on sustainable goals. These goals are typically linked to executive remuneration rather than employee salaries due to the executives' strategic decision-making role, higher level of responsibility, influence on organisational culture and greater impact on ESG performance, as well as the administrative complexity of incorporating numerous ESG metrics for all employees.

There is a consensus among investors and senior leaders on the importance of linking ESG to pay, even though priorities may differ[128]. Yet, the integration of ESG metrics into executive remuneration is not the sole method of achieving these goals. Organisations can also reward the achievements of ESG objectives via promotion, hiring decisions, spot bonuses and firm-wide recognition outside of incentive plans. In other words, if ESG metrics are used in remuneration, it needs to be done in the correct way. Metrics should be carefully chosen to align with the organisation's strategy and business model[129].

ESG metrics and KPIs

For the successful integration of ESG KPIs into remuneration, it is crucial that these indicators align with the organisation's strategy, address its most significant issues and are clear, understandable and genuinely ambitious. It is crucial to have a compelling reason when introducing new goals into a remuneration programme, e.g., to transform organisational culture, manage business risks or grasp ESG-related opportunities. Understanding shareholder perspectives on the role of ESG in executive remuneration is another important aspect to this decision-making process[130].

Remuneration Committees face the challenge of striking a delicate balance when navigating the limited space for targets and metrics in executive reward systems. On one hand, they need to link ESG goals to executive remuneration to incentivise sustainable behaviours and performance. But on the other hand, it's equally important that they maintain simplicity in their reward systems, so that they are understandable in order to effectively motivate and retain executives.

Investors closely examine proposals that aim to link ESG metrics and remuneration while understanding that the determination of such ESG KPIs and metrics are the responsibility of the Remuneration Committee. Whether the latter is ready to incorporate ESG metrics into the executive remuneration plans depends on the organisation's ESG maturity[131].

The effective implementation of a reward system that links ESG KPIs to remuneration requires careful attention and planning, as there is no universal approach. Key considerations for an effective implementation are shown in figure 23.

After finalising the selection of ESG KPIs, the next step involves determining the weighting assigned to each of these indicators. This weighting is a strategic decision that reflects the organisation's priorities and helps communicate the relative importance or significance of different ESG metrics based on their relevance to the organisation's sustainability goals and stakeholder expectations.

Based on this, it is unsurprising that the allocation or weighting of ESG KPIs varies considerably between organisations according to analysis of remuneration policies[132]. The differences in weighting emphasise the customised nature of remuneration policies, reflecting varying organisational priorities, industry considerations and stakeholder expectations when incorporating non-financial and/or ESG criteria into their reward systems.

Figure 23: Key considerations for the effective implementation of ESG KPIs to remuneration.

Input measure	Output measure	Comments
This focuses on the efforts and resources invested by the organisation to address ESG issues. They quantify the commitment and actions taken rather than the direct outcomes or impacts (e.g., percentage of funds allocated to sustainability initiatives).	This assesses the tangible results or outcomes achieved as a result of an organisation's ESG initiatives. They reflect the direct effects and impacts of the implemented sustainability practices. (e.g., a reduction in carbon emissions measured in tons).	Output targets are often preferred by investors because of their objectivity and tangible assessment. However, both perspectives contribute to a comprehensive evaluation of an organisation's performance and strategy.
Quantitative	Qualitative	Comments
These are measurable and expressed in numerical terms. They involve specific, quantifiable metrics that can be objectively assessed (e.g., a reduction of 10% in energy consumption).	These are descriptive and often involve subjective assessments or qualities that may be challenging to measure precisely in numerical terms (e.g., fostering an inclusive workplace culture).	Quantitative measures tend to be favoured by investors as they are more easily measurable and objective than qualitative KPIs. However, qualitative measures are also recognised for capturing important aspects that may not be easily quantifiable.
Individual KPIs	Scorecard	Comments
Specific metrics or indicators that focus on a single aspect of performance and are assessed independently (e.g., percentage of women in leadership roles).	Instead of assessing individual metrics in isolation, a scorecard aggregates multiple KPIs into a holistic assessment, assigning scores or ratings to each category (e.g., a combination of metrics, such as carbon footprint, diversity ratios and board composition).	Investor preferences vary based on their specific investment strategies, values and priorities. The trend, however, is toward a more holistic and integrated approach, where a scorecard provides an overview of overall ESG performance, complemented by attention to specific individual KPIs that align with the investor's particular concerns or focus areas.
Scale target	Underpin	Comments
Thresholds with minimum and maximum levels that, when achieved, lead to escalating rewards (e.g., the achievement of specific milestones in the reduction of carbon emissions).	Minimum performance level(s) that executives are expected to meet (i.e., the baseline) to be entitled to a bonus or incentive (e.g., employee safety).	Underpin targets are usually used when a particular ESG factor is considered a minimum requirement. While underpin objectives are appreciated by investors, they are uncommon in practice.
External	Internal	Comments
Performance indicators defined or established by third-party organisations, indices or standards (e.g., sustainability indices like the Dow Jones Sustainability Index (DJSI) or the Global Reporting Initiative (GRI) standards).	Performance indicators that an organisation defines and tracks internally based on its own specific goals, values and priorities.	The choice between external and internal KPIs often depends on the organisation's objectives, stakeholder expectations and the desire for external recognition and benchmarking.

ESG KPIs and variable remuneration

Whether ESG KPIs should be connected to STIs or LTIs mainly depends on the time horizon of the ESG goals and risks associated with them. Short-term ESG goals that can be achieved within a one-year time frame can logically be incorporated into STIs. Therefore, STIs offer more flexibility, allowing organisations to adjust ESG goals annually based on evolving priorities and circumstances.

On the other hand, ESG goals with a more extended time horizon will be connected to LTIs. However, the common three-year measurement periods for LTIs might not effectively capture the 5 to 10-year (or more) window for some ESG objectives[133]. The primary purpose of a LTIP is to provide support for a long-term action plan with extended objectives, such as achieving a net-zero carbon footprint by 2050. The milestones and KPIs established within the LTIP would then be measured on an annual basis over a predetermined period.

In practice, non-financial KPIs, and in particular ESG indicators, are more frequently used for STI rather than LTI. This could be because it is more challenging to set meaningful ESG targets for LTI as LTI targets are frequently more output driven. It is also preferable to have ambitious and well-designed short-term objectives rather than vague long-term goals. As a result, organisations start by establishing ESG metrics in STI and progress step by step[134].

Challenges in linking ESG goals to executive remuneration

Boards and Remuneration Committees often face challenges when integrating ESG metrics into incentive plans, primarily due to their inherent complexity. The proliferation of ESG KPIs further increases difficulties in measuring ESG goals objectively and in a standardised way. These complexities need to be managed, especially due to the lack of clear rules on how to link remuneration to sustainable performance.

There is a risk of executives simply 'checking the box', where they achieve the ESG goals without addressing the underlying issues (e.g., achieving a gender quota in the board without addressing the gender pay gap of the organisation). Other challenges include the risk of incentivising the wrong behaviours, setting inappropriate targets, setting overly attainable strategic targets (i.e., perceived as a guaranteed bonus), sending unintended signals to the executive team or investors, gathering and trusting ESG-related data, exercising discretion in remuneration matters and finding the right balance between ESG and financial performance[135]. All of these may impact executive motivation, create difficulties in evaluating and calibrating ESG objectives and add complexity to executive reward systems.

The PwC's 2023 Annual Corporate Directors Survey further emphasises a gender disconnect on ESG issues, as female directors seem more likely to see ESG issues as linked to the organisation's strategy with a financial impact on organisation performance[136]. This differing perspective from female and male directors on ESG issues highlights the importance of promoting greater diversity in boardrooms in order to ensure a more comprehensive understanding and consideration of ESG factors.

Female directors who acknowledge the financial impact of ESG issues may advocate for the inclusion of ESG metrics in performance evaluations and executive remuneration plans. They may also push for LTIs that align with sustainable and responsible business practices. By incorporating ESG metrics and LTIs, organisations can incentivise executives to focus on ESG goals and achievements, ultimately promoting sustainable and responsible business practices.

Current ESG and remuneration trends[137]

Executive performance is still largely measured in relation to financial performance, with financial KPIs representing, on average, at least two thirds of the weighting criteria for short term incentive plans (STIPs) and LTIPs[138]. However, there are a growing number of shareholder and investor proposals that urge organisations to integrate ESG objectives into their executive reward systems. These proposals are being incorporated into executive remuneration, although organisations often find it challenging to achieve a balance between financial and non-financial KPIs.

The organisations that have incorporated ESG KPIs into their incentive plans have found it easier to link them to STIPs. The integration of ESG KPIs into LTIP is expected to grow in the future.

Social measures are popular in ESG performance indicators. While some social goals are not necessarily new to remuneration plans (e.g., customer satisfaction and safety), there is a rapid adoption of diversity and equity-related goals. It is worth noting that even though social indicators are used more frequently than environmental or governance indicators, they tend to have a lower weight in the overall scoring.

The trend towards ESG KPIs is also visible in the growing number of legislative interventions and requirements for non-financial disclosure. One example of this is the corporate sustainability reporting directive (CSRD) which requires organisations to report on the environmental and social impact of their activities to help investors, consumers and other stakeholders to evaluate the organisation's non-financial performance and encourage a more responsible approach to business.

3.1.5. Remuneration disclosure

Transparency, including remuneration disclosure, in executive reward systems is crucial for building trust among stakeholders, shareholders and the public. This involves openly sharing information about executive remuneration structures, performance metrics and the reason behind remuneration decisions. When an organisation decides to incorporate ESG goals into executive remuneration, it necessitates transparent communication about the reasons for doing so, as well as how remuneration is determined based on ESG performance, including the chosen ESG KPIs and the evaluation methodology.

While remuneration disclosure can enhance accountability and align incentives, the increased transparency also exposes executives to heightened scrutiny. Stakeholders, including shareholders, the media and the public, may closely analyse disclosed remuneration figures. If there is a perceived misalignment between executive remuneration and organisation performance or industry standards, it can lead to criticism and negative publicity. Executives may find themselves in the spotlight, and their decisions and actions subject to more intense evaluation. Furthermore, executives, like many individuals, value a certain degree of privacy. Detailed remuneration disclosure may lead to concerns about the invasion of their privacy and potentially impact the negotiation power of executives in their remuneration discussions.

3.2. Non-executive remuneration

The remuneration levels for non-executive board members should mirror the time commitment and responsibilities associated with the role. They are not allowed to receive remuneration directly linked to the organisation's performance. Instead, remuneration can be provided in the form of shares, excluding stock options.

The remuneration of non-executives typically comprises a combination of one or more of the following components:
- Annual fee for Board-related activities;
- Fee per Board meeting;
- Annual fee for Committee-related activities;
- Fee per Committee meeting; and
- Other fees (e.g., member nomination, pension plan, warrants, seating in ad-hoc committees, travel fee and communication fees).

An annual fee is most frequently reported for both Board-related and Committee-related remuneration (respectively 53% and 31%)[139].

In conclusion, the distinction between narrow-based and broad-based reward is pivotal in designing effective incentive structures. As executive remuneration faces increased scrutiny, there is a growing imperative to connect ESG goals to remuneration, fostering accountability for sustainable achievements. However, the effective implementation of ESG metrics in executive remuneration presents inherent challenges, necessitating careful consideration and strategic solutions to ensure meaningful impact and alignment with corporate values.

After investigating the most effective strategies for the reward system's scope, we now turn our focus to how to position a reward strategy in the market.

Figure 24: Remuneration mix for Board-related and Committee-related remuneration.

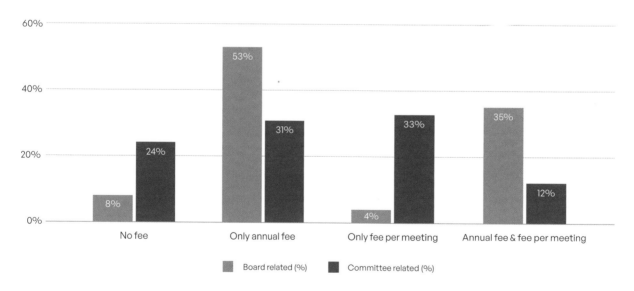

6.
Reward
architecture

Key takeaways

1. Reward architecture, including a clear architecture framework, is the foundation of an effective reward system.

2. Job definitions within the framework support career development, performance and HR processes.

3. Job evaluation frameworks objectively assess job importance using methods such as point-factor, ranking, skill-based and market-based grading.

4. Job evaluations are becoming more skill-based, data-driven, agile and holistic.

5. Benchmarking helps organisations to stay competitive and make informed decisions about reward.

When it comes to structuring a reward system, keep in mind an expression used by the Romans: Festina lente, or make haste slowly. This emphasises the importance of carefully considering which actions to take and making deliberate decisions that ensure the organisation is correctly positioned before moving forward - towards victory on the battlefield or in its reward system.

This chapter starts by looking at reward architecture, which forms the framework for a reward system, before turning to benchmarking to see how to position the organisation in its market.

1. Reward architecture

An effective and consistent reward system starts from a solid foundation. In order to construct this, the organisation needs a clear job architecture.

It is important to note that a job architecture framework is much more than an organisational chart with job descriptions. A well-balanced job architecture framework supports the organisation as a whole, highlighting the organisation's willingness to invest in its employees by giving them new career opportunities, developing their competencies and boosting their performance. Additionally, a job architecture framework can be set up in all types of organisations: large or small, local or international, matrix or not, newly formed or well established.

1.1. The foundation

A job architecture framework organises jobs within an organisation both vertically, for jobs that share similar skill and competency sets, and horizontally, for jobs with a similar complexity and accountability. The job architecture framework is the foundation for aligning jobs within the organisation.

By investigating the work and tasks performed by the organisation and its employees, the organisation develops a holistic, streamlined and scalable framework with work clustered in job families and/or functions and jobs. The job definitions enable the organisation to allocate a relative value for each job based on its classification, grading or levelling.

1.1.1. Organisational capabilities

The starting point for the job definitions used by the architecture is the business strategy, purpose and operating model, which defines which organisational capabilities are needed. While these capabilities are all interlinked, certain competencies and skills are very rare, requiring the organisation to use job crafting to adapt jobs and organisational structure based on the resources available[140].

Job crafting can be very beneficial for both employers and employees because when an employee can tailor their job to their interests and passions, they are more likely to be motivated, with improved productivity and performance. However, employers should ensure that the job crafting is in line with organisational goals. If the employee focuses too much on tasks and responsibilities that are not aligned with the overall strategy, it can be detrimental to the organisation. This means that there needs to be a balance between the tasks to be performed and the flexibility given to the employee for job crafting.

Developing job definitions offers benefits for both the organisation and employees. From an employee engagement perspective, executives and employees face consistent expectations, reducing role ambiguity, clarifying expectations and providing the foundation for career development. It also simplifies performance management processes and empowers employees to better manage their own careers through better understanding of cross-functional opportunities and skills gaps.

Job definitions also help to increase the availability and accuracy of HR data, improve daily reporting as well as strategic workforce analytics for more effective processes. This enables more effective employee development and deployment through a standardised foundation for organisation-wide career and performance frameworks.

Lastly, from an administration efficiency perspective, job definitions reduce the time spent on transactional and administrative tasks, empowering HR to spend time on value added and strategic activities. Job definitions also reduce the number of job codes needed, improving how job data can be used and what it can be used for, as well as supporting standardised pay administration and governance around pay decisions globally.

Figure 25: Talent architecture components moving from a business perspective and strategy to competencies and skills.

1.1.2. Employee role descriptions

The organisation's strategy, purpose and operating model define the required capabilities that the organisation needs for its daily operations and to meet its future ambitions. These capabilities form the basis for the level-based competencies and skills needed for a job or job family. From here, the technical and behavioural skills are described in the job description. While the resulting job descriptions can range from very generic to very specific, there are advantages and disadvantages to both ways of working.

Generic descriptions are easier to maintain as they cover a multitude of jobs and HR does not need to update the job description when something small has changed or been added or withdrawn. They also help employees to build career paths through the organisation. However, employees do not always recognise themselves in this type of job description, especially for functions lower in the hierarchy. Additionally, generic job descriptions are not popular with union delegates and some executives as they can make it challenging to explain jobs and the differences between them.

Specific job descriptions are popular with union delegates as they can easily 'defend' their employees as the tasks and responsibilities are described in detail. This also enables employees to easily recognise their job. However, the detailed descriptions need to be updated and reviewed every time something changes within a role. Furthermore, this individual approach makes it difficult to build career paths within the organisation.

Before deciding how much detail to include in a job description, the organisation should focus on their job architecture framework which encompasses job functions, families and/or levels.

- Job families and/or functions create a transparent, consistent and strategically focused job function/family structure for effective talent management. Job families include sales, finance, legal, HR and operations.
- Job levels (also known as job grades or buckets) enable employees to progress vertically and/or laterally through the organisation, empowering

HR to effectively manage talent, reward and performance.
- Jobs define critical elements of job profiles and/or descriptions, reconciling redundancies or differences across similar jobs.
- Job attributes and related data includes job codes, job titles, job summaries, job descriptions, pay rate types, remuneration grades, exemption status, job categories, workers remuneration codes, job classifications, skills and competencies.

The illustrative job architecture framework example in figure 26 gives an overview of the different elements.

Figure 26: An example of the different elements found in a job architecture framework.

	What's included in the framework*?		
JOB FUNCTION A collection of job families	Human resources		
JOB FAMILY A cluster of jobs that share common tasks and responsibilities	Human resources generalist	Compensation and benefits	
	Talent acquisition	Payroll	
CAREER TRACK Potential progression through the organisation	Management		Employee
JOB LEVEL Relative position of the job internally/externally	Executive	Director	Analyst
JOBS Duties, responsibilities and the scope at which they are done	Executive, Human resources generalist	Director, Payroll	Analyst, Compensation and benefits
JOB CODE Job specifications	06563	06554	06574

*Framework items represent PwC's perspective of a job architecture framework and what is generally considered leading practice in the market

1.2. Job evaluation frameworks

After defining the organisation's structure, jobs need to be structured and evaluated to objectify their relative importance. This involves assessing jobs against predefined criteria or factors such as responsibilities, impact on the organisation and the knowledge and/or experience required to do the job. By using the same set of factors, jobs can be evaluated in a consistent and objective manner. However, this depends on the quality and completeness of the information delivered to the job evaluator and their ability to remain objective.

It is possible for organisations to avoid this pitfall by evaluating jobs via a panel of evaluators instead of just a single individual. Alternatively, the evaluator can interview different job holders and stakeholders, challenge the gathered information and review job evaluations regularly.

Most job frameworks include job levels that group jobs with similar characteristics and requirements together, enabling the organisation to establish clear hierarchies and structure. This helps to determine the appropriate salary and benefits per level, as well as helping career progression, performance management, succession planning and talent management strategies.

Overall, the objectives of job evaluation frameworks are to create a fair, transparent and consistent system for evaluating and classifying roles within an organisation, facilitating talent management and future organisational development.

1.2.1. Evaluation methods

There are different ways for an organisation to assess its job evaluations, but most are either analytical schemes that break jobs down into their core components or non-analytical schemes that look at the entire job. In general, analytical schemes offer greater objectivity by looking at details, while non-analytical schemes are simpler, cheaper and quicker.

It is important to find a scheme that meets the organisation's needs and objectives regarding the weighing of jobs, qualitative descriptions, time commitment and cost awareness.

- Point-factor method
  This quantitative methodology based on a predefined set of criteria[141] is often used by global organisations. The job evaluator defines the criteria for their organisation, e.g., technical knowledge, problem solving or responsibilities, before evaluating each job based on the criteria

and attributing points for each. The total number of points determines the job level.

While the point-factor method isn't as flexible as STRATA (see later in this chapter), it is a very systematic, objective and qualitative approach. Also, as it defines and translates the criteria based on the organisation, the methodology is easily accepted by employees. However, it can be time consuming.

- Ranking method or paired comparison
  In this methodology, jobs are paired and compared to each other. For each pair, the most impactful job is chosen leading to a forced ranking of all jobs. While this approach is only recommended for smaller organisations, it could be applied to larger organisations if the jobs are first mapped to a generic list of jobs. However, this is a more qualitative approach to weighing jobs, making the results more difficult to explain to stakeholders.

- Skill-based grading frameworks
  This methodology evaluates jobs based on the required skills and competencies, rather than traditional job roles. Compared to other methods that try to be as objective as possible, this is a more person-related methodology that recognises employee contributions to the business goals, which adds to its flexibility. However, as it is linked to employees, it can be seen as being more subjective.

- Market pricing or market-based grading
  With this methodology, jobs are graded according to the market rate[142]. The organisation benchmarks its jobs against external market data to determine appropriate remuneration levels. This methodology is more outward focused, reflecting market realities. However, it is not always straightforward to find the data for a relevant job in the market data. Also, the market value might not match the internal equity that the job holds for the organisation. Lastly, as this methodology combines the weight of the job with its market value, it can be less stable as it follows fluctuations in the labour market.

1.2.2. Prerequisites for successful evaluations

When selecting an appropriate evaluation method, there are a number of important prerequisites that need to be considered in order to ensure successful job evaluations.

- Organisational objectives
  Closely align the chosen methodology with the organisation's objectives and resources. This will ensure that it is accepted more easily by all of the organisation's stakeholders.

- Consistency
  Ensure that the chosen methodology is applied consistently throughout all jobs in the organisation so that employees know what is expected of them in their current and (potential) future roles.

- Clear evaluation criteria
  Establish clear and well-defined criteria for evaluating jobs. Depending on the chosen job evaluation methodology, these criteria can include skills, responsibilities, complexity and qualifications.

- Scalability and flexibility
  Design a job evaluation system that is scalable and adaptable to changes in organisational structures, roles and market conditions. Flexibility is crucial for the long-term effectiveness of the process.

- Information quality
  Develop detailed and accurate job descriptions for each role to be evaluated, as well as clear organisational charts. Each job description should clearly outline the responsibilities, required skills, qualifications, reporting relationships and other relevant factors that contribute to the job's value. When job descriptions are not available, interview executives and employees.

- Job evaluators
  Properly train the job evaluators so that they fully understand the chosen methodology, criteria and importance of consistency in evaluations. By involving several job evaluators in the process, it is possible to double check evaluations to ensure that the information has been understood correctly.

- Legal compliance
  Ensure that the job evaluation process complies with applicable labour laws and regulations, including equal pay and non-discrimination laws. Legal compliance is essential for the validity and fairness of the process.

- Reviews and updates
  Regularly review and update job evaluations to keep pace with industry trends, organisational changes and evolving job responsibilities. This ensures that the job evaluation process remains relevant over time.

1.3. STRATA methodology

PwC has its own classification methodology called STRATA, which works well for organisations of all sizes and types. By using a point system to objectively weigh and grade jobs, the methodology enables external comparisons while ensuring the classification is simple and transparent to all stakeholders.

Each job is evaluated with points being assigned to the same set of eight criteria, prioritised in order of importance. The total number of points determines the wage rate for the job, with jobs with similar point totals placed in similar grades.

By using the same set of criteria, STRATA is a universal language. However, the method can be adapted to the specifics of each organisation, for example, size or complexity. This means that the definitions of the criteria and the wording of the definitions can be adapted to the organisation.

Even though the STRATA methodology is easy to use, it is important to provide stakeholders with the necessary information about the system at the start of the project to prevent misunderstandings and ensure full transparency about what the system aims to achieve.

1.3.1. STRATA criteria

STRATA uses eight predefined criteria and dimensions, which are grouped into three themes (knowledge and skills, identifying and solving problems and influencing and taking responsibility) to evaluate roles and jobs. These criteria can be tailored to the organisation's size and/or complexity, with additional criteria being added if necessary[143].

Here is an example of STRATA criteria being used in an organisation.

Knowledge and skills
- Technical knowledge and skills:
  Breadth, depth and diversity of technical, business, process and general management knowledge, as well as the necessary professional experience.
- Knowledge of the business:
  Level of complexity of knowledge and awareness related to an organisation's business, markets, goals, policies, processes and procedures.
- Management of relationships and staff:
  Ability to persuade and motivate others, including aspects of communication, leadership and cultural integration.

Identifying and solving problems
- Scope of thinking:
  Intellectual requirements to be able to develop concepts and procedures for solving the tasks set.
- Degree of difficulty:
  Complexity of problems and uncertainty of information in the evaluation and development of solutions.

Influencing and taking responsibility
- Discretion to make decisions:
  Autonomous decision-making scope with direct reference to the level of thinking (follows hierarchical structure).
- Amount of influence:
  Amount of resources that are both directly controlled and indirectly influenced.
- Influence on achievement of objectives:
  Amount of influence the position has on the target achievement via the organisation's indirectly influenced resources.

1.3.2. Scales

Each of the eight STRATA criteria has its own pre-defined scale. It should be noted that the definitions and the scale itself, both its length and the number of levels, can be altered to fit the organisation's requirements.

Figure 27 shows an example of levels for the technical skills criteria, with each scale moving from the lowest requirement level to the highest level conceivable within the organisation. The requirements are clearly defined and cover all functions.

Even though the intermediate pair levels (e.g., A2 and A4) are not described explicitly, they are used in the same way as the other levels, allowing the evaluators to express nuances in the job requirements between functions, especially when evaluating several functions within one organisational unit.

The scales are customised to the organisation's requirements. This enables easier adoption throughout the organisation as employees and executives recognise themselves in the methodology. However, this requires a time commitment from the organisation, as they will need to do some testing with actual roles before rolling it out for all jobs.

Figure 27: Example of technical knowledge and skills levels.

LEVEL	DEFINITION	EXPLANATION
A1	No specific technical knowledge: Simple, function-related basic knowledge which can be communicated by means of simple, formal briefing and/or practice on the job.	• Very simple tasks that can be learned in a few days/ weeks and communicated by means of simple instructions.
A2		
A3	Limited technical knowledge: Subject-specific knowledge for simple or standardised work processes which has been acquired by means of a training process and/or practical experience on the job.	• Simple or standardised tasks. • Systematic induction in the workplace over several months. • No formal training course (vocation training) required.
A4		
A5	Competent technical knowledge Practical or systematic skills acquired through formal vocational training or several years of practical experience and additional training.	• 2 to 3 years' formal training (e.g., vocational training) and up to 6 months' practical experience, or • Secondary school education without formal training, but several years' experience and additional training courses which lead to a comparable level of knowledge.
A6		
A7	Advanced technical knowledge: Technical knowledge acquired through intensive practical experience which normally builds on methodical professional training and additional qualifications.	• Completed vocational training (A5) plus • A minimum of 5 years' practical experience plus additional professional development (seminars, certificated specialist courses such as Meister (master), Techniker (technician), Fachwirt (Senior technician), or Bachelor degree.
A8		
A9	Method-based technical knowledge: Mastery of technical/theorical interrelationships or practical and systematic aspects of a subject based on comprehensive practical experience or formal university education.	• Master's degree ('know why') plus 2 to 3 years' practical experience or doctorate, or • Professional in practice who has mastered the 'know how' based on technical training and many years' (at least 10 years) practical experience, as well as certified professional development.
A10		
A11	Mature technical knowledge: Mastery of technical/theorical interrelationships and mature knowledge about how to handle complex areas of work professionally: Specialisation in one subject (depth of knowledge) or integration of several subjects (breath of knowledge).	• Professional specialist with background knowledge of the theory (degree course) and many years' experience (8 to 10 years) or 5 to 7 years after doctorate as a high-level specialist in one subject. • Generalist with comparable theoretical and practical background knowledge in various subject disciplines.
A12		
A13	Outstanding technical knowledge: Outstanding, comprehensive mastery of a subject in theory and practice (top specialist) or integration of many subjects with great depth of knowledge (top generalist).	• Top specialist ('subject guru') with recognised outstanding subject expertise in one specialist area (depth of knowledge), or • Top generalist who is part of the management of a large national or small international business (breadth of knowledge).

1.3.3. Evaluating jobs

While organisations often focus on the methodology, they tend to underestimate the job evaluation process, which should be clear and detailed, with clear milestones, with process steps and with the involvement of different stakeholders. The rest of this section focuses on the standard methodology, but this can be adapted to meet the individual requirements of each organisation.

It is important to involve stakeholders from the beginning of this process via personal interviews, workshops and other internal communication methods. Personal interviews enable the organisation to create buy-in from employees and executives, as well as generating more detailed information on actual jobs and roles. Executives in particular are able to provide useful information about the positions to evaluate, the organisational structure and the responsibilities of one job compared to another. These high quality job descriptions ensure consistency and completeness, which is important when connecting the job architecture framework to other processes.

Figure 28: Extract of a job interview guide.

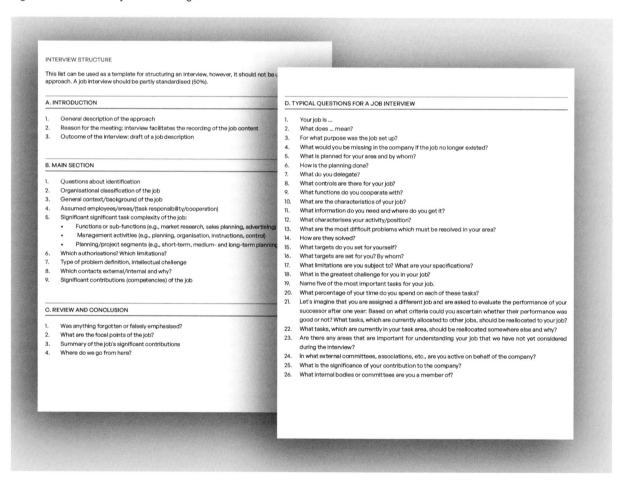

INTERVIEW STRUCTURE

This list can be used as a template for structuring an interview, however, it should not be used as a rigid approach. A job interview should be partly standardised (50%).

A. INTRODUCTION

1. General description of the approach
2. Reason for the meeting: interview facilitates the recording of the job content
3. Outcome of the interview: draft of a job description

B. MAIN SECTION

1. Questions about identification
2. Organisational classification of the job
3. General context/background of the job
4. Assumed employees/areas/(task responsibility/cooperation)
5. Significant significant task complexity of the job:
   - Functions or sub-functions (e.g., market research, sales planning, advertising)
   - Management activities (e.g., planning, organisation, instructions, control)
   - Planning/project segments (e.g., short-term, medium- and long-term planning)
6. Which authorisations? Which limitations?
7. Type of problem definition, intellectual challenge
8. Which contacts external/internal and why?
9. Significant contributions (competencies) of the job

C. REVIEW AND CONCLUSION

1. Was anything forgotten or falsely emphasised?
2. What are the focal points of the job?
3. Summary of the job's significant contributions
4. Where do we go from here?

D. TYPICAL QUESTIONS FOR A JOB INTERVIEW

1. Your job is ...
2. What does ... mean?
3. For what purpose was the job set up?
4. What would you be missing in the company if the job no longer existed?
5. What is planned for your area and by whom?
6. How is the planning done?
7. What do you delegate?
8. What controls are there for your job?
9. What functions do you cooperate with?
10. What are the characteristics of your job?
11. What information do you need and where do you get it?
12. What characterises your activity/position?
13. What are the most difficult problems which must be resolved in your area?
14. How are they solved?
15. What targets do you set for yourself?
16. What targets are set for you? By whom?
17. What limitations are you subject to? What are your specifications?
18. What is the greatest challenge for you in your job?
19. Name five of the most important tasks for your job.
20. What percentage of your time do you spend on each of these tasks?
21. Let's imagine that you are assigned a different job and are asked to evaluate the performance of your successor after one year: Based on what criteria could you ascertain whether their performance was good or not? What tasks, which are currently allocated to other jobs, should be reallocated to your job?
22. What tasks, which are currently in your task area, should be reallocated somewhere else and why?
23. Are there any areas that are important for understanding your job that we have not yet considered during the interview?
24. In what external committees, associations, etc., are you active on behalf of the company?
25. What is the significance of your contribution to the company?
26. What internal bodies or committees are you a member of?

Additionally, workshops enable employees across the organisation to get better acquainted with the methodology so it becomes part of the organisation's structure and future. Workshops also enhance the consistency of job descriptions through cross-checks and additional evaluation, plus group workshops are more cost efficient than individual sessions. This is because group evaluations can highlight different measures and standards used by evaluators, leading to discussions during the session and reducing the amount of time needed for cross-comparisons. Another issue is some executives evaluate their positions too highly, creating a tendency towards overvaluation. To eliminate these issues, an experienced moderator is essential.

Before starting to evaluate jobs, it is important to gather all relevant information including a list of jobs to be evaluated, organisational charts and existing job descriptions. By analysing this information, the aim is to update existing job descriptions, create job descriptions for new jobs and remove job descriptions that no longer exist.

Depending on the organisation's needs, the updated job descriptions could be either generic or highly specific, only contain the minimum information needed for the job or have information for other HR purposes, such as career development, training or reward categories, detailed reporting lines or the N+1 reporting structure.

There are advantages and disadvantages to each of these approaches. In organisations with a fast pace of changes in terms of organisational structures or job content, it might be better to have a basic job description with a minimum amount of information to avoid numerous reviews. In a more established organisation that has a slower rate of change, a more specific approach where employees easily recognise their job might be more appropriate.

1.4. Implementation

After selecting a methodology, it needs to be implemented. This involves a clear process, buy-in from stakeholders and good communication.

- Organisational goals
  Successful job evaluation exercises align with the overall goals and strategies of the organisation. It is crucial to ensure that the job evaluation methodology and process support the broader organisational objectives, such as attracting and retaining talent, enhancing internal mobility and controlling costs.

- Clear communication
  Communication throughout the entire organisation is critical during the job evaluation process as it touches upon the foundation of the employment contract. Additionally, transparent communication helps to manage expectations and build trust, making it especially important when other HR processes are linked to the overall job architecture framework.

- Stakeholder involvement
  Involving key stakeholders, including HR professionals, executives and employees is vital for encouraging collaboration, input and buy-in, as well as ensuring a comprehensive and well-accepted outcome.

- Continuous process
  The job evaluation process requires regular reviews and updates to keep up with organisational changes and needs, evolving job responsibilities and industry trends. For example, trends such as digitalisation, AI and agile ways of working are already impacting the jobs and competencies organisations need today and in the future.

- Flexibility and scalability
  Organisations need to ensure that their job evaluation system is sufficiently flexible to handle expected change, as well as scalable to accommodate organisational growth and evolving business needs.

- Information quality
  Successful job evaluation exercises rely on data and analytics. This can be qualitative and quantitative information from job descriptions, organisational charts, interviews and workshops. It is also important to document every rationale that leads to each evaluation score to facilitate comparisons.

- Human factors
  While the job evaluation process uses information from a number of sources, it touches the foundation of the employment contract which can make it a sensitive topic. For that reason, it is important to evaluate the current job and not the performance of the job holder, their current remuneration level or planned changes to the job. Furthermore, the job holder should not evaluate their own job role.

- Organisational design
  As the job evaluation process assesses and ranks jobs within the organisation based on responsibilities, skills and complexity, certain inconsistencies are identified, such as duplication of jobs, no clear distinction between roles or too many levels of management. These observations can support recommendations for changes in the organisational design.

1.5. Links to HR processes

Designing a new or revised job architecture framework via a job evaluation process represents a large investment of time and resources. Therefore, it is important to optimise its use by considering other HR processes during the design phase.

- Remuneration and benefits
  As job families and levels are defined, organisations can assign fixed salary ranges to each job family and level. Other benefits can also be linked to each job family and level, ideally balancing with internal and external expectations (see benchmarking). The combination of the job and the employee will define the final level of remuneration[144].

- Optimisation of personnel costs
  Job evaluations provide structure which helps to ensure clarity, transparency and comparability regarding the comparative worth of each job within the organisation. By using the connection with remuneration and benefits, the organisation can gain a better control of their personnel costs. Additionally, tight personnel budgets can be distributed in a more optimal and consistent manner, avoiding discretionary decisions.

- Workforce and succession planning
  The job evaluation exercise can help with future workforce planning to identify personnel overlap or skill shortages for jobs that are critical to the organisation's future success. This can lead to increased internal mobility and re- and upskilling where there is an overlap of functions, an action plan for hiring new employees with the required skills or introducing targeted training and development programmes to cover the skill shortages within the current workforce.

- Internal mobility
  The job architecture framework can clearly define career paths to attract and retain employees. As employees' skills and competencies grow in line with job families and levels, they are more likely to participate in employee rotation programmes that align with their career aspirations and organisational goals.

- Performance management
  Clear job descriptions facilitate goal setting as employees understand what is expected from each job, as well as its added value. This ensures that employee performance goals contribute to the overall success of their team and the organisation.

1.6. Trends in job evaluations

In order to understand the current trends in job evaluation methodologies, it's useful to go back in history. Job evaluation dates back to the early 20th century when experts like Frederick Taylor focused on time and motion studies to optimise efficiency[145]. Taylor broke each job into steps before altering each step to minimise the time needed to complete it. This change threatened to deskill and accelerate the speed of industrial work, and led to worker resentment[146]. Working in the same time period, Frank and Lillian Gilbreth focused on workers' mental and physical condition[147].

Originally job evaluations were seen as rigid and static, not evolving much over time. However, jobs began to evolve and diversify, with organisations adopting systems to meet their specific needs. Modern job evaluation methods can incorporate quantitative and qualitative analysis and consider factors such as skills, working conditions and responsibilities. However, the underlying principle of job evaluations remains a fundamental aspect of human resource management.

Looking to the future, market trends include skills-based job evaluations, data-driven evaluations, technology integrations, agile structures and using a holistic approach.

1.6.1. Skills-based job evaluations

There is a shift towards evaluating jobs based on required skills and competencies, rather than just the traditional factors. However, there is the risk that more personal information will be included in the evaluation, decreasing objectivity. To mitigate this risk, a clear distinction must be made between the skills necessary for the job and the personal skills of the job holder.

Skills-based evaluation supports a dynamic and adaptable workforce, putting the emphasis on continuous learning and development as being key for employee and organisational success. Employees are encouraged to develop a diverse skill set, enabling them to pivot and contribute across various functions within the organisation as they navigate the complexity of a rapidly changing business environment. In this way, organisations recognise that the value an employee brings to the organisation extends beyond the boundaries of a predefined job role. This is particularly important in industries where agility is paramount, allowing organisations to respond swiftly to market shifts, technological advancements and unforeseen challenges.

1.6.2. Data-driven evaluations

Data-driven evaluations represent a transformative approach to evaluating and classifying job roles within organisations. Departing from traditional, subjective methods, the data-driven evaluation methodology uses quantitative and analytical techniques to harness the power of data analytics to inform and enhance the job evaluation process. This results in more objective and unbiased evaluations that minimise the inherent biases that are prevalent in traditional evaluation systems.

One of the key advantages of data-driven evaluation is its ability to promote fair reward practices where remuneration decisions are based on quantifiable metrics, such as skills, performance and responsibilities.

Ultimately, data-driven evaluations align with the broader goals of creating inclusive and equitable workplace environments. They enhance the accuracy of job assessments and foster an organisational culture that values objectively, transparency and fairness in reward systems.

1.6.3. Technology integrations

The implications of integrating technology, particularly artificial intelligence (AI) and automation, into job evaluation practices are far-reaching, creating a landscape where efficiency, reduced bias and sophisticated job evaluations are prominent features.

One significant implication is the enhancement of efficiency in job evaluation processes. Automation streamlines data collection, analysis and decision making, significantly reducing the time and resources traditionally associated with manual evaluations. The speed and accuracy afforded by technology enable organisations to respond swiftly to changing workplace dynamics and business needs, fostering agility and adaptability.

1.6.4. Agile structures

Agile structures are designed to adapt to dynamic work environments, offering a framework that allows organisations to respond easily to market changes and technological advances. They also foster a culture of continuous improvement, with teams inside the structure being empowered to experiment, iterate and innovate, promoting a proactive mindset and a feeling of ownership.

Organisations that embrace agile structures become proactive agents in the face of change. This adaptability not only supports their short-term responses, it also cultivates a culture of innovation that is essential for long-term sustainability and success. Job architecture methodologies need to be able to incorporate agile organisational structures.

1.6.5. Holistic approach

Organisations are increasingly moving towards a more holistic and integrated approach for job evaluations. This is particularly important as job evaluations often form the basis for other HR processes such as remuneration and benefits frameworks, performance management, talent acquisition, succession planning, diversity and inclusion policies and learning and development programmes. This ensures consistency and alignment across these functions, creating a cohesive and interconnected HR framework that increases employee engagement and facilitates the retention of employees.

2. Benchmarking

Conducting remuneration and benefits benchmarking is vital for organisations aiming to maintain competitiveness in today's talent market, especially in the face of challenges such as attracting and retaining employees in a tight labour market and evolving work trends like remote and hybrid working.

This challenge is particularly tough as it takes place at the intersection of two seemingly conflicting drivers: on one hand, a strong position in the talent market is crucial for the organisation to achieve its ambitions, and on the other hand, organisations must prioritise cost-effectiveness, both now and in the future.

Reward benchmarking plays a pivotal role in achieving these objectives. Through a comprehensive reward benchmarking study, organisations gain valuable insights into their current standing compared to the market concerning remuneration and benefits, with a specific emphasis on the total reward as opposed to total wellbeing. Furthermore, organisations can leverage benchmark information to strategically adjust their market position and redesign their remuneration and benefit policies to align with industry standards and remain competitive.

2.1. Employee and employer interests

Remuneration benchmarking impacts both the employee and employer, and both have a vested interest in the outcome.

From an employee perspective, fair and competitive remuneration contributes to positive employee morale and engagement. This involves the organisation transparently communicating about remuneration practices, supported by benchmarking data, to foster trust among employees and reduce concerns about fairness. The result is when employees feel that they are fairly compensated compared to industry standards, they are more likely to be satisfied and committed to their work.

And from an employer perspective, organisations can reduce the risk of losing valuable employees to their competitors. Competitive salaries are a significant factor in attracting top talent to an organisation, and accurate remuneration benchmarking enables organisations to compare their remuneration practices with those of similar organisations. By aligning reward practices with candidate expectations, the organisation becomes more appealing to qualified candidates, as well as facilitating the retention of existing employees.

Understanding industry salary trends and benchmarks supports organisations in their strategic workforce planning. It allows organisations to make informed decisions about hiring, promoting or restructuring roles based on remuneration data and market demands. Remuneration benchmarking is often linked to performance management as it helps organisations determine how to reward high performers, ensuring that salary adjustments and bonuses are in line with both internal and external benchmarks.

Finally, remuneration benchmarking provides valuable insights for budget planning. Organisations can allocate resources more effectively by understanding the market rates for different roles and adjusting their budget accordingly.

2.2. Benchmarking exercise

2.2.1. Guiding principles

When conducting a benchmarking exercise, there are certain guiding principles that should be followed.

- Define the scope
  Before starting, make a list of all the job roles that are in scope. Use the job architecture information which defines the role, responsibilities, level, job family and reporting lines. This is an important step even though benchmark data will never be an exact match for the organisation's roles. Also, as job titles vary between organisations, comparing matching job roles will require investigating the details of each role, using for example, the job description, organisational charts, contracts and reporting lines.

- Gather internal data
  For each of the functions in the scope, gather and check all reward data, ideally on a monthly and annual basis. This data should cover all reward components, i.e., fixed, variable and benefits.

- Personal data
  Gather extra information that can be linked to the job holders in the scope. For example, employee age, years in service, years of experience and performance reviews.

- Total recognition versus total reward
  It is important to note that benchmarking often gives a monetary based result. However, total recognition is more than just the total reward. Non-monetary components, including amount of holidays, career opportunities and training and development possibilities, are gaining in importance. This is why organisations should keep a holistic view of their total recognition package instead of focusing solely on reward for new hires and current employees (see chapter 7 on reward mix for more information about total reward and total wellbeing).

- Use common sense
  Benchmarking is not an exact science. It is a methodology that compares an organisation's reward practices to the market in order to support management decisions. In other words, quantitative data needs to partner with qualitative common sense.

2.2.2. Important factors

The most important factors to consider during a benchmarking exercise are:

- Market or industry
  Which market or industry is important for the organisation? Salary benchmarking is a very helpful tool as long as the organisation compares itself against the right competition. This includes paying attention to the organisation's size and location.

- Job families
  Salary benchmarking often structures data based on job families like HR, operations, sales and finance. When comparing internal and external data, this should be taken into consideration.

- Function levels
  Different job levels and career paths, like experts, administrative support and managers, can vary between organisations, so organisations need to be cautious when comparing this external data to their internal data.

2.2.3. Results

After gathering all the internal and external data, the organisation can start to map its job roles to the generic external roles. This should generate a comparison of each component of the reward package, highlighting where the organisation is positioned in the market. Based on these results, organisations can define the positioning they would prefer for each job role.

It is important to note that, as well as these external market conditions, the organisation should also consider its internal strategy. This includes its values, cost containment, non-monetary reward and employee preferences.

3. From architecture to content

This chapter has focused on the importance of a solid reward architecture as a basis for other HR processes and the reward system itself. It has demonstrated that in order to ensure a sustainable reward and job architecture, a number of primary conditions need to be fulfilled: relevant role descriptions and a job evaluation framework, such as STRATA, that is capable of capturing all relevant information about the business for consistency throughout the organisation.

When a solid job architecture is implemented, organisations can begin to assign fixed salary ranges and other benefits to each job family and level. To ensure consistency across their market and industry, as well as internally, organisations can undertake a benchmarking exercise. This enables organisations to compare internal and external data in order to position themselves competitively.

The next step in the process of developing an effective and optimised reward system is to decide on the combination of reward to offer employees and executives. This is covered in the next chapter on reward mix.

7.
Reward mix

Key takeaways

1. Organisations need to find the right balance between financial and non-financial reward in order to remain competitive in the war for talent.

2. Customised reward packages, effective communication of benefits and monitoring preferences are key components of an effective total reward strategy.

3. A typical reward mix consists of a base salary, short-term incentives, long-term incentives, financial benefits and non-financial benefits.

4. Base salary structures are impacted by the EU directive on minimum wages, living wages, equal pay regulations and age discrimination.

5. Geographic differentials and remuneration adjustments for remote employees based on the cost of living are increasingly important considerations for organisations.

6. Employee preference studies that align reward with the values of both the organisation and employees can improve hiring, reduce attrition and enhance customer service.

One crucial question when designing an effective reward strategy is what to offer employees. In this respect, it is key that the offered reward mix strikes the right balance between financial and non-financial reward. This chapter delves into the importance of achieving this equilibrium and explores the key components that contribute to a successful total reward strategy in terms of reward mix, as we follow the evolution of remuneration from purely financial reward to total reward to total wellbeing, a state-of-the-art holistic reward strategy. This chapter also looks at the importance of customisation and the need to align changing employee preferences for reward with the organisation's values in order to remain competitive in the talent market.

1. From financial reward to total reward

Total reward covers both the financial and non-financial incentives that an employee can earn by working in an organisation. By rewarding the employee, the organisation signals to them that they did a good job. However, reward is not limited to just cash.

As we saw in chapter 1, financial or extrinsic reward covers all reward components that can be assigned a monetary value, such as base remuneration, variable remuneration (short and long term) and benefits in kind (e.g., contributions to a healthcare or pension plan, mobility allowances, discounts on products, gym membership). And non-financial or intrinsic reward is achieved by the employee experiencing a feeling of achievement in their job. This includes a better work-life balance, recognition from their supervisors, involvement in challenging work, growth opportunities, expanding their competences in a particular area, an attractive work environment, being part of a good team and the organisation's sense of purpose.

Figure 29: An inclusive view of total reward.

	COMMON EXAMPLES	REWARD ELEMENTS	DEFINITION
INTRINSIC Internal value	• Leadership • Values • Employer's reputation	Psychological alignment	TOTAL REWARD
	• Work-life effectiveness • Workability • Recognition • Job content • Building for the future • Work atmosphere • Quality of work • Job security • Talent and performance management	Engagement factors	
EXTRINSIC Everything we can assign a monetary value to	• Tangibles • Cars • Clubs • Discounts	Active benefits	TOTAL REMUNERATION
	• Retirement • Health and wellbeing • Holidays	Passive benefits	
	• Share plans • Long-term incentives	Long-term variable pay incentives	TOTAL DIRECT COMPENSATION
	• Annual incentive compensation • Bonus	Short-term variable pay incentives	TOTAL CASH
	• Base salary	Base cash based upon job description	

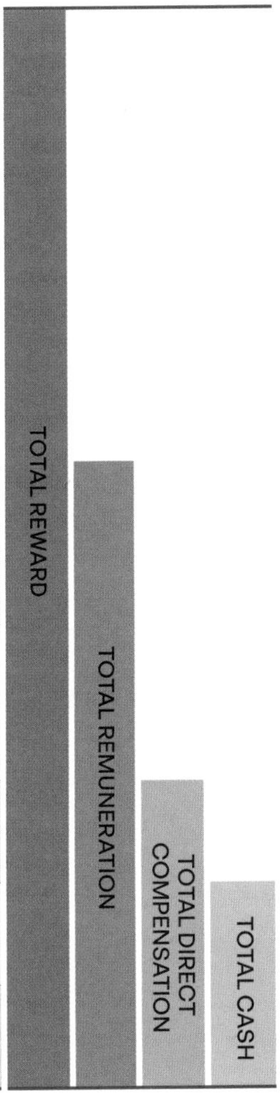

Even though the relative importance of financial benefits remains high, there has been a significant increase in the importance of other (non-)financial benefits such as medical, dental, vision and life insurance, wellbeing and supplemental health benefits, work-life balance options, training and career development.

It is a challenge to find the right balance between financial and non-financial benefits that also aligns with the employee's preferences. However, finding this balance plays a crucial role in an organisation's ability to remain an employer of choice in today's market. Not only will a carefully designed total reward strategy help to attract and retain the right talent, it can also improve the alignment of employees and business outcomes for the organisation. Furthermore, it is important for the organisation's employee value proposition (EVP), in other words the benefits that employees gain when they join and stay in an organisation.

In light of the changing talent landscape, organisations are encouraged to focus on the following four elements when creating an effective total reward strategy[148]:

- Data and insight
  Understand employees through comprehensive data and insights from engagement surveys and preference analytics. Cross-reference with demographics, locations and career development goals to enrich the generated insights.

- Customise and innovate
  Personalise total reward packages and offer deals that bundle types of reward, benefits and experience. Research indicates that if employees feel they have choice and control, they place greater value on the overall offering. Today, reward can even include choices involving environmental impact or time with the family.

- Communicate and implement
  Align with employee expectations, provide user-friendly processes and communicate the benefits offered by the organisation.

- Monitor and evolve
  Remain agile as employee preferences and the talent landscape evolves. By regularly monitoring and evolving, organisations can create a competitive advantage in the war for talent.

Transitioning from focusing on financial reward to embracing total reward improves recruitment and retention objectives, reduces costs and improves profitability. By strategically reallocating reward in a more cost-effective manner, organisations can strengthen their comprehensive reward system, elevating the perceived value of reward in the eyes of their employees. This holistic approach fosters a more comprehensive and satisfying employee experience, which contributes to a more sustainable and prosperous corporate environment.

1.1. Job base salary

Base salary serves as the foundation for an employee's remuneration and plays a crucial role in attracting, retaining and motivating employees, as an employee who is unsatisfied with their base salary is more likely to leave their job. Base salary is a fixed cost for organisations, and should reflect internal and external equity. This means that the base salary is primarily determined by the job they do within the organisation (internal factors) as well as being attractive, market competitive and compliant with national regulations (external factors). See chapter 6 on internal job architecture and external benchmarking for more information on this.

1.1.1. Internal factors
Job analysis
It is vital to understand the specific jobs within the organisation in order to determine the base salary. This means systematically gathering and analysing information about specific jobs and job families, including essential duties, responsibilities, needed skills, competences and qualifications.

Job evaluation
After analysis and descriptions, the jobs are evaluated to determine their value within the organisation to obtain internal equity. This enables a systematic comparison between job values to establish a grading base salary structure.

1.1.2. External factors
Benchmarking
Also known as market analysis, benchmarking assists organisations to develop a pay structure that is competitive to the external market. This involves comparing their pay practices with similar employers in the same industry and/or local market to determine similar rankings for jobs and job families.

The regulatory environment
A competitive base salary not only needs to be competitive to the external market, it also needs to be compliant with national laws and regulations, which vary significantly from country to country.

Minimum wages

The regulations regarding minimum wages are a critical aspect in determining base salary. Countries often have mandated minimum wage levels that serve as the baseline for remuneration packages, where the minimum wage is the lowest wage that employers are legally obliged to pay their employees per hour, week or month. The minimum wage amount is usually set after consultation with social partners or by a national intersectoral agreement.

The national minimum wage usually applies to (almost) all employees, with exceptions in some countries for some types of employees, such as younger employees, apprentices or employees with disabilities. As income tax and social security deductions vary between countries, gross amounts are reported to facilitate comparisons. Minimum wage laws contain provisions for regular reviews, often involving tripartite negotiations among government, unions and employers, to reflect changes in prices, wages and other economic factors. The minimum wage may be subject to automatic reassessments (indexed to the consumer price index (CPI) or economic growth) or to discretionary increases (via legislation)[149]. In January 2024, monthly minimum wages in the EU Member States range from € 477 in Bulgaria to € 2,571 in Luxembourg[150].

Figure 30: Minimum wages in January 2014 and January 2024. Figures are in € per month and average annual growth in %[151].

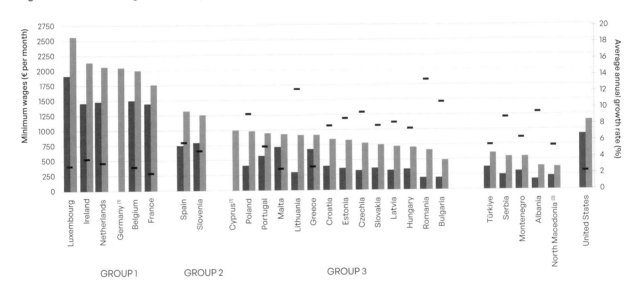

■ Minimum wages, January 2014 (left hand scale)
■ Minimum wages, January 2024 (left hand scale)
— Average annual growth rate, January 2014 to January 2024 (right hand scale)

Note: Denmark, Italy, Austria, Finland and Sweden have no national minimum wage.
(1) January 2014 and average annual rate of change not available.
(2) Minimum wage in force on 1 July 2021

The EU has established a new Directive that promotes adequate statutory minimum wages in Europe, helping to achieve improved working and living conditions for employees. The final text of the directive on adequate minimum wages was adopted by the Council on October 4, 2022, and does not aim to impose the same level of remuneration throughout the Member States nor to establish a uniform mechanism for fixing minimum wages.

The result of this Directive is not a single European minimum wage. This is because the EU's competences in social matters are limited. Additionally, it would have a negative effect on the economy. For example, if Bulgaria were to raise its minimum wage to the same level as in Luxembourg, its economy would become non-existent.

Instead, the aim of the EU Directive is to guarantee that the minimum wage offers a dignified standard of living to those who receive it, while ensuring that it remains a national competence[152].

To achieve this aim, Member States have to ensure that their national minimum wages enable employees to live decently, taking into account the cost of living and different levels of wages. In order for the minimum wage to be adapted to the cost of living, Member States must encourage collective bargaining which involves significant mobilisation of social partners. In countries where less than 80% of employees are covered by collective bargaining, Member States, in collaboration with social partners, need to establish an action plan to increase this coverage[153].

Each Member State also needs to establish a control system with reliable monitoring and field inspections to ensure compliance with the Directive and combat abusive subcontracting, false self-employment, undeclared overtime or increased labour intensity[154].

Living wages
With the Corporate Sustainability Reporting Directive (CSRD) prompting businesses to increase their focus on social issues, there is a noticeable surge in awareness about organisations paying living wages globally. The concept of a living wage is defined as the remuneration level that enables an individual and their family to cover all essential needs, meet necessary tax obligations and set aside savings for emergencies, enabling them to live with dignity and well-being, which, in most cases, exceeds the required statutory minimum wage (where one exists).

According to a recent survey, 67% of organisations believe that paying a living wage is a priority for their business. Even more, this survey states that "*the statutory minimum wage is below what is calculated to be a living wage and therefore what is considered as the minimum necessary to meet the basic needs of the employee and their family. This is where meeting the living wage will have the most impact for employees and economies alike, and addressing this gap will have an impact which transcends global regions, industries and geographies. Striking a balance between offering competitive pay and adhering to these minimum standards is an intricate task that requires meticulous attention*"[155].

Equal pay
Furthermore, equal pay regulations play a pivotal role in shaping base salary structures. Organisations are obligated to ensure that employees are remunerated fairly, regardless of gender, ethnicity or other protected characteristics. To address this issue, the EU's Pay Transparency Directive[156] aims to establish equal pay for equal work or work of equal value. By promoting pay transparency, the objective is to empower employees to assert their right to equal pay. Member States have until June 7, 2026, to incorporate this directive into their national legislation. See chapter 10 for more information on the Pay Transparency Directive.

In addition to minimum wages and equal pay, anti-age discrimination laws also come into play. Some jurisdictions have stringent regulations to prevent discrimination based on age, mandating that employees are compensated fairly irrespective of their age bracket. This adds an additional layer of complexity for remuneration professionals, as they must consider age-related factors when structuring base salary to remain in compliance with the law.

1.1.3. Base pay structuring and development

Base salary structuring involves defining the bandwidth of a salary scale for certain jobs and job families, by positioning the minimum, midpoint and maximum salary limits for each job level. This enables organisations to monitor the required behaviour and performance, bring order and clarity to managing salary rises and career development and ensure internal fairness.

Most organisations perform an annual review of their salary bands based on benchmarking. Employees within a specific salary band may be eligible for a salary increase or development allowance, contingent upon factors such as the length of service, acquired skills, competencies and individual or organisational performance.

Typically, employers manage their pay increases through merit increases, which boost employee salary based on their performance. Moreover, employers can manage the size and frequency of merit increases within a salary band. The compa-ratio tool is useful for this, comparing the relationship of the employee's actual salary to the midpoint of a specific level. For example, if a manager has a salary of € 75,000, but the midpoint for that job is € 80,000, then the compa-ratio is 0.94.

Typically, organisations strive to pay their high performers 90-110% or 95-105% of the midpoint[157]. A high-performer who is located at the bottom of the salary band will receive a higher pay increase in comparison to a high performer who is located at the top of the salary band.

Indexation

Certain countries, including Belgium, use automated salary indexation to adjust base salaries to consumer price increases. Salary indexation mechanisms need to be considered in the organisation's reward system as they play an important role in the way that base salary increases are determined in local markets. See chapter 5 for more information on salary indexation.

Working from anywhere (WFA)

New ways of working are empowering employees to work from anywhere and organisations are facing the reality that a growing number of employees are embracing remote work. This means that employees can execute their work from countries other than the headquarters of the organisation, which needs to be reflected in the organisation's reward system.

One critical consideration concerns remuneration for employees that work remotely: should they be remunerated based on the standards of the organisation's headquarters or should their salary ranges be adjusted to align with the specific location where they reside? The latter approach involves aligning remuneration to the local cost of living, which could be higher (or lower) than at the headquarter location. Either way, employers are now required to have a strategic reward system with a clear pay methodology for both employees who work locally and remotely. There are four main ways to achieve this.

Figure 31: An example of a salary increase matrix using the compa-ratio approach.

PERFORMANCE	COMPA-RATIO			
	0.75 - 0.87	0.88 - 1.00	1.01 - 1.13	1.13 - 1.25
Outstanding	6% - 7%	5% - 6%	4% - 5%	3% - 4%
Above average	5% - 6%	4% - 5%	3% - 4%	2% - 3%
Average	3% - 4%	2% - 3%	1% - 2%	0.5% - 1%
Below average	1% - 2%	0.5% - 1%	0.25% - 0.5%	0.1% - 0.25%
Unsatisfactory	0%	0%	0%	0%

- Align all remuneration with the headquarters
  This approach values the job role, regardless of the employee's geographical location. Remuneration is determined according to the headquarters location, so all in-office and WFA employees are paid according to the main reward system. This means that a remote employee who lives in a location with a low cost of living will have higher purchasing power than an in-office employee at headquarters due to the difference in the cost of labour in the headquarter's country and the country where the remote employee resides.

- Use current market-level salaries for the employee's location
  Unlike the first approach, salaries are determined based on the current market level salary for the remote employee's specific location. Organisations set remuneration levels for particular jobs by benchmarking against similar organisations in that location. However, implementing this approach requires time and financial resources to gather and analyse the necessary databases and surveys, which are sometimes limited or unavailable making this task more challenging.

  It is crucial to recognise that market-level pay, which is determined by supply and demand within a specific location, may not align with the concept of WFA, but it does consider global supply and demand to take broader market dynamics into account.

- Develop a geographic differentials structure
  The third approach lies in the middle of the one-size-fits-all first approach and the individualised second approach. By implementing a geographic differentials structure, organisations establish a reward structure that is based on competitive remuneration at their headquarters or specified base locations. Alternatively, organisations can utilise cost of living information instead of competitive salary data to determine geographical differences.

After deciding whether to use competitive remuneration or cost of living information, the organisation can create as many reward structures as they wish, with each structure linked to a specific work location determined by the organisation. This approach simplifies the concept of market-based remuneration.

- Remuneration based on the cost of living
  In the last approach, organisations use their remuneration structure based on competitive salaries for the headquarters location. This is then adjusted, using cost of living data, for the location where the remote employee lives. This approach is similar to the third one, except that here organisations focus on the individual employee's situation.

1.2. Short term variable pay incentives

After establishing a base salary programme in line with the market, organisations can then add a variable incentive to it.

Lasting a year or less, short-term incentive plans (STIPs) motivate employees to achieve certain goals in line with the organisation's objectives, where the goals are achievable, easy to measure and have a concrete impact on the organisation.

When designing a STIP, the employer needs to decide which employee behaviour will help the overall organisation to achieve its objectives. In return for reaching their goals through excellent performance or achievements during the reference period, employers should offer reward. Even though there is a risk that the employee won't receive the full amount of the variable reward, it is also important that employees feel a sense of control over these short-term goals. Without that feeling of control, the incentive plan is ineffective and the desired behaviour is unlikely to happen.

1.2.1. Eligibility

When implementing a STIP, it is vital to define who is eligible for it. Most organisations that offer a STIP typically grant it in line with the job level, so employees at higher levels tend to receive higher bonus amounts. STIP awards are often defined as a percentage of the employee's base salary.

Executives and salespeople typically have separate STIPs. Executive STIPs for quoted organisations are governed by corporate governance rules in most jurisdictions. Shareholders play an active role in shaping their design, aligning with the 'say on pay' principle which emphasises the importance of shareholder input in executive remuneration arrangements.

Salespeople, who play a pivotal role in revenue generation, often have their own tailored STIPs to recognise and reward their performance in driving sales and contributing to the organisation's bottom line. Overall, remuneration for salespeople emphasises variable remuneration, unlike the fixed remuneration structures commonly found in other roles. This approach aligns with the nature of their responsibilities, where performance and achievement of sales targets play a central role.

1.2.2. Performance KPIs

For the STIP to be successful, it is important to select the right (financial or non-financial) performance KPIs. On one hand, employers need to design KPIs that motivate employees to behave in a certain way that results in the desired outcomes for the organisation. On the other hand, employees need to have control over the KPIs. This means that the KPIs need to be specific and measurable, as well as being linked to the employee's daily activities.

A suitable KPI is aligned with organisational strategy. This requires the employer to define how achieving the KPI directly supports the organisation's strategic goals and mission. The KPI will also be quantifiable and can be measured objectively in a complete and approachable manner. Ideally, the granularity of the available data within the organisation enables employees to have control over the KPI, particularly across different organisational layers.

Organisations often use a balanced scorecard to define performance KPIs. It considers a number of financial and non-financial performance indicators to set objective and measurable goals on different levels of the organisation. The balanced scorecard

Figure 32: KPIs linked to the four dimensions of the balanced scorecard.

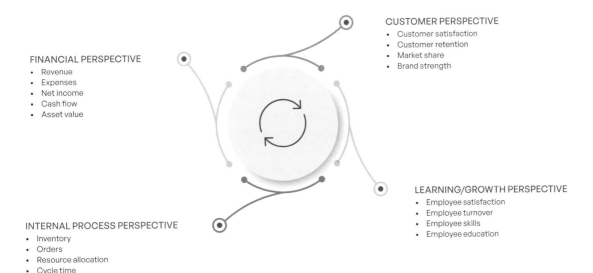

FINANCIAL PERSPECTIVE
- Revenue
- Expenses
- Net income
- Cash flow
- Asset value

CUSTOMER PERSPECTIVE
- Customer satisfaction
- Customer retention
- Market share
- Brand strength

INTERNAL PROCESS PERSPECTIVE
- Inventory
- Orders
- Resource allocation
- Cycle time
- Quality control

LEARNING/GROWTH PERSPECTIVE
- Employee satisfaction
- Employee turnover
- Employee skills
- Employee education

typically comprises four dimensions of organisational performance, encompassing customer interactions, employee learning and development, internal business processes and financial metrics.

Even though the employee should have control over the KPI, it should still be challenging. Behavioural research suggests that individual creativity and initiative is maximised when people are under a reasonable amount of pressure to perform. Remove the pressure, and performance and creativity slow to a more relaxed pace. Therefore, performance KPIs should be challenging, but not perceived as either too easy or unreasonably difficult.

For example, a 5% increase in profit may be relatively easy to achieve, while a 35% increase in profit may be extremely difficult. When put into a graph (see figure 33), we can see that if the goal is too easy to achieve, employees are not challenged and the motivational effects are dampened. As the goal becomes more difficult, the effort increases and employees find ways to rise to the challenge. In this example, employees are working at their full potential to meet a goal of 17%. However, at a certain point, the goal seems unreasonably difficult and employees begin to give up. They believe that achieving the goal is either impossible or not worth the effort leading to a fall in motivation and effort as the goal passes 18%.

Figure 33: An example that compares motivation to achieve a goal to the difficulty of the goal.

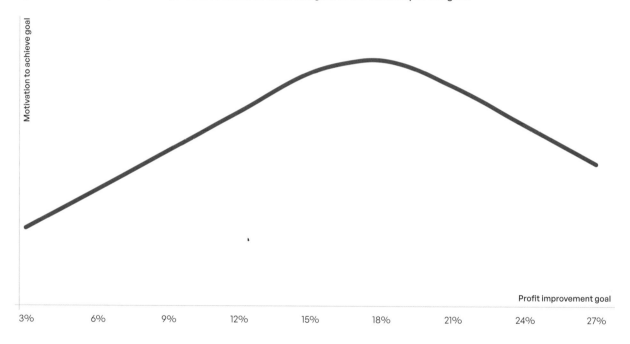

1.2.3. Target reward

The target reward from a short term incentive (STI) is usually expressed as a percentage of the employee's base salary. For example, if an employee meets their performance goals, they earn an additional 10 or 20% of their base salary as variable remuneration. But what happens if the employee does not meet or if they exceed the performance goal? Organisations often decide to introduce a threshold and a cap to determine the minimum and maximum levels of performance required to earn the incentive.

The threshold represents the minimum level of performance that an employee must achieve in order to qualify for any variable pay, serving as a baseline expectation and ensuring that employees meet a certain standard before being eligible for additional remuneration. It is typically set based on the minimum acceptable level of performance required to contribute to the organisation's success.

At the other end of the spectrum, the cap represents the maximum level of performance, beyond which

an employee cannot earn any additional variable pay. It sets a limit on the amount of remuneration an employee can receive, even if they exceed their performance targets by a significant margin. The cap is usually determined based on factors such as budget constraints, fairness considerations and the organisation's overall remuneration philosophy.

An alternative to using a percentage of an employee's base salary to determine the variable pay is to either set the variable remuneration as a fixed amount or as performance tiers. In the latter approach, employees are categorised into different performance levels, each with a different level of variable remuneration. This means that employees who achieve the highest performance level have a higher target amount compared to employees in the lower performance levels.

Most organisations also use benchmark data to determine the STI target. This ensures that variable remuneration targets are aligned with market practices.

Figure 34: An example of a linear pay-out curve for STIPs with a threshold of 80% and a cap of 140%.

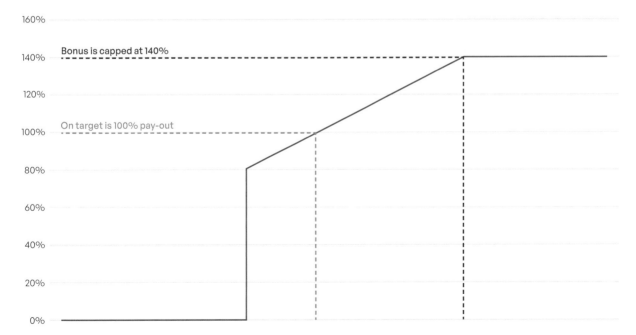

1.3. Long term variable pay incentives

In addition to STIPs, organisations can implement long-term incentive plans (LTIPs) as part of their total reward system to attract, motivate and retain key executives and align their financial interests with those of shareholders.

Using LTIPs to attract and reward key executives has become a very common market practice. In fact, they can make the difference when prospective executives assess the attractiveness of job offers[158]. To be competitive on the talent market, organisations either need to include LTIPs as part of their total reward system or offer other reward components or base salaries and bonus levels that are above market levels, but may not support shareholder value creation in the same way as an LTIP[159]. In a competitive talent market environment where the trend is for the vast majority of organisations to use LTIPs, it is extremely difficult to buck this trend and still attract the talent the organisation needs.

Motivation is another driver for granting LTIPs. This relies on the shareholder expectation that executives will perform better if they are properly incentivised[160]. Although executives' interests do not always align with those of shareholders, equity-based incentives may cause a better alignment for executives[161]. As LTIPs enable executives to obtain higher remuneration when the organisation outperforms in the long run, they encourage executives to take the appropriate management decisions to improve business performance and sustain shareholder value.

Lastly, LTIPs help organisations to retain talent during the ubiquitous war for talent. Organisations can defer remuneration with LTIPs, encouraging executives to stay at the organisation while it is performing well or until the date the LTIP award vests. As leavers lose their unvested awards, they forfeit a significant portion of their LTIP value by leaving. This may encourage executives to reassess leaving, or at least the timing for their departure[162]. However, market fluctuations in the organisation's stock price may affect the LTIP's value and, therefore, their ability to retain executives[163].

1.3.1. How long term incentives work
Executive LTIPs

Executive LTIPs take many forms, including stock options, restricted stocks, restricted stock units (RSUs) and stock appreciation rights (SARs).

Stock Options
Stock options provide the right to purchase shares over a fixed period of time (the exercise period) against a price (the exercise price), which is generally the grant share price (i.e., the value of the share at the time the options are granted, also known as the grant date). Stock option arrangements have an average lifetime of 5 to 10 years.

Together with RSUs, stock options are the most common form of LTIP. Like SARs, they are leveraged financial instruments which may provide an important pay-off for the executive. Stock options offer the executive the opportunity to benefit from any share price increase from the grant date to the option's exercise date. Additionally, executives are not exposed to the risk that the share price plummets below the exercise price, as options are generally granted at no cost, apart from the tax cost in jurisdictions that tax options at grant.

In general, stock option agreements include a step-in vesting period that describes when they become exercisable over the vesting period. For example, if the vesting period is four years, the stock options typically vest in four equal instalments on the anniversary date of the grant date, subject to the executive remaining at the organisation, creating a retention effect. Alternatively, the stock options can all vest together, in a one-cliff vesting, but this can hold a lower perceived value for executives, reducing its motivational impact. Additionally, the amount of options that vest may be subject to achieving certain performance conditions.

As the executives' risk profile for share price fluctuations does not match that of the shareholders, executives holding options may take management decisions that exceed the shareholders' risk appetite. For this reason, organisations may prefer LTIPs that mix stock options with restricted stocks and RSUs.

Restricted stocks and RSUs

Restricted stocks are shares that are transferred, along with all shareholders' rights, to an executive on the grant date. There are restrictions on the shares, such as they cannot be transferred during a contractually agreed period (i.e., the vesting period) and they are forfeit if the executive leaves the organisation before the agreed vesting date. The executive is also entitled to the dividend distributions, paid either during the vesting period or at the expiry of the vesting period.

Like stock options, restricted stocks may either gradually vest over the vesting period (step-in vesting) or all vest together at the expiry of the vesting period (one cliff-vesting). However, one-cliff vesting some years after the grant date may result in the executive having a lower perceived value of the award, reducing its motivational and retention role.

Unlike restricted stocks, RSUs are a promise made at the grant date to allocate shares to the executive for free on the agreed vesting dates. This means that the shareholders' rights are not transferred prior to the vesting dates.

Vesting of RSUs works in a similar way to restricted stocks, with step-in vesting or one-cliff vesting. The vesting is sometimes subject to performance conditions, with the amount of transferred shares being calibrated with the achieved performance over the vesting or performance period.

A key difference between restricted stocks and RSUs is their tax point for employment tax purposes. RSUs are generally taxed on their vesting date, while the tax point for restricted stocks in most jurisdictions is their grant date. Because restricted stocks are forfeitable shares (i.e., the restricted stocks may be clawed back for no consideration by the organisation in case of employment termination prior to the vesting date), their taxation at grant for employment tax purposes means that organisations generally opt for RSUs. Indeed, with RSUs there is no risk that the executive will lose the shares once employment taxes have been paid. Another difference is that RSUs can be settled in shares or in cash, while restricted shares can only be settled in shares on the grant date. During the RSU vesting period, the executive is generally entitled to dividend equivalents (i.e., amounts equivalent in value to dividends, but not treated as dividends from a legal or tax perspective as the executive is not a shareholder prior to the vesting date). Instead, the dividend equivalents are treated as employment income.

Unlike stock options, restricted stocks and RSUs give the executive a risk profile that is closer to the shareholders' risk profile. Both restricted stocks and RSUs track the share's value, supporting the alignment of the executive's financial interests with those of the shareholders during the vesting period. Therefore, executives with restricted stocks and RSUs are more likely to be aligned with shareholders than executives that exclusively hold stock options. In practice, organisations tend to combine stock options with either restricted stocks or RSUs.

Stock appreciation rights

SAR agreements have the same economic features as stock options, including a vesting period during which the SARs vest, as long as the employee remains in service at the organisation. When exercised, SARs entitle the recipient to obtain the spread value at exercise, which is measured as the difference between the fair market value (FMV) of the exercised SAR shares at the time of the exercise and the value measured when the SARs were granted. That spread value is either settled in cash or in shares. If the SARs are settled in shares, the executive receives an amount of shares computed by dividing the spread value at exercise by the share price at exercise.

While some organisations use SARs, they are not as common as stock options and RSUs.

Broad-based employee stock purchase plans

While LTIPs are heavily concentrated among executives and rarely extend to other employees, an employee stock purchase plan enables non-executives to become shareholders[164].

Employee stock purchase plans (ESPPs) offer employees the opportunity to acquire shares at a discount after an agreed saving period which usually lasts for a period of three to twelve months[165]. ESPPs encourage employee ownership, aligning the interests of employees with those of shareholders[166].

The discount applied to the purchase price varies depending on the ESPP, but can be as high as 15%[167]. Certain ESPPs have a 'lookback' provision that bases the purchase price on the lower of either the discounted price at the start of the saving period or the discounted price at the end of the saving period[168]. Some ESPPs may require the employee to keep the shares for an agreed period, usually over a year.

Measuring LTIP costs

Shareholders can use accounting treatments to quantify the financial costs of granting stock options and other long term incentives (LTI). LTIP-related costs are reflected in the organisation's financial statements, so shareholders can better assess whether their costs are worth their expected benefits, which was not the case for all LTIPs prior to the 2002 financial crisis, and can calibrate LTIP grant sizes and features at an acceptable cost.

Accounting of LTIPs also provides shareholders the opportunity to benchmark their LTIP costs against those of their competitors and the market, enabling them to make informed decisions about the LTIPs they offer.

On February 19, 2004, the International Accounting Standards Board (IASB) issued the International Financial Reporting Standard 2 (IFRS2) Share-based payment[169]. For the first time, organisations were required to quantify the effect of LTIPs in their financial statements (i.e., share-based payment transactions), including the expenses associated with transactions where stock options are granted to executives and employees[170]. Previously, these transactions were not recognised in the organisation's financial statements, although they were disclosed in the notes when reporting earnings to capital markets[171]. This resulted in shareholders having poor information about stock option-related costs, so they were unlikely to be able to properly assess whether they were market conforming and worth their costs.

IFRS2 applies to all share-based transactions, including equity-settled and cash-settled share-based transactions, as well as transactions with a choice of settlement[172]. It requires all share-based transactions to be recognised as an expense.

The accounting method used depends on the nature of the transaction: equity-settled, cash-settled or a choice of settlement. In principle, the organisation measures the goods or services received in connection to a share-based payment and the corresponding increase in equity (equity-settled) or liability (cash-settled) at fair value[173].

For equity-settled share-based transactions, the fair value of the granted equity instruments is measured and fixed at the grant date. This means that the expense is charged to the profit or loss over the vesting period.

For cash-settled awards, the fair value is measured at the grant date and subsequently remeasured at each reporting date for changes in fair value until the settlement date[174]. This means that a change in the fair value results in a change in value. For example, if the underlying share price increases, the share-based payment expense also increases.

For both equity-settled and cash-settled awards, the number of awards expected to vest is estimated at each closing date over the vesting period.

For share-based transactions which provide one party (either the entity or counterparty) with the choice of settlement, the recognition and valuation of such transactions depends on whether the entity or counterparty has the choice of settlement. The accounting treatment of this type of transaction is outside the scope of this book.

Organisations are more inclined to opt for equity-settled LTIPs rather than for cash-settled LTIPs. This is because the carried liability for cash-settled LTIPs is remeasured for subsequent changes in fair value until the settlement date of the LTIP award, and if the underlying share price increases, the share-based payment expense also increases. For equity-settled LTIPs, the expense is measured and fixed at the grant date and spread over the vesting period. This means that equity-settled LTIPs are less volatile from an accounting perspective, which is generally preferred by organisations and shareholders.

1.3.2. LTIPs in practice

Choosing the right LTIP for an organisation can be challenging, but when performance remuneration is managed carefully, it aligns executive and employee behaviour with the organisation's strategy to drive better performance[175]. Organisations tend to use publicly available data on executive remuneration (e.g., corporate governance and executive salary reports) to benchmark executive remuneration. However, this may be too complicated for smaller, unquoted organisations as there is often not enough publicly available data for them to benchmark their reward offering[176]. While benchmarking has many advantages, it is worth noting that some experts believe it has led organisations to offer ever-increasing levels of remuneration[177].

Finding appropriate LTIPs that promote the growth of executives and the organisation's capabilities requires deviating from benchmarking to focus on the business and the people. Strategic thinking is essential to align incentives policies with both the organisation's ambition and HR strategy to deliver the full potential of LTIPs[178].

When it comes to deciding which incentive strategies to use, it is important to have a deep understanding of the type of business (quoted versus unquoted), the maturity of the organisation (mature versus start-up) and the executives' expectations.

To give an example of how these factors influence the choice of incentive strategy, consider the needs of mature organisations and start-ups. Mature organisations are well established in their industry with a well-known product offering, however, they may face slower or steady growth at some point[179]. Start-ups are on the other end of the spectrum, often having a disruptive business model or a unique or innovative product offering that makes them stand out in the market and can lead to a rapid growth of their organisation[180].

As a leveraged product offering high reward potential, options appear to be best suited for start-ups rather than mature organisations with a declining product offering and a less significant growth potential. In mature organisations, giving stocks is a better alternative in order to maintain the status quo. The value of stocks fluctuates depending on the organisation's performance and growth, so a reasonable amount of growth from the organisation will reward the shareholders and LTIP-holders with dividends.

To simplify administration, some organisations tend to standardise their LTIPs[181]. However, duplicating an incentive programme from another organisation without considering internal reactions is unlikely to work and can be expensive for shareholders who expect the LTIP to drive performance and organisational growth[182].

Even though a PwC survey showed that the majority of executives are risk averse, their attitudes to risk differ in developed and emerging markets[183]. Even so, LTIPs can only be effective if the organisation strongly considers how the potential beneficiaries of the LTIP actually perceive them. This is why organisations should customise their LTIP strategies to their particular situation. Organisations need to evaluate the possibilities of their industry, investigate their executives' attitude to risk and focus on maintaining some flexibility to adapt LTIPs to meet their executives' preferences, which could involve offering multiple LTI instruments[184]. For example, some organisations already offer the choice between restricted stocks and options, with the results generally showing a higher perceived value, which could outweigh the administrative cost of implementation[185].

See chapter 8 for more information on LTIPs in mergers, acquisitions and spin-off organisations.

1.4. Financial benefits

Financial benefits occupy a central place in an organisation's HR strategy, playing a crucial role in employee motivation and remuneration. The benefits offered by organisations, such as competitive salaries, bonuses, benefits and other forms of remuneration, are fundamental to attracting and retaining qualified talent. These benefits contribute to employee satisfaction by meeting their financial needs and improving their quality of life. Additionally, financial benefits promote employee motivation, boosting productivity and engagement within the organisation.

These benefits also contribute to competitiveness in the job market, reinforcing the organisation's image as an attractive employer and aligning with organisational objectives to create an environment conducive to collective success. In this context, financial benefits are not simply monetary incentives, but strategic levers that shape the dynamic between the organisation and its employees, promoting growth and organisational sustainability.

1.4.1. Mobility

A company car is often considered a financial benefit for employees, as it allows them to benefit from a vehicle, provided by their employer, in both their personal and work lives. It enables employees to reduce their transportation costs as the employee does not pay the costs of purchasing, renting, insuring, maintaining or repairing the vehicle. These savings can be significant and help improve the employee's financial situation.

Driving electric vehicles (EVs) is becoming an increasingly viable and attractive option thanks to advances in technology, increased charging infrastructure and growing environmental awareness. Organisations are helping to push this trend forward by encouraging their employees to only drive electric vehicles, which has the added benefit of reducing the organisation's CO_2 emissions, helping it to achieve its net-zero emission ambition or other sustainability targets.

A fleet of EVs can enhance the organisation's brand image, attracting environmentally conscious customers, business partners and talented potential employees who value organisations committed to environmental protection. Additionally, EVs are seen as symbols of technological innovation and progress. Encouraging their use can foster a culture of innovation and adaptability to new technologies within the organisation.

Providing company cars with reduced emissions is a strategic move for employers, particularly in light of PwC's recent Trust Survey where 86% of employees stated they wanted to be employed by an organisation that aligns with their values. Additionally, 53% of the over 2,000 employees surveyed emphasised the significance of their employer's purpose and values being congruent with their own[186].

Both company bikes and public transport offer a sustainable and efficient alternative to traditional company cars, providing an efficient, cost-effective and environmentally friendly mobility solution while improving employee quality of life and promoting a healthier lifestyle. By encouraging the use of these alternatives, employers can play a key role in promoting sustainable transportation and reducing the carbon footprint of their employees and society as a whole. This underscores corporate responsibility and positions the organisation as an ideal workplace for those who prioritise environmental values.

1.4.2. Occupational pension plan

Pensions in a reward context tend to be an occupational pension plan which is generated as part of the relationship between the employee and employer. This typically ensures that when the employee reaches retirement age, they receive an additional layer of financial benefits on top of the statutory pension benefits that they accrued under the national social security system.

As a result, such pension plans can be seen as deferred remuneration. In practice, different types of plans exist, such as a defined benefit plan, a defined contribution plan and a hybrid of the two. See chapter 11 for detailed information on occupational pension plans from a Belgian perspective.

1.4.3. Development and training

Organisations can attract committed employees by emphasising skill development, career advancement and ongoing learning. This involves the organisation developing clear career paths that help employees to understand why they should invest in their careers, opportunities for new projects that strengthen employee skills and training that broadens and deepens employees' skills and knowledge. In this way, the organisation goes beyond employer branding to create meaningful relationships with their employees.

1.4.4. Flexibility

There is no one-size-fits-all solution to attract and retain employees, which explains the importance of flexible and innovative benefit structures such as personalised packages or cafeteria plans, also known as a flexible benefits plan.

A cafeteria plan empowers employees to choose from a menu of different benefits or remuneration options. This involves offering employees the ability to tailor their benefits to better suit their unique circumstances, such as health insurance, meal vouchers and additional vacation days. This personalised, bottom-up approach places the employee at the core of a redefined and flexible reward system, which puts their needs and preferences first in order to foster employee engagement and motivation. Furthermore, the customisation of the reward system not only improves the overall employee experience but also supports employee wellbeing and improves their work-life balance.

1.5. Non-financial reward

As we saw in chapter 1, employees are motivated by more than just financial remuneration. Since the early days of sociology and organisational psychology, experts have studied the non-financial components that drive social relationships, helping us to understand the complex social relationships within the workplace[187]. These frameworks and explanations describe how employees and employers are motivated by both financial and non-financial reward.

Effective leaders know the value of recognition for engaging and motivating their employees, even in challenging economic or contextual situations. For example, numerous organisations distributed various gifts to their working from home (WFH) employees during Covid-19 lockdowns. These gifts recognised the huge effort made by employees when they suddenly switched to working fully remotely, as well as encouraged their connection and engagement with the organisation.

This section focuses on non-financial reward that recognises, engages and motivates employees, distinguishing between means (what is used as a reward) and schemes (how the reward is used)[188].

1.5.1. Means of recognition

There has been a lot of research carried out on different means of recognition, and their effectiveness as an incentive. There are three categories of means of reward: emotional reward, semi-financial reward and developmental reward.

Emotional reward

This category contains all types of recognition that do not have a monetary value. Common examples include a simple "thank you" during a team meeting, a mention or photo in the organisation's newsletter or a dedicated feature in the organisation's external communication.

> *EOM programmes as reward*
> *A widely spread example is employee of the month (EOM) programmes that can be found on workfloors around the world and aim to acknowledge the exemplary behaviour of one employee to serve as an example for the other employees[189]. Although these programmes aim to provide positive examples of good organisational practices, it can also spark a negative, or even hostile, team culture. As various authors point out, employees may be engaging in undesirable behaviours to produce the results, including undertaking unethical or illegal actions. Furthermore, the criteria for earning EOM is often vague, resulting in employees being unclear about how to get the reward or what the reward programme is about[190].*

Semi-financial reward

Reward in this category tends to have a limited and symbolic financial value. Even though the value of the reward might be perceived as substantial by the recipient, such as a high-end fountain pen or watch for a significant work anniversary, the reward's main characteristic is the symbol behind it, not the pure financial value.

> *SPOT awards as reward*
> *One example of a semi-financial reward is SPOT awards, also known as special performance or on-the-spot awards, which is a type of recognition immediately given to employees when exceptional performance occurs or a milestone is achieved such as demonstrating outstanding teamwork, solving a challenging issue or going above and beyond in customer service. While the criteria for receiving a SPOT award tends to vary depending on the organisation and its specific recognition programme, they are used to motivate and reward employees for their hard work, dedication and contributions by recognising and reinforcing desired behaviours and outcomes. Used correctly, SPOT awards can boost employee morale, engagement and motivation, as well as foster a positive work culture.*

Development reward

This type of reward includes anything that primarily aims to acknowledge and improve the skill that led to the achievement that is being recognised, or to unlock additional skills that will further upgrade the employee. As access to learning and development and opportunities for growth is becoming increasingly important over the different generations at work (see chapter 1), the impact of this type of reward should not be underestimated.

> *Training as reward*
> *Examples of training as a reward include team workshops to recognise extraordinary team achievements or a nomination for an exclusive training or networking event. These types of reward can be seen as win-win, as strong performers engage further with a growth path that benefits themselves and the organisation. Especially when granted collectively to a team, it can reinforce both positive behaviour on an individual level as well as the positive culture within the team on a collective level.*

1.5.2. Recognition schemes

Despite their low financial value, it is important for employers to understand how the means and the scheme of the reward work together. In other words, the different ways that reward can be perceived by recipients and their peers depending on when and how the reward is distributed.

For example, nominating an employee for an exclusive training event can recognise their current skills or it could give the recipient the impression that their skills are not up to par. Organisation-branded plastic merchandising distributed throughout the organisation could give employees a feeling of belonging, but it could imply that the employer does not consider sustainability to be important. A personalised "thank you" message will motivate the recipient, while a standard one handed out on random occasions will make employees question its authenticity. This shows that the reward's purpose, which is generally to improve the recipient's intrinsic motivation, is important when considering how to deliver reward linked to recognition. This connection has been illustrated by numerous studies that link recognition with engagement.

As the value of the reward is often of limited financial value, it becomes crucial to get the emotional value right. In other words, the recipient's perception of the recognition largely determines its success. To achieve a positive outcome, employers should consider the total experience for schemes that grant recognition by following the TAPAS model (timing, authenticity, participative, aligned and social).

Timing

Considering its limited value, recognition should happen shortly after the behaviour that the employer wants to positively reinforce occurs. Used in this way, it is an ideal complement to the regular performance bonus system, which is often an annual exercise. If a recognition reward followed a similar timeline, it would lose its differentiation against the standard performance cycle and not deliver an exceptional experience. Instead, the recognition award should be timely, prompt and appropriate for both the situation and the employee[191].

It is important to understand that introducing a recurring recognition reward can be both an opportunity and a risk. While recognising employees gives them positive reinforcement, it can easily become an automated exercise, which removes the gesture's authenticity. This does not mean that recurring recognition cannot become part of the organisation's culture, as many organisations have an award for 'employee of the month' or recognising achieving a milestone event or the start of a new period[192]. However, it is key to ensure that there is a discretionary element in the process, that includes a personal touch in the decision-making process.

Authenticity

Authenticity should not be underestimated, with research identifying it as the most important factor of best practice recognition as it influences the way that the recipient believes they are perceived in the organisation, what their future there will bring and the organisation's values[193].

As simple as it may seem, authenticity can just as easily go well as it can go wrong. This is because it is assessed by the perception of the recipient, not the good intentions of the employer. Imagine an employee being thanked for their hard work by a manager who pronounces their name incorrectly. This is likely to do more harm than good.

A positive example that was broadly cited in the international media was Taylor Swift's handwritten thank you note for the crew that worked on the logistics of her 'Eras' concert tour. Although combined with a significant bonus payment, the fact that the artist had gone to the trouble to write personal and individual notes only added to the exceptional experience, and pictures of the notes were widely spread on social media[194].

Participative

It is essential to embed recognition in the organisation's culture, ensuring that all levels of the organisation participate in recognition schemes, both as recipients and as grantors.

Involving different layers of the organisation can reinforce the effectiveness of a reward. Research has shown that the most memorable recognition comes most often from an employee's manager (28%), followed by a high-level leader or CEO (24%), the manager's manager (12%), a customer (10%) and peers (9%)[195].

This doesn't mean that recognition should come only top-down. Peer-to-peer recognition is even stronger when a team nominates a member from amongst them, as it expresses the team culture, highlights positive behaviour for that group and enhances the feeling of belonging to the team.

Some organisations use reflective recognition to help the manager understand how to best personalise recognition and reinforce the positive perception for the recipient by making them participative in the process[196]. Managers use reflective techniques in individual conversations or team meetings to encourage team members to share what they are proud of. This can uncover achievements that may otherwise go unnoticed and it also enables the manager to get a better understanding of what their team members value most.

Aligned

Recognition makes certain behaviours stand out, emphasising what the organisation finds important and identifying heroes of the organisation's culture. This means it is vitally important to carefully select recipients based on alignment with the organisation's values as their highlighted behaviour will spread.

However, it is important that the recognition itself aligns with the organisation's values. For example, sustainability is important to consider. It can be detrimental for the reward's internal authenticity and the organisation's external brand when the organisation promotes its environmental efforts but distributes a recognition reward to its employees that is heavily packaged or made from single-use plastic. Instead, this can be given a positive spin, for example, by using vouchers that support the local economy or community[197].

Social

The last part of TAPAS is the social aspect of recognition which underscores the importance of fostering a sense of community and shared success within the organisation.

When recognition is made public, whether through organisation-wide announcements, social media posts or shared during team meetings, it amplifies the positive impact on the recipient and inspires others to strive for excellence. This public acknowledgment helps to cultivate a culture of appreciation, reinforcing the organisation's values and vision and celebrating people and contributions at all levels.

It encourages a communal spirit, where achievements are collective wins that contribute to the overall goals and success of the organisation. Furthermore, social recognition strengthens connections among team members, enhancing teamwork and collaboration. By acknowledging achievements in a social context, organisations can create an environment where employees feel genuinely valued and part of a supportive community, leading to increased engagement, loyalty and motivation.

However, the social aspect may also turn into a political aspect, resulting in envy or strategic behaviour, thus leading to value destruction for the organisation[198]. As illustrated earlier, to avoid the reward from backfiring, selecting the recipient and the subject of the recognition should be a well considered decision that takes into account the organisation's values and context as well as individual preferences.

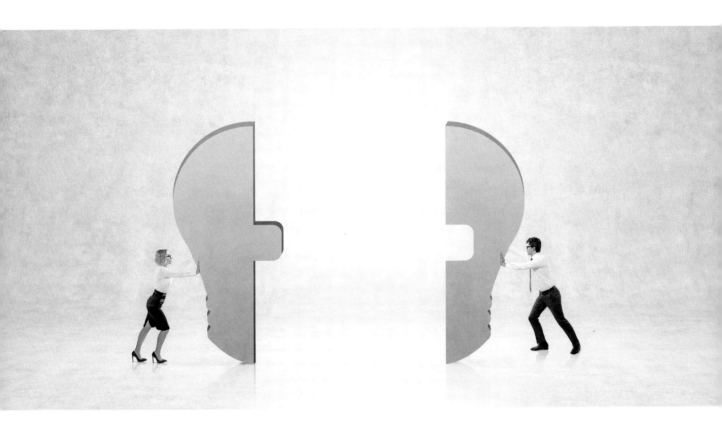

1.5.3. Total wellbeing

Non-financial reward, including recognition, is a vital component of total wellbeing within the organisational culture. This holistic approach to employee engagement encompasses the employee's physical and financial wellbeing, as well as their emotional, social and professional development.

Organisations can significantly enhance the total employee experience through strategic and thoughtful implementation of recognition programmes, including emotional, semi-financial or developmental reward and using the TAPAS model for recognition schemes. In turn, this fosters a more engaged, motivated and cohesive workforce, where employees feel genuinely valued and supported in all aspects of their professional and personal development.

By integrating recognition into the broader concept of total wellbeing, organisations elevate individual employee experiences while cultivating a thriving, resilient and inclusive workplace culture that values and celebrates every contribution. This holistic view benefits individual employees and propels organisations towards greater success, demonstrating the profound impact of recognition beyond the immediate moment of acknowledgement, towards the sustained engagement and wellbeing of all employees.

2. From total reward to total wellbeing

Figure 35: Moving from total reward to total wellbeing.

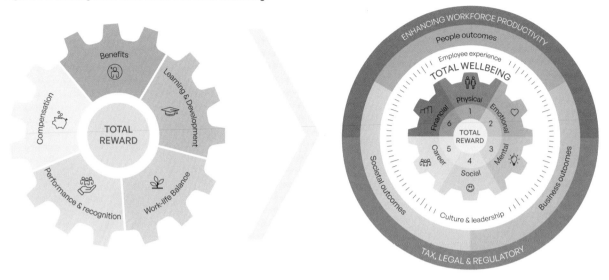

Reward systems continue to move forward, finding new ways to attract, motivate and retain talented employees. After moving from financial reward to total reward, organisations are starting to elevate their reward systems further by using a bottom-up approach to offer total wellbeing.

As previously discussed, total reward uses a top-down approach to add non-financial reward to the financial reward that organisations traditionally offered. Total wellbeing places the employee at the centre of a reframed, flexible approach to the total reward equation, creating a framework that organisations will use to deliver personalised reward to their employees in the future.

Traditionally, when there is a shortage of talent in the market, organisations are expected to offer more competitive remuneration and benefits packages[199]. However, providing higher salaries and larger benefit packages, sometimes at the cost of eroding profitability, is not sustainable in the long run. Especially as larger salaries are not enough to stop some employees from leaving their employer.

In today's competitive and inflationary environment, many organisations are focused on containing costs, yet they also realise that they need to do their utmost to attract and retain the best talent. This makes it increasingly important to optimise the return on their investment in reward.

Employees want to work for organisations that prioritise their employees' wellbeing and create a work environment that stimulates feelings of connection, commitment, belonging and growth. These considerations are becoming increasingly important as more employees pay attention to the compatibility between their own values and those of the organisation they work for, as well as to their general mental and physical wellbeing. Organisations are learning that, in order to attract and retain the best talent, they need to focus on the person as a whole, rather than just the employee at work.

2.1. Total wellbeing components

PwC's total wellbeing approach goes beyond the traditional focus on financial wellbeing to bring the employee's physical, social, emotional, career and mental-related wellbeing to the fore. These six wellbeing components create an employee experience that attracts, motivates and retains qualified employees, as well as helping the organisation to fully realise its productivity and performance potential.

2.1.1. Physical wellbeing

By providing access to resources and incentives for physical activities, employers can promote a healthier lifestyle and improve the physical wellbeing of their employees. This can include offering gym memberships and/or fitness reimbursement programmes or organising fitness challenges to encourage employees to engage in regular exercise. A relatively simple change to implement is to encourage employees to take regular breaks and be physically active during the workday.

Additionally, organisations can provide financial support for preventive healthcare services, such as annual check-ups or vaccinations, or making healthcare more accessible with (on-site) health screenings to help employees maintain their physical health. Programmes that address nutrition, stress management and ergonomics are also increasingly offered. This type of investment in the physical wellbeing of employees is resulting in reduced healthcare costs, decreased absenteeism and improved overall productivity for organisations.

2.1.2. Social wellbeing

In addition to diversity and inclusion initiatives, the social wellbeing component fosters a sense of belonging, which can involve creating affinity or employee resource groups to enable employees to connect with others who share similar backgrounds or interests. For example, creating communities, such as expats, young mothers or LGBTQIA+ can improve the social cohesion and wellbeing for employees.

Social wellbeing also promotes flexible work arrangements for a healthy work-life balance that strengthens social connections by enabling employees to spend more time with family and friends outside of work.

2.1.3. Emotional wellbeing

Employees deserve to be appreciated, so recognition and feedback should follow the TAPAS model (timing, authenticity, participative, aligned and social, see above) in order to have the greatest impact on employee emotions, morale and motivation. Implementing mindfulness practices into the work culture can help reduce stress and improve emotional resilience among employees, while mental health support resources, such as employee assistance programmes (EAPs) and counselling services, demonstrate the organisation's commitment to their employees' emotional wellbeing.

2.1.4. Career wellbeing

Career development is important for employee motivation and retention. Regular performance evaluations and career planning discussions can help employees track their progress and identify areas for growth, while aligning their career goals with the organisation's mission and values. This is an ideal opportunity for the organisation to support employee career wellbeing with training programmes, mentorships and tuition reimbursement that develop the employee's skills and advance their career. The result is employees that have a greater sense of purpose and fulfilment in their work.

2.1.5. Mental wellbeing

Work should be a safe environment, both physically and mentally. From a mental wellbeing perspective, organisations can encourage a healthy work-life balance by setting realistic workload expectations and providing resources that promote time management. It is also important for employers to create a culture of psychological safety at work where employees feel comfortable speaking up about mental health concerns without the fear of stigma, repercussions or retaliation, and managers are trained to recognise the signs of burnout or distress in their team members and provide the support and accommodations they need.

2.1.6. Financial wellbeing

The last component of wellbeing builds on the financial reward traditionally offered by organisations. Organisations should care about their employees' financial wellbeing, as financially-stressed employees tend to be more distracted, less engaged and more likely to look for another job. And this is becoming increasingly important as inflation hit hard in 2023, causing rising levels of financial stress as employees navigate higher prices, uneven wage growth and record credit card debt. More than ever before, employees are looking to their employers for help.

PwC's 2023 employee financial wellbeing survey shows that 60% of full-time employees are experiencing financial stress, which is slightly higher than the number of people who were stressed about their finances during the peak of the pandemic. Furthermore, this financial stress has a significant impact on various aspects of employee health and wellbeing, including sleep and self-esteem[200].

In this environment, financial benefits play a crucial role in attracting and retaining employees, promoting their wellbeing and providing financial security both during their working years and in retirement. This can include benefits such as a pension, group insurance and medical coverage. Pensions provide employees with a retirement income, based on their years of service and salary history. Group insurance offers employees access to various types of coverage, such as health, dental, vision and life insurance, often at lower costs compared to individual plans. Medical coverage ensures that employees have access to healthcare services and helps cover the costs of medical treatments and procedures. Additionally, financial wellbeing programmes that provide training on budgeting, saving and investing can help build trust and loyalty among employees.

2.1.7. A holistic approach

Employers who take a holistic approach to employee wellbeing and comprehensively address these six components will be rewarded with increased employee job satisfaction, productivity and retention.

It is important to note that, while all six components have an impact on employee wellbeing, it is extremely challenging to get excellent scores across all six components for all employees. Therefore, employers should strive for the best overall score. However, scoring extremely high on one or two components will not compensate for low scores on the other components. Paying insufficient attention to multiple components will result in employees feeling under-appreciated and could lead to them leaving the organisation.

Unfortunately, a standardised approach is unlikely to lead to an optimal result as employee populations become increasingly heterogeneous. Instead, organisations should try and understand individual preferences with a list of reward options that reflect an understanding of the wellbeing needs of individual employees, not just employee groups. Furthermore, organisations need to understand that individual preferences will change over time, so the total wellbeing strategy should evolve to meet changing employee needs. This is covered in more detail below in the section on employee preferences.

2.2. Ignoring total wellbeing

Failing to address total wellbeing can have a negative impact on employees, leading to undesirable effects for the organisation, and even for society. Experience shows the following negative effects may occur when total wellbeing is neglected:

Physical wellbeing: It has been proven that physical health affects productivity. Employees who are physically inactive, compared with those who are active, report a higher prevalence of cardiovascular diseases, fair or poor health status and absenteeism from work.

Social wellbeing: Employees who don't feel a sense of belonging in their organisation are less productive. Additionally, less engaged employees experience significantly more stress, anger and health problems.

Emotional wellbeing: Employees experiencing poor emotional wellbeing are less resilient and less able to cope with stress. Furthermore, they may struggle to deal with and learn from failure, crises or disappointment.

Career wellbeing: Lack of future career development remains a key driver of employee attrition and is often cited by departing employees as a dissatisfying factor in their job.

Mental wellbeing: Poor mental wellbeing often results in higher levels of absenteeism. It can also negatively impact productivity, as employees who are stressed or anxious may struggle to concentrate on work and daily activities.

Financial wellbeing: Financial stress can lead to distractions and reduced productivity among employees. Moreover, financially stressed employees are likely to seek job opportunities elsewhere.

With this in mind, rethinking total reward to deliver total wellbeing can only benefit the organisation in the long run. Together, the six components deliver better results for employees in the form of motivation, retention, employee engagement and productivity, for the organisation as a better return on investment, more customer satisfaction and higher financial performance, and for society with burnout prevention, improved governance and better compliance with regulations.

3. Employee preferences

As organisations strive to foster and maintain a culture of employee engagement and productivity, the significance of understanding and recognising employee preferences is increasingly important, especially when the supply of talent becomes scarce (see chapter 2 for more information on the demand and supply of talent).

Understanding and implementing employee preferences help organisations to stand out from their competition in the talent market. Employee preferences describe the attributes that job seekers and current employees want most in their employment relationships. These include job characteristics, the organisation itself, manager and co-worker relationships, remuneration, benefits and working conditions, such as flexible work schedules[201].

Organisations that prioritise understanding and meeting the diverse needs of their employees are better positioned to attract top talent as well as to retain and harness the potential of their existing employees.

When implementing a reward system based on employee preferences, it is important to note that a one-size-fits-all approach does not work as employees have unique backgrounds, aspirations and values. As we saw in chapter 1, employees can be motivated in different ways, including satisfaction from challenging projects and opportunities for personal growth (i.e., intrinsic motivation) and recognition, financial incentives and a healthy work-life balance (i.e., extrinsic motivation). Recognising and respecting these diverse preferences is pivotal in creating a workplace where employees feel valued, heard and empowered to contribute their full potential.

3.1. Employee experience (EX) and employee value proposition (EVP)

Every organisation sets the primary parameters of its products/services and makes decisions on the basis of the expectations and/or reactions of its customers to its products/services. Customers and their behaviour are top priority of an organisation.

When organisations turn this around to view their employees as their customers, they find themselves doing their best to create an attractive and compelling EX. Research has shown that improving EX is likely to drive a strong customer experience[202], meaning that improving EX is in an employer's vested interest. Employees are uniquely positioned to transmit an organisation's brand message directly to customers and other stakeholders because when they feel good at an organisation they represent it to customers enthusiastically, proudly and honestly, which delivers an outstanding experience to their audience.

EX is defined as the sum of everything an employee experiences throughout their connection to the organisation, from their first contact as a potential hire to their last touchpoints after their employment ends[203]. While EX requires a holistic, focused and purposeful approach, most organisations design and manage it as a set of discrete elements of employment, e.g., flexible work arrangements, reward and recognition programmes or wellbeing initiatives. However, this way of thinking is outdated as EX is created through the overall organisational culture.

It is more than just employee engagement, as it focuses not only on retaining and motivating key employees, but also on attracting future talent. EX takes into account the messages that job seekers are receptive to, where they would like to work and what their preferences are. At the same time, the messages communicated on the talent market to attract talent must be in line with the actual daily experience of the organisation's current employees. In other words, EX must be aligned with employer branding.

In practice, this means that when an organisation formulates its employer brand message, it must be aware of the target group's employee preferences, its own organisational culture and the commitment of its employees. On the basis of this awareness, the organisation must consciously manage EX. An organisation must be able to both attract and retain talented employees, while encouraging their commitment and motivating them.

An organisation's employer brand represents its reputation from the employees' point of view, reflecting the organisation's value proposition, as opposed to a more general approach where an organisation's brand is primarily associated with its reputation and value-creation for customers. In fact, the employer brand is an image of the organisation as perceived by its current employees and external stakeholders (active and passive candidates, customers and other key stakeholders). Where a customer brand proposition is used to describe a product or a service, the EVP is used to describe what an organisation offers to its employees.

An effective (re)design of the EVP combines four perspectives: the employer, employee, financial impact and external market. In other words, the EVP needs to have a clear people value proposition (PVP) designed by the employer. This needs to take employee preferences into account within the budgetary framework and principles of the organisation, all compared to and supported by the relevant external market.

Organisations are increasingly recognising the importance of standing out in the talent market. It is no longer sufficient to make innovative products, use the latest technology and have a good cafeteria plan. The organisation's strategy has to be aligned with its EVP in order to create an EX that attracts and motivates employees, allowing them to reach their full potential and act as representatives of the organisation's mission and brand.

3.2. Employee preference study

As well as the challenge of finding and attracting employees, organisations are facing the greater challenge of retaining skilled employees due to the intense competition for top talent. What is regarded as a genuine retaining factor varies from organisation to organisation and from employee to employee.

An employee preference study enables organisations to gain insight into the preferences and needs of their employees so they can optimise their reward system based on how employees value different options and the cost to the organisation. For example, flexible work arrangements are often considered extremely valuable, but cost the organisation relatively little. This type of knowledge is useful for attracting and retaining employees, as well as showing that the reward system lives up to the organisation's brand promise.

3.2.1. Different preferences
Executives
In order for the organisation to create an EVP that supports its strategy, it is important to know what the strategy is. How does the organisation intend to win in the marketplace? What segments of the workforce are the most critical for growth? What does the organisation most want to be known for? Talking to executives will get to the heart of these issues.

Current employees
Employees are valuable sources of information for several reasons. In order to retain top talent, it is important to know what (if anything) about the current EVP appeals to them. Employees can describe what is unique about the organisation, both positive and negative. They are also knowledgeable about whether the leadership's stated values are effectively communicated and acted upon.

Potential employees
In addition to current employees, it is important to know what candidates value, how competitors are trying to win them over and what the organisation's reputation is. Unfortunately, this information can be difficult to obtain.

3.2.2. What to measure
The decision on what the employee preference study should measure depends on the organisation's goals. For example, will the results be used for an upcoming benefits cycle, an EVP or a cafeteria plan? The focus of an employee preference study can also be narrow or broad, i.e., looking at the full reward system or just job attributes such as organisation culture, colleagues and leadership, remuneration, benefits and work-life balance. The study can also consider the future to ask about attributes that are not currently emphasised or even offered, but could be important to (future) employees. This can be useful for the total reward scheme, where offerings may require periodic adjustments to meet the needs of an ever-evolving workforce.

Figure 36: The four perspectives required for an effective (re)design of an organisation's EVP.

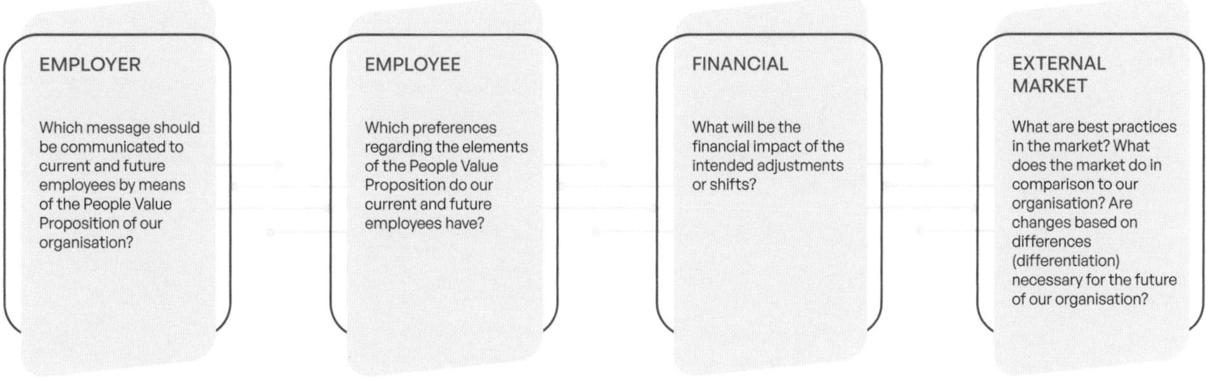

EMPLOYER

Which message should be communicated to current and future employees by means of the People Value Proposition of our organisation?

EMPLOYEE

Which preferences regarding the elements of the People Value Proposition do our current and future employees have?

FINANCIAL

What will be the financial impact of the intended adjustments or shifts?

EXTERNAL MARKET

What are best practices in the market? What does the market do in comparison to our organisation? Are changes based on differences (differentiation) necessary for the future of our organisation?

3.2.3. How to conduct an employee preference study

An employee preference study involves gathering data to understand which financial and non-financial attributes are valued by current employees. While there are different ways to conduct an employee preference survey, most methods have four steps: preparing the data collection and interviewing employees, conducting the survey, analysing the data and implementing the results.

Preparing the data collection

Generally, data are gathered by means of an email survey, sometimes supplemented with personal interviews.

Before the survey is sent out, it is important to customise its content and design. The organisation should analyse its current reward system and decide which components to focus on. As such, it is important to consider the survey's strategic goals (should it focus on cost reduction, brand positioning or another goal?) in order to challenge general beliefs and habits (i.e., are certain benefits really important or have they just become expected?) and model alternative decision scenarios.

The survey can then ask for preferences and attitudes to the selected group of items that are currently offered, as well as for financial and non-financial components that could be offered in the future.

Conducting the survey

Employees should be provided a personalised link to the survey. While this link ensures the employee's anonymity, it should give some demographic information which can be used to filter results afterwards and generate new insights.

The questions should ideally enable employees to rate each reward component, giving both absolute (very important/not important) and relative (item x is more important than item y) preferences.

The survey also gives organisations the opportunity to re-communicate about their current remuneration plan, often giving employees a positive surprise ("I was not aware that I received all these benefits").

Analysing the data

The survey results are in principle compiled in an advanced database that the organisation can use to generate insights. The database should empower the organisation to examine the preference ranking (and ideally the perceived value of different components) for all employees or filtered according to other criteria, such as demographic data, locations, levels, organisational unit or length of service. Additionally, with an advanced database, organisations can generate insights into the cost impacts of the surveyed benefits.

Figure 37: The four typical stages of an employee preference study.

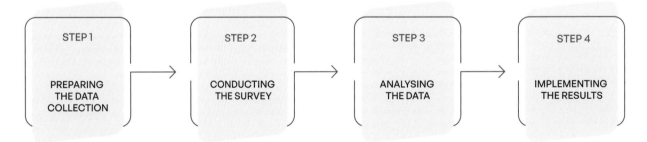

Implementing the results

Ideally, the information in the database includes a wide range of real-time data on employee preferences related to all aspects of the EVP. Organisations can play around and use this information to improve employee experience, satisfaction and engagement as well as increase retention and their attractiveness on the market. Furthermore, the insights can potentially reduce costs and streamline their reward system, while maintaining, or even increasing, the preference of the new reward system compared to the previous one, at a lower cost.

3.3. Changing employee preferences

An employee preference study is vital for developing a reward system that is relevant for today's employees. However, it cannot be seen as a one-off occurrence. Employee preference studies should be repeated regularly to ensure that the organisation maintains its position as an employer of choice.

With this in mind, the PwC network has been conducting research on employee references around the world for the past several years. Here are some of the results showing the background for the preferences of certain demographics.

3.3.1. PwC workforce preference study in the Netherlands (2023)[204]

The 2023 study looked at 3,000 Dutch people aged 18-35, including students and starters and found that young people find (financial) security, leisure activities and recognition very important.

Figure 38 shows the top 10 preferences in 2023 and compares them to their ranking in the 2022 study (right hand column). For example, the preference for base salary has increased one place to the top spot in 2023.

Figure 38: The top 10 preferences in the 2023 employee preference study in the Netherlands and their position change compared to the year before.

TOP 10 ITEMS	Position compared to last year
#1 Base pay	+1
#2 Vacation days	NEW
#3 Permanent employment contract	NEW
#4 Work that is interesting and challenging	-3
#5 Salary increase	NEW
#6 Colleagues	-3
#7 Good transport access to workplace	+10
#8 Approachable managers and leadership	-1
#9 Face-to-face recognition	NEW
#10 Pension benefits	-1

The study shows a notable shift in the priorities of young talent, moving from a desire for 'work that is interesting and challenging' to a greater emphasis on (financial) stability. Base salary now ranks at the top of the list. This change in mindset can be partly attributed to the rising cost of living, which is driven by increasing inflation rates.

Furthermore, there is a growing assertiveness among young individuals in their pursuit of career progression and faster promotions. This phenomenon can be explained by the tight job market. If young talent does not find the right career opportunities at their current employer, they may be inclined to seek them somewhere else. Young talent may also feel the need to take on work that is above their current level and seek recognition for their extra efforts and responsibilities. They are eager to prove themselves and demonstrate their capabilities.

It is worth noting that societal impact (e.g., diversity and inclusion and commitment to sustainability) is not a top priority when choosing a job. Furthermore, on average, the younger generation values their work-life balance and may not be willing to work longer hours. In order to continue to attract and retain young talent, it is important to recognise and address these changing priorities of young professionals.

3.3.2. PwC workforce preference study in Europe and South Africa (2020)[205]

In order to gain more insight into the workplace preferences of the workforce of the future, PwC assessed the expectations of students and career starters from all educational levels (age 16 to 28) in 10 European countries and South Africa. The sample of respondents revealed a number of shared values across the covered countries, as well as regional differences.

From this survey it is clear that young job seekers are looking for more than an attractive financial reward package. In all the countries surveyed, transparency, fairness, a good reputation and flexibility were found to be key to successfully recruiting and retaining talented employees. Moreover, the study shows that interesting and challenging work, together with work-life balance are the top priorities in Western and Southwest Europe. In many respects, the study results might be a wake up call for employers who do not believe that non-financial factors play an important role in keeping the workforce of the future motivated.

Figure 39: A selection of the top 15 relative preferences taken from the PwC 2020 workforce preference study in Europe and South Africa.

Survey highlights: selection out of the top 15 relative preferences

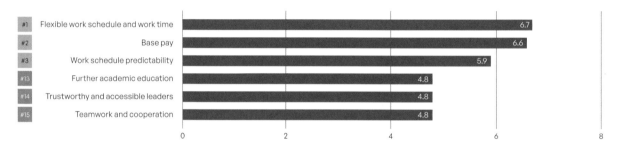

3.3.3. PwC workforce preference study in Belgium (2020)[206]

In 2020, PwC Belgium conducted research into the expectations of target employees, including Generation Y and Generation Z, to see what they are looking for and expect from their (future) employers.

The results showed a number of differences depending on, for example, the region or job (context). As well as a good base salary, other preferences for the workforce of the future include interesting and challenging work and a flexible work schedule and work times, highlighting the importance of non-financial factors.

When looking at responses before, during and after the Covid-19 lockdown, it seems that organisations with a culture that encourages innovation are more likely to attract talent.

Furthermore, the study suggests that organisations located outside the Brussels Capital-Region may need to reconsider their value propositions or risk no longer being competitive compared to job opportunities outside Belgium.

Figure 40:
Relative preferences for employees in Belgium based on the results of the 2020 PwC workforce preference study.

Highlights of the 2020 Survey - Relative preferences

#1	Interesting & challenging work
#2	Flexible work schedule & work time
#3	Base pay
#7	Performance-based promotion with credible and fair performance evaluation
#9	Transparent business operation: open & honest leadership communication
#15	Digital skills development
#51	Other benefits: Extra facility services
#52	Corporate brand name
#54	Sabbatical (career break)

4. Reward evolution

This chapter has shown how organisations are increasingly shifting their focus from purely financial reward to a more comprehensive approach known as total reward, or even beyond to total wellbeing. This evolution has encompassed various components beyond base salaries, such as short-term incentives linked to immediate performance goals and long-term incentives connected to sustainable achievement and organisational growth.

Additionally, financial benefits such as healthcare and pension plans form an integral part of total reward, ensuring employees' financial security (see chapter 11 for more on occupational pension plans). Non-financial reward and recognition, including opportunities for career development, work-life balance initiatives and appreciation programmes, are also critical contributors to employees' overall satisfaction and engagement.

The chapter also encourages organisations to rethink their total reward practice to deliver total wellbeing via a bottom-up approach. Total wellbeing goes beyond traditional benefits to look at emotional wellbeing, physical wellbeing and more. These types of benefits can be seen as a reward for being a member of the organisation, in contrast to being a reward for performance like a classic pay component. In practice, too many organisations pay too little attention to the employee benefits and perquisites that can affect their employer brand when faced with a shortage of available talent.

After focusing on the reward mix balance, the next chapter looks at the context for reward, in particular for organisations going through a merger, acquisition or spin-off, or are financed by private equity.

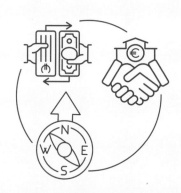

8.
Reward in transactions

Key takeaways

1. Transactions, such as mergers, acquisitions, spin-offs, IPOs and private equity buy-outs, call for specific types of reward for key employees and executives.

2. Long-term incentive plans (LTIPs) are effective in retaining key talent during organisational changes. This is why it is important to assess long-term incentive plans pre-, during and post-deal.

3. Analysing existing retention incentives and aligning them with the new organisation's goals is crucial.

4. Management incentive plans (MIPs) in private equity-backed organisations involve executive investments, such as co-investment, sweet equity and ratchet instruments. Modelling MIPs helps executives to understand their financial implications, incentivising them to achieve the organisation's goals.

When developing or redesigning a reward system, it is important to have a clear understanding of the transactional context of the change, as well as identifying the reasons behind it. This will enable organisations to tailor their reward system to address their specific organisational challenges and objectives.

Organisations typically use transactions as a moment to reward key employees, regardless of their situation, e.g., when going through a merger or acquisition, forming a spin-off or participating in a private equity (PE) buy-out.

However, the type of reward transaction depends on the organisation's situation. For example, post-deal actions vary based on the type of deal, whether it's a standalone acquisition, merger or another transaction. Organisations need to be aware of the potential need to harmonise remuneration and benefits packages across several legal entities when implementing a buy-and-build strategy related to a merger or standalone acquisition.

In the context of transactions, the focus is on alignment and calibration, as well as the retention of key employees and executives. In an ideal world, the best talents are retained, but the reality may be different. Competitive incentive plans certainly contribute to motivating directors and executives to work toward a joint vision and keep them engaged, but is that enough to guarantee a successful deal and the smooth continuation of the business?

When used effectively, reward can work for an organisation as it undergoes a change in situation. This chapter looks at ways to use LTIPs for mergers, acquisitions and spin-offs and MIP in the private equity environment, starting by investigating transaction and retention bonuses, including when and how much to pay.

1. Transaction and retention bonuses

While both transaction and retention bonuses are typically linked to the successful completion of a deal and the terms are often used interchangeably, there is a clear distinction between the two terms.

Retention bonuses are bonuses paid upon the contingency that the employee remains with the organisation until a predetermined date. With a retention programme, the acquirer of the organisation has time to become familiar with the talent in their acquisition and build a relationship.

Transaction bonuses are any bonus specifically related to a transaction. They are paid out for more than just their retention aspect, for example, they can be connected to specific milestones or the successful completion of the deal. While there are many reasons why these bonuses are granted, the most common are a support or completion bonus, covering the additional work required by certain employees during the deal process, and a share value bonus, which is based on the final closing price to entice key employees (usually executives and directors) to do their utmost to increase the sale value of the organisation or negotiate a lower acquisition price.

1.1. Bonus payment schedule

The deal process can be a burdensome process which requires a lot of time and effort from several employees within the organisation who will need to perform these tasks on top of their normal work. Organisations should dedicate sufficient time and resources early in the deal life cycle in order to avoid ongoing frustration both internally and externally at the counterparty.

There are two main reasons to pay out a bonus. Firstly the expectation of fair remuneration. Employees typically expect fair remuneration for their commitment during the transitional phase. The clarity of communication regarding the structure, timing and conditions of cash bonuses is crucial. Employees may also expect transparency about how the bonus aligns with their role and contribution to the success of the merger or acquisition.

Secondly, an effectively communicated and structured cash bonus can be used as a powerful motivator for employee loyalty. Employees expect recognition for their contributions and value proposition, and a well-structured cash bonus programme addresses these expectations by directly linking financial reward to their commitment and performance.

Typically retention bonuses are paid to the key talent that is required for the operation of the organisation. Certainly in distressed organisations, where the KPIs from the normal bonus plans might not or only partially be met, retention bonuses can convince key talent to remain on board until a plan is put in place to turn around the distressed organisation. In certain instances, a rather limited retention bonus is paid to all employees who remain employed after completion (often with a requirement to stay in service for at least a year). This bonus is sometimes also referred to as a welcome bonus.

Due to the reasons behind their introduction, retention and transaction bonuses are paid out on differing timeframes.

Retention bonuses are typically time-based rather than performance-based, meaning employees receive them for their continued service rather than achieving specific performance metrics. This design is intended to encourage employees to stay with the organisation until the specified timeframe is completed. The exact structure and duration over which these bonuses are earned varies, for example, paying out the bonus in full at the end of a specified retention period or paying out portions of the bonus at certain milestones, such as on completion of (part of) the deal with the remainder at a later date.

Transaction bonuses are typically paid out at completion of (part of) the deal, but can be delayed in case part of the transaction bonus is related to, for example, the post-deal integration.

For both types of bonuses, it is important to note that the longer it takes for the bonus to be acquired and paid, the lower the deemed value will be in the hands of the beneficiary. In case of retention bonuses this also significantly decreases the retention aspect of the bonus.

1.2. Bonus size

As well as the perceived value, there are several reasons why organisations pay out cash bonuses. Firstly, the utilisation of cash bonuses in mergers and acquisitions (M&A) serves as a tangible and immediate financial incentive for employees. Unlike other forms of remuneration, such as equity, cash bonuses provide a direct monetary benefit. This can be particularly effective in aligning the interests of employees with the goals of the acquiring organisation, fostering a sense of immediate reward for commitment during the transitional period.

Cash bonuses offer flexibility and liquidity for employees. In contrast to equity-based incentives, cash is immediately accessible and can be used at the discretion of the employee. This can be appealing in scenarios where employees prioritise liquidity or have immediate financial needs.

Lastly, bonuses can also help to mitigate the uncertainty that often follows M&A transactions. Knowing that a financial reward is guaranteed at the end of the retention period provides a level of reassurance, which enhances employee morale and commitment during a potentially challenging transition.

In essence, the choice of a cash bonus is rooted in its immediacy, flexibility and capacity to address employee expectations for tangible recognition and reward during M&A transitions. Clear communication and fair structuring are pivotal to ensure that cash bonuses effectively serve their intended purpose of retaining key talent.

When it comes to the amount of the bonus, it is generally expressed as a percentage of the beneficiary's annual salary. Surveys show that the median reward in 2021 is 60% for executives and directors and 30%

to 40% for other employees, which are higher than in previous years. However, several organisations paid executives and directors a reward of two or more times their annual salary, with retention bonuses being paid out over a period of at least 2 years[207].

While the overall budget allocated for retention bonuses is often 1% to 2% of the total purchase price, the survey results show that over 25% of acquirers answered that they did not set a specific budget[208]. In practice, it is rare that retention bonuses surpass 50% of the beneficiary's annual salary. If higher bonuses are granted in scope of a transaction these are often completion bonuses based on a certain sale price being met or the successful completion of the deal. As these bonuses come on top of the normal short term incentive plans (STIPs) and LTIPs, it can be argued that employees with a LTIP that already covers the organisation's share price are already incentivised to achieve the highest possible value for the organisation during the deal.

2. Long term incentive plans (LTIPs)

When an organisation agrees to a deal such as a merger, acquisition, spin-off or initial public offering (IPO), this exit event should be seen as both the end of one chapter and the start of a new one for the organisation(s) involved in this process. The post-deal landscape brings opportunities and challenges, especially concerning executive remuneration and integration within the new structure of the organisation[209]. But given the dynamics of the deal at stake, employee LTIP, typically comprising equity instruments such as stock options and restricted stock units (RSUs), are usually deeply affected during the process. This is why it is key to analyse the retention incentives already put in place before determining what should remain and/or be created after the deal takes place. In practice, there are several ways to manage LTIPs during the deal, depending on the type of deal[210].

For more information on how LTIPs work and their use in mature organisations and start-ups, see chapter 7.

2.1. Mergers & acquisitions

In the event of a merger (the consolidation of one entity with another in order to create a sole entity) or an acquisition (one entity acquires the control of another), organisations can decide to continue, accelerate, replace or cancel their LTIPs.

The most common way to handle LTIPs in an M&A is to continue the plan. In the scope of an acquisition, where the acquired organisation remains a standalone entity, this is relatively straightforward. In mergers, it is a bit more difficult as the number of shares (relating to the reward) and the exercise price (in case of stock options) need to be adjusted to obtain economic neutrality, taking into account the features of the restructured entity post deal. However, there is no accelerated vesting of any reward.

LTIPs can also be accelerated via a single or a double trigger. With single trigger acceleration (or protection), the vesting of the reward is accelerated based on one single trigger event, e.g., a change in control or dismissal of the beneficiary. However, single-trigger acceleration is rare as it means that the beneficiary receives the full benefit of the reward, removing its retention aspect. As such, investors typically are less interested in organisations with single trigger acceleration clauses in their LTIP unless it is in a private equity environment where it is expected that the new owner will implement their own plan and the original management is required to reinvest.

Double trigger acceleration (or protection) requires two trigger events to occur, typically both a change in control and the dismissal of the beneficiary. This ensures that the beneficiary has protection against being dismissed by the new owner. Double trigger acceleration is generally granted for a limited period of time, such as 1-2 years. An example of this is a beneficiary who is dismissed within a year of a change in control. Their reward is then accelerated and they receive the benefit as if they had stayed until the end of the normal vesting period.

Instead of continuing or accelerating reward, it is also possible to cancel the existing reward and replace them with reward from the restructured entity. However, this could be an unwelcome change if the moment at which the beneficiaries will receive any benefits is delayed, for example, due to the implementation of a longer vesting period than the remaining vesting period under the old system.

In most countries this would not cause any taxation issue as taxation is typically deferred until vesting (i.e., the moment the shares are delivered), but there could be consequences if taxation occurred at grant, for example under the Belgian law of March 26, 1999.

The last possibility is to cancel all or part of the unvested reward. In most equity plans the organiser of the plans has a lot of freedom to do as they please with reward. However, due to obvious reasons, it is extremely rare that no compensation is granted for a cancelled reward.

2.2. Spin-offs

In the event of a spin-off[211], where an organisation separates a portion of its operations or assets to create a new organisation, the equity instruments can be translated and divided between the remaining organisation and the new one that was created through the spin-off, or they can be translated exclusively into one organisation's equity, depending on where the employee's role or position lies within the divided entities.

In both cases, there will be differences in the values of equity instruments pre- and post-deal. This requires the organisation to make a valuation in order to determine the amount of cash and/or shares the equity holders are entitled to, notably taking into account the volatility of the equity instruments, which may be impacted by the deal. Indeed, corporate events like spin-offs may introduce uncertainties in the market until the value of both the organisation and the spin-off fully stabilise.

The Belgian ruling commission requests that the translation of equity instruments should be 'economically neutral'[212]. In practice, there are several admissible ways to undertake the post-deal valuation.

Taking all this into account, it is key to understand how equity instruments are treated post-deal. The restructured organisation needs to decide whether the existing LTIP will continue to vest under the new structure, after translation to take into account the new post-deal features, or if there will be a cash-out of the existing LTIP, potentially before issuing new equity instruments under the restructured organisation.

The advantage of continuing the existing LTIP is that the reward continues to vest unchanged. However, in the case of a cash-out, where the plan is cancelled and a new one is introduced, a retention/incentive may arise as employees would have to respect a certain vesting period before receiving any reward from the new plan, while they were probably already getting something out of the current plan on a regular basis. This situation could lead to a lack of motivation for key employees and executives, which could have an influence on post-deal value creation.

This means that continuing the existing incentive plan can be beneficial for executives who have vested rights or are close to vesting milestones. It ensures that their efforts and commitment to the organisation's growth aren't reset or undervalued due to the exit event leading to the post-deal situation. This continuity can be a strong motivator for key executives to remain engaged and focused during a potentially turbulent period of transition. Indeed, as the initial purpose of the deal is to create and deliver growing value to the shareholders, it is very important to keep incentivising key employees and executives who play an important role in this.

In order to keep key employees and executives interested in the success of the deal, organisations also foresee specific incentive plans directly linked to certain metrics of the post-deal structure[213]. This aims to align managerial goals with the objectives of the deal to foster commitment to the success of the transition. Indeed, properly designed LTIPs can safeguard against short-term profit seeking behaviour that may harm the organisation in the long-term[214].

Deciding between keeping the initial LTIP or cashing-out before introducing a new plan involves carefully balancing honouring existing commitments, aligning incentives with new objectives, retaining key talent and negotiating terms that benefit all parties involved. The decision also needs to take into account the specifics of the deal and the strategic direction of the restructured organisation.

A one-size-fits-all solution doesn't exist when it comes to post-deal equity instruments. What is important to keep in mind is that every action should aim to facilitate a successful transition post-deal, ensuring that key executives are motivated, retained and aligned with the new organisation's goals and values.

3. Management incentive plans (MIPs)

Incentive arrangements for executives working for PE-backed organisations (i.e., an organisation held by a private equity fund) differ from those used in quoted organisations and family businesses. These incentive arrangements are aligned with the PE strategy of buying and developing businesses to achieve an outstanding return on investment over an average period of five years.

Typically a PE house funds its acquisitions through a combination of external debt and equity, possibly also using shareholder debt. When a PE house acquires a business (the target), they set up an acquisition structure to acquire the shares of the target organisation.

3.1. Management investments

As per market practices, the executives at the target organisation and its subsidiaries are required to invest in the new acquisition structure, usually in the entity that is expected to be sold upon exit.

This executive investment aligns their financial interests with those of investors and incentivises them. This investment requirement forms an integral part of the management reward package, as it is recognised to be a motivational reward tool, driving executives to create shareholder value, just like LTIP do in quoted organisations.

The size of the executive investment is calibrated to align the executives' risk with that of investors. While this investment should be a significant amount for the executives, it should also give executives the opportunity to realise significant capital gains upon exit. Usually, the investment is 1-3 years' salary for directors and 1-2 years' salary for executives, but a different range can be negotiated during the commercial discussions.

This investment is divided between a co-investment (in the form of strip instruments) and incentive instruments (such as sweet equity and ratchet instruments).

The strip instruments are a combination of ordinary shares and preferred instruments. Preferred instruments can be preferred shares, shareholder loans or a combination, where both preferred shares and shareholder loans have a fixed annual return. Executives typically invest pari passu in strip instruments together with investors. This means that executives and investors invest at the same rate and in the same proportion in the ordinary shares and preferred instruments embedded in the strip instruments. This investment is called a co-investment.

The sweet equity is an additional amount of ordinary shares that is subscribed by executives without them further investing in preferred shares. The higher the proportion of sweet equity in the ordinary equity, the more the executives will be incentivised.

Figure 41: The incentivisation level as captured by the envy ratio.

The higher the envy ratio (see figure 41), the higher the leverage on the sweet equity and the executive incentivisation. The envy ratio will depend on the deal size, but an envy ratio in the range of 3 to 10 is not uncommon.

Ratchet instruments, typically in the form of ratchet shares, are shares that entitle executives to additional exit profits above agreed hurdles (i.e., the minimum rates of return), generally defined as a combination of agreed multiple of money (MoMs) and internal rate of return (IRR). Ratchet shares have the features of option-like instruments.

The sweet equity and ratchet instruments can be structured as options on instruments where this is more tax-friendly, such as in Belgium. However, such structuring adds a layer of complexity, so investors may prefer a typical MIP set-up with sweet and ratchet shares.

3.2. Modelling MIPs

Modelling incentive arrangements, such as MIPs, results in executives understanding and managing their financial implications from the outset, ensuring that incentives are market-competitive and supportive of value-creating behaviour.

It should be common practice for executives to properly understand their MIP from its implementation. Without this understanding, the perceived value of the incentive as part of their total reward package could be either under- or overestimated.

Together, the MIP model and the business plan create the link with the KPIs that the executives can influence, showing them how their actions can impact their MIP's value. If the executive is unclear about the impact of their actions on the organisation's value, equity value and their MIP value, then the MIP isn't meeting its key objective of supporting controlled shareholder value creation.

3.3. Leavers

When an executive leaves the organisation, their investment in the MIP is subject to leaver conditions which aim to keep executives on board until an exit point. It is logical that if an executive terminates their activities within an organisation, they do not keep their MIP shares or benefit from shareholder value creation that they have not contributed to. The dissuasive effect of the leaver conditions is created by requiring that the financial instruments held by leaver are transferred back, in part or in full, to investors.

Executives and investors negotiate leaver conditions during their commercial discussions. While executives push to have favourable leaver conditions, investors want to maximise the likelihood that the executives will stay on board.

There is a spectrum of types of leavers, with 'good' leavers at one end and 'bad' leavers at the other. A good leaver is generally identified as an executive who terminates their activities for the organisation due to death, permanent disability or retirement at the legal age. It may extend to executives who are dismissed without cause and can include leavers that investors decide to consider as a good leaver at the time of their departure.

A bad leaver, on the other hand, is generally any other executive who decides to leave. This includes executives who voluntarily resign, are dismissed for cause or leave under similar circumstances.

In between these two extremes, investors and executives may agree on other categories of leavers, such as intermediate leavers, to better differentiate the types of leavers. This enables better customisation of the conditions at which shares are repurchased (i.e., the timing and price of the repurchase) to the specific circumstances of the leaver event.

The repurchase conditions of the leaver's instruments will depend on the timing and circumstances of the leaving event, with the repurchase conditions of bad leavers' investments being more detrimental than those applying to good leavers.

3.4. Reserve

During the time that the MIP is running, some financial instruments are held in reserve for executives that join after its inception. This reserve can grow when instruments are re-purchased from leavers, as well as shrink as new executives join the MIP. For tax purposes, it is key that executives acquire the instruments at the fair market value (FMV) prevailing at the time they are acquired. This also means that new executives should invest in the instruments at the FMV that prevails when they join the MIP.

3.5. Transferability

As a rule, the financial instruments held by executives are not transferable except for the reasons listed in the shareholder agreement, such as for legal succession, to implement the leaver conditions and tag-along and drag-along rights in case of an exit or an agreed liquidity event.

3.6. Exit

Upon an exit event, investors and executives will dispose of their shares and capture their share in the sale proceeds of the organisation. An exit event is generally a change of control where more than 50% of the equity or voting rights is transferred to a third party, there is an IPO of the organisation (i.e., a listing of the organisation on a regulated stock exchange) or there is a sale of the business assets.

Tag-along and drag-along rights refer to both investors and executives being expected to sell their shares in the same proportion to the buyer upon an exit or liquidity event. The drag-along right empowers investors to require executives to sell their shares in the same proportion as investors, while tag-along rights enable executives to sell their shares alongside investors so that they can capture the shareholder value embedded in their shares and are not stuck with their shares.

Lastly, a roll-over will generally occur in case of a secondary buy-out (i.e., the sale of the business to another private equity player) and executives are usually requested to re-invest part of their sale proceeds into the business alongside the new investors.

3.7. Results

The organisation's management is required to invest a significant amount in the organisation, putting them at risk, just like the investors are, and further enhancing their commitment to the business. This perspective uses specific financial leverage mechanisms structured through sweet equity, and possibly ratchet instruments, to further incentivise the executive team to achieve the large shareholder returns that were originally agreed with investors.

This does not mean that equity incentive arrangements in private equity backed organisations are more effective than standard LTIPs, but their nexus with shareholder objectives is more obvious, making them extremely supportive of an outperforming management team.

4. Optimising effectiveness

The chapter on reward in transactions emphasises the importance of understanding the transactional context and reasons behind the change in order to tailor the reward system to address the specific challenges and objectives facing the organisation.

Transactions are used as reward for key employees and executives during organisational changes such as mergers, acquisitions, spin-offs and PE buy-outs. However, remuneration and benefit packages need to be harmonised across legal entities in buy-and-build strategies related to mergers or standalone acquisitions.

When it comes to LTIPs, it is important to analyse existing retention incentives and align incentives with new objectives to retain key talent and foster commitment to the organisation's goals. Similarly, with MIPs in PE-backed organisations, it is vital for executives to understand the financial implications of their incentives to optimise their effectiveness.

Considering the context of designing effective reward systems in various organisational contexts, the next chapter focuses on reward for partnerships, as well as the differences for quoted and unquoted organisations.

9.
Reward
in different types
of organisations

Key takeaways

1. Each type of organisation faces different challenges and considerations which shape their approach to remuneration.

2. Within partnerships, the partner evaluation and income systems determine their reward system and internal culture.

3. Market forces, industry benchmarks and investor expectations influence (executive) remuneration.

4. Quoted organisations face stricter regulatory requirements and higher transparency standards compared to unquoted organisations.

5. Remuneration structures in unquoted organisations have more flexibility in design.

What impact does the organisation's structure have on its potential reward system? For the reward system to be effective, it is necessary to carefully consider the organisational structure, recognising that this can significantly impact the overall strategy. With this in mind, this chapter looks at how different partnership structures can impact the reward system, as well as the distinction between quoted and unquoted entities when it comes to reward.

1. Reward in partnerships

The organisation's structure provides the foundations of the reward system. The best-known structure is corporate organisations, where ownership and control are separate. Ownership is in the hands of the shareholders who collectively own the business, but the shareholders are not directly involved in the organisation's daily decision making. Instead, shareholders elect a board of directors to make key strategic decisions and the board-appointed executives run the organisation. The capital comes from outside the organisation and the reward system only needs to focus on the executives and employees. Corporate organisations are also characterised by their hierarchical structure and centralised decision making.

But not all businesses are run via a corporate organisation. Professional service organisations, such as lawyers, accountants, consultants and medical practices, are often structured as a partnership[215]. Within a partnership, the partners effectively manage the business, while maintaining both ownership and control. A partnership is characterised by shared ownership, collective decision making and joint liability between partners.

Figure 42: The structure of a corporate organisation.

Figure 43: The structure of a partnership.

Designing a reward system for the workforce within a partnership (i.e., the staff, whether it is employees, fee-earners, executives or directors) is similar to the reward system required by the workforce of a corporate organisation. However, certain particularities linked to the business must be taken into account. For example, lawyers in law firms based in Belgium must always be self-employed under current legislation, which means that some typical reward components cannot be provided, such as employer funded pension schemes, company cars and costs proper to the employer.

Even so, the general principles for drawing up a reward system as described in the previous chapters also apply to partnerships. There is one major difference: as the partners are also co-workers, the way profits are distributed between the partners determines their reward system as well as the culture within the partnership.

Partner evaluation and income systems (PEIS) play an important role in the dynamics of partnerships. They ensure equity and fairness, motivate partners, stimulate collaboration and support the longer-term sustainability of the partnership. Depending on the type of partnership, the PEIS will accommodate and drive different behaviours.

1.1. Building blocks of effective partnerships

Ensuring equity and fairness in a partnership is essential for maintaining a healthy and sustainable collaboration. Partnerships are sensitive ecosystems where the following building blocks play a key role.

1.1.1. Clear communication and expectations
Establish open and transparent communication channels from the beginning of the partnership. Clearly define roles, responsibilities and expectations for each partner. This ensures that everyone understands their contributions and the value they bring to the partnership.

1.1.2. Equal decision making
Promote equal decision-making power among partners. Encourage active participation and input from all partners when making important decisions. This helps prevent power imbalances and ensures that decisions are made collectively, considering the perspectives and interests of all partners.

1.1.3. Fair evaluation criteria
Establish fair and objective evaluation criteria to assess partner contributions and performance. This can include factors such as expertise, effort, results achieved and value added to the partnership. Regularly review and update these criteria to reflect the evolving needs and dynamics of the partnership.

1.1.4. Transparent financial reporting
Maintain transparency in financial matters by providing regular and detailed financial reports to all partners. This includes sharing information about revenue, expenses, profits and losses. Transparency builds trust and allows partners to have a clear understanding of the financial health of the partnership.

1.1.5. Equitable income distribution

Implement an income distribution system that is fair and aligns with the contributions and value provided by each partner. This can be achieved through various models, such as equal income distribution, proportional income distribution or performance-based income distribution (discussed later in this chapter). Choose a model that best suits the partnership's goals, objectives and individual partner circumstances.

1.1.6. Conflict resolution mechanisms

Establish effective conflict resolution mechanisms to address any disputes or conflicts that may arise. Encourage open dialogue, active listening and mediation to find mutually agreeable solutions. Having a fair and transparent process for resolving conflicts helps maintain equity and fairness within the partnership.

1.1.7. Regular evaluation and adjustment

Regularly evaluate the partnership's performance, including the effectiveness of the income distribution system and the collaboration's overall equity and fairness. Seek feedback from partners and make necessary adjustments to ensure ongoing equity and fairness.

1.1.8. Legal agreements

Consider drafting a partnership agreement or contract that outlines the terms and conditions of the partnership, including provisions for equity and fairness. This legally binding document can help protect the interests of all partners, providing a framework for resolving any disputes.

By implementing these strategies, partners can foster an environment of equity and fairness, ensuring that each partner feels valued, respected and motivated to contribute to the partnership's success.

1.2. Equity versus non-equity

Partnerships can (and often do) make a distinction between equity and non-equity partners. There are many reasons for this, including maintaining the ownership balance or providing key employees the opportunity to access the partnership at a younger age. However, there are differences between equity and non-equity partners.

1.2.1. Ownership

Equity partners have ownership stakes in the business. They contribute capital and share in the profits and losses based on their ownership and the income system. Non-equity (or salaried) partners do not have ownership stakes and typically do not share in the profits and losses, although their income usually depends on the organisation's results.

1.2.2. Decision making

When it comes to formal decision making (i.e., voting), only equity partners are entitled to participate in such decisions. Typically a 'one partner one vote' model applies, but voting rights may also depend on their ownership percentage. Non-equity partners may be informed about planned decisions, but do not have voting rights so do not have a say in the actual decision making.

1.2.3. Liability

Equity partners may be exposed to unlimited liability, meaning they are personally responsible for the debts and obligations of the business. Non-equity partners typically have limited liability. In practice this all depends on the legal structure of the partnership. In the case of limited liability, the personal assets of the partner are protected to some extent.

1.2.4. Capital contributions

Equity partners contribute capital to the business in exchange for their ownership stake. Non-equity partners do not usually provide any capital. However, when they do contribute capital, it is not directly tied to ownership. Capital contributions may be used to fund the partnership's operations or for other purposes such as investments, as agreed upon by the partners.

1.2.5. Exit strategy

Non-equity partners do not hold shares and therefore do not have to transfer them upon exit. For equity partners, this depends on the partnership model. In the case of a 'naked in, naked out' system, partners do not have to buy shares upon entry but then they cannot sell them upon exit. Other systems can apply, for example, where an equity partner is required to buy into the partnership (compared to paying goodwill) and can sell their shares upon exit.

Again, it is important to note that the specific terms and arrangements of partnerships can vary depending on the agreement between the partners, as well as the legal jurisdiction in which the partnership operates.

1.3. Models of partner evaluation and income systems

Several models of partner income systems exist, each with its own advantages, challenges and suitability for different partnership contexts. International partnerships add complexity as they range from integrated partnerships with full profit sharing to international networks without any legal connectivity other than membership to a global network agreement. In the case of full profit sharing, this can again range from the allocation of profits per territory to a globally integrated partner evaluation and income system, where each partner is assessed under the global model.

Let's first discuss the most common profit distribution models[216], before diving into the cross border sharing of profits.

1.3.1. Equal income distribution

With equal income distribution, partners receive an equal share of the partnership's income, regardless of their individual contributions or roles. This approach promotes fairness and equal ownership among partners. However, it may not account for variations in effort, expertise or investment made by each partner. Depending on the moment in time where a partner enters the partnership, this model may require the partner to pay a significant amount of goodwill to obtain alignment with the other partners.

1.3.2. Proportional income distribution

Under this model, partners receive income in proportion to their contributions or ownership stake in the partnership. It considers factors such as capital investment, time commitment, expertise and revenue generated by each partner. Proportional distribution aligns income with individual efforts and can motivate partners to contribute more. However, it may lead to disparities if partners have unequal resources or contributions.

1.3.3. Seniority-based income distribution

Although individual performance will be taken into account in this model, the seniority of the partner will determine the majority of their income. In the seniority-based income distribution model, all partners typically pay the same amount of capital but develop their goodwill over time, so the seniority compensates for their increased experience and assumed contribution. As this model is less performance based, it may lead to tensions with hard working younger partners who feel their contributions are undervalued.

This model is also known as Lockstep and has two variations: a Pure Lockstep which only takes seniority into account and a Modified Lockstep which combines the lockstep with a performance assessment at specific moments in time. While these Lockstep distribution methods were embedded in most traditional partnerships, most organisations have moved away from them, preferring a performance-based system that gives partners credit for the origination of work (lead generator) and billing of work (billing attorney).

1.3.4. Performance-based income distribution

The performance-based income distribution model ties income distribution to specific performance metrics or outcomes achieved by each partner, rewarding partners based on their individual performance, such as sales targets, client acquisition or project completion. Performance-based systems incentivise high performance and can drive motivation. However, they require clear and measurable performance criteria and may create internal competition or strain relationships if not managed effectively.

An extreme application of performance-based income distribution is the so-called 'eat-what-you-kill' method where individual turnover is the only important measure: every partner receives the net revenue which they generate with their team.

Performance-based income distribution in practice
With this type of partnership, the experience, responsibilities and expected performance of each partner is categorised (e.g., A, B, C, D), with a number of levels in each category and a number of points per level. In this way, every partner is mapped to a category and a level within that category, resulting in a number or range of points. The value of these points depends on the distributable profit. At the start of the financial year, the distributable profit is based on the budget for that year, which leads to the target income of each partner. This target income should then allow the partner to receive regular advances (or drawings).

At the end of the financial year, the performance of each partner is evaluated. If they maintain the current mapping, i.e., their target points equals their actual points, then their points are multiplied by the final point value. If the partner over or under performs, the number of points is higher or lower than their target. In the following year, the partner is mapped again based on their performance in the previous year(s). Usually, the mapping increases over time as the partner's contribution rises, but it may vary in case of inconsistent performance or remain fairly flat if the partner has, for example, an expert role which does not evolve much.

1.3.5. Hybrid income distribution

A hybrid model combines elements of different income distribution approaches to create a customised system that suits the specific needs and goals of the partnership. It may involve a combination of equal distribution, proportional distribution and performance-based incentives. This model allows flexibility and can accommodate varying partner contributions and circumstances. However, it requires careful design and ongoing evaluation to ensure fairness and alignment with partnership objectives.

It is important to note that the choice of income distribution model should be based on the partnership's specific context, goals and the preferences and agreements of the partners involved. Regular evaluation and open communication among the partners are crucial to ensure that the chosen model remains fair, equitable and aligned with the evolving dynamics of the partnership.

1.4. Cross-border partnerships

When profit sharing takes place within a local (single territory) partnership, it remains fairly straightforward. Tax, legal and accounting aspects are all local, making them easy to manage once the profit distribution has taken place. The only potential complexities are the assessment of whether the partnership is transparent or opaque and whether the partners operate as individuals or through personal service organisations.

Things become more complicated in the case of cross border profit sharing. As well as the complexity of the nature of the partnership (transparent or opaque) and the status of the partners (individual or organisation), the tax treatment differs depending on the countries involved.

1.4.1. Branch offices in other jurisdictions

Organisations, especially international law firm partnerships, operate in different countries through branch offices either of the main partnership or a separately created partnership. As a branch office is a direct extension of the organisation in another location, the main organisation still has direct and complete control of the foreign office, making this structure often preferred to a foreign subsidiary. The latter is a separate entity, making direct control less obvious.

Although a branch office is often preferred for international law firms, the existence, requirements and restrictions of all relevant regulations should be checked. While there are few restrictions in Belgium, other countries, such as France and Germany, are more strict. Furthermore, within the branch structure, international partnerships often establish a branch of a separately created partnership instead of the main partnership to limit liability. Within the regulatory restrictions, there are different options available depending on the needs and preferences of the partners.

Since the local office is not a separate entity, equity partners are partners of the local office, plus they participate in the worldwide profits, leading to the necessity of complying with international tax rules. Besides the fact that these regulations often lead to individuals, not personal service organisations, being accepted as equity partners, they also determine the tax situation of the office and individual partners.

The tax consequences for the branch office will depend on where the head office is established (so called 'lex societatis') in function to whether or not the partnership is regarded as a separate legal entity according to the law where it is established. To the extent that the partnership is regarded as a separate legal entity, the branch office will probably follow the same taxation rules as a corporation. Special rules may be foreseen in case the local profit is insufficient to finance the local partners' profit share, i.e., the so-called valve arrangement where a valve opens to enable participation in the profits of an affiliated partnership. However, if the partnership is not regarded as a separate legal entity according to the law where it is established, a branch office may be regarded as transparent for tax purposes.

A tax transparent entity implies that each equity partner is considered to have a fixed base in the country where the office is established outside the country of the main partnership. Typically, the income derived through the local office is consequently taxed in that country. On a case by case basis and for each country where the main partnership has activities, the organisation needs to check whether the income is taxable and if so, when (e.g., the date at which each partner has actually drawn their profit share or another date such as the closing date of the financial year) and what formalities need to be fulfilled (e.g., advance tax payments, withholding taxes and separate or joint tax returns). Moreover, it needs to be verified whether the taxable basis is determined on an accrual or modified cash basis.

In practice, not all partners of the partnership reside in the same country. This means that for tax purposes, an equity partner can be a tax resident of country B and a non-resident of country A, while the situation for another partner may be vice versa.

Typically an equity partner who is resident in country B needs to report their worldwide income in country B. The equity partner then needs to verify whether county B has concluded tax treaties with the countries from which the partner has derived partnership income to prevent double taxation. Foreign source income from a non-treaty country is likely to be effectively taxed in the country of residence (see figure 44 and 45).

Tax compliance also includes VAT and accounting obligations. As the local VAT and accounting regulations must be met, cross border activities also lead to increased complexity.

Figure 44: Partnership is opaque in country A where it was established.

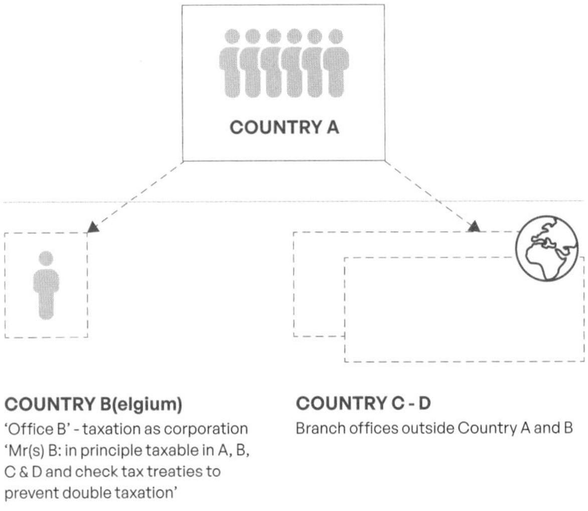

Figure 45: Partnership is transparent in country A where it was established.

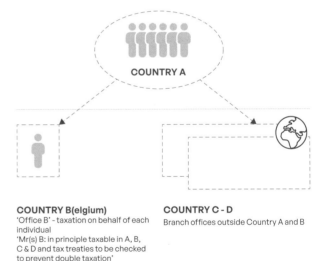

COUNTRY B(elgium)
'Office B' - taxation as corporation
'Mr(s) B: in principle taxable in A, B, C & D and check tax treaties to prevent double taxation'

COUNTRY C - D
Branch offices outside Country A and B

COUNTRY B(elgium)
'Office B' - taxation on behalf of each individual
'Mr(s) B: in principle taxable in A, B, C & D and tax treaties to be checked to prevent double taxation'

COUNTRY C - D
Branch offices outside Country A and B

1.4.2. Local incorporated organisations

For each local incorporated organisation, partners need to be nominated as directors of the incorporation. The partners need to determine whether or not the partners that also act as directors are additionally remunerated for their director activities or only remunerated as a partner of the main partnership.

In contrast to a transparent setup, partners are not subject to personal income tax in principle if they are not a resident, not nominated as a remunerated director of the local entity and not physically working in the local country where the incorporation took place. This is because the local activities are carried out via a separate and opaque legal entity for tax purposes.

However, an incorporation triggers specific formalities. It is expected that the corporation will be subject to local accounting law and corporate income tax, for which a corporate income tax return needs to be filed. It is important to note that when paying dividends, interests and royalties, the local entity may be required to withhold withholding taxes and corresponding formalities. Moreover, depending on the jurisdictions, VAT formalities may need to be complied with.

1.5. Equitable and successful partnerships

In conclusion, partner income systems are crucial in fostering equitable and successful partnerships. By implementing fair income distribution models and considering various factors that influence partner income, individuals and organisations can promote collaboration, trust and long-term sustainability.

This section has provided a comparative analysis of different partnership types and income distribution models, highlighting their significance and potential impact on partnership dynamics. It is clear that apart from the PEIS, tax and other compliance formalities may quickly require specialist knowledge, especially when the activities are carried out in different jurisdictions and/or partners of the partnership reside in different jurisdictions.

2. Quoted versus unquoted organisations

Corporate governance is of vital importance for quoted (also known as public or listed) organisations, and it is becoming more relevant for unquoted (also known as private or unlisted) organisations. Corporate governance is a framework of rules, practices, processes and structures by which an organisation is directed, controlled and held accountable. It involves the relationships between an organisation's management, board of directors, shareholders and other stakeholders. The primary goal of corporate governance is to ensure that the organisation operates ethically, transparently and in the best interests of its stakeholders.

The G20/OECD provides a clear statement of what an effective corporate governance framework is intended to achieve: *"The purpose of corporate governance is to help build an environment of trust, transparency and accountability necessary for fostering long-term investment, financial stability and business integrity, thereby supporting stronger growth and more inclusive societies"*[217]. Quoted organisations are subject to greater external pressure as the need for transparency, accountability and alignment of long-term interests has increased due to the dispersed ownership structure and the demands of the public market.

2.1. Remuneration and corporate governance

Remuneration is important in corporate governance as it plays a crucial role in aligning the interests of various stakeholders, incentivising the desired performance, managing risks associated with executive behaviours, enhancing shareholder value and ensuring that the organisation operates effectively and ethically. Furthermore, offering competitive and fair remuneration is key to engaging skilled executives and employees, which is crucial for the organisation's long term success.

Quoted and unquoted organisations operate under distinct corporate governance regulations. For example, the reward system for unquoted organisations often offers a level of flexibility, while quoted organisations face increased external scrutiny from various stakeholders, including investors, regulators and the general public.

For unquoted organisations, corporate governance is typically voluntary, meaning they are not legally obligated to adhere to specific governance standards. Instead, it is considered a strategic tool that can enhance resilience and provide a framework for addressing broader societal challenges, including those related to environmental, social and governance (ESG) considerations. Nevertheless, there is a growing trend towards increased transparency expectations for unquoted organisations. This is reflected in some regulations that are applicable to organisations based on their size instead of their shareholding's structure (e.g. CSRD and the EU Pay Transparency Directive). In anticipation of these trends, unquoted organisations are encouraged to proactively adopt transparent practices and engage with relevant stakeholders. This enables them to secure their long-term success by aligning with emerging expectations and reducing the risk of being exposed to policy makers' decisions in the future.

2.2. Unquoted organisations

The European Confederation of Directors' Association (ecoDa) released a guide on corporate governance principles for unquoted organisations in Europe[218]. This guide comprises a set of recommendations and promotes a phased-approach that considers the organisation's specific characteristics in terms of size, complexity and maturity. The ecoDa principles differ from the conventional 'comply or explain' principle commonly found in corporate governance codes for quoted organisations.

Phase I from ecoDa establishes the universal principles applicable to all unquoted organisations. These recommendations are considered foundational governance principles, ensuring a baseline level of governance. It includes Principle 5, that states: *"Levels of remuneration should be sufficient to attract, retain, and motivate executives and non-executive board members of the quality required to run the company successfully"*[219].

Phase II introduces more sophisticated measures that become relevant for larger or more complex unquoted organisations. It is particularly applicable to organisations with significant external financing or organisations preparing for a future public listing.

In essence, the ecoDa principles represent a dynamic and adaptive approach to corporate governance, acknowledging the diverse needs of unquoted organisations. The phased approach ensures that governance practices are tailored to the specific characteristics and objectives of each organisation, providing a roadmap for their governance journey.

The remuneration guidelines for unquoted organisations are in harmony with the corporate governance framework applied to quoted organisations, notably the 2020 Belgian Code on Corporate Governance. In particular, the report identifies several elements that constitute good practice in designing executive remuneration.

These elements include maintaining a balance between fixed and variable remuneration, while linking variable remuneration to predetermined performance criteria and long-term goals with a clawback clause. There should also be a minimum vesting period for share-based remuneration and a limit on severance remuneration.

For more mature unquoted organisations, effective engagement with shareholders and stakeholders, presenting a balanced assessment of the organisation's position and preparing for media attention and shareholder votes on executive remuneration are critical components of good governance[220].

2.3. Quoted organisations

As a fundamental principle, and unless otherwise specified in the articles of association or decided otherwise by the general meeting at the time of their appointment, directors receive remuneration for the execution of their mandate[221]. As previously indicated, quoted organisations are subject to specific regulations and increased scrutiny, resulting in a need for a more structured and transparent approach to executive remuneration. The remuneration policy should align with the organisation's business strategy, long-term interests and sustainability ambitions, and explain how it contributes to these objectives[222].

2.3.1. Elements of the remuneration policy

The remuneration policy is required to be clear and comprehensive, encompassing the following elements[223]:

- Remuneration components
  A clear description of both fixed and variable components, including bonuses and other forms of benefits for directors and executives, with an indication of their relative proportion.

- Working conditions
  A comprehensive explanation of how remuneration and employment conditions were taken into account when establishing the remuneration policy.

- Variable remuneration criteria (if awarded)
  Clear, comprehensive and varied financial, non-financial and corporate social responsibility criteria, including how these criteria contribute to the organisation's strategy, long-term interests and sustainability ambitions. It should also describe how these criteria are measured. Additionally, the policy should provide information on deferral periods and the organisation's ability to reclaim variable remuneration.

- Share-based remuneration (if awarded)
  Clear vesting periods and, where applicable, retention of shares after vesting. The policy should also explain how the award of share-based remuneration contributes to the corporate strategy, long-term interests and sustainability ambitions.

- Contractual arrangements
  The duration of contracts or arrangements and the applicable notice periods, main characteristics of supplementary pension or early retirement schemes, termination terms and payments linked to termination.

- Decision-making process
  A clear description of the decision-making process for determining, reviewing and implementing the remuneration policy, including measures to avoid or manage conflict of interest and the role of the Remuneration Committee or other committees where applicable.

In this context, benchmarking is a critical practice for quoted organisations, particularly in the context of executive remuneration, as it helps establish competitive and fair pay structures. Identifying an appropriate peer group and accurately classifying functions are essential steps. Additionally, understanding an organisation's position relative to its peer group and ensuring pay for performance alignment are key components of effective benchmarking, contributing to the organisation's ability to attract, motivate and retain top talent in a competitive market. See chapter 6 on job architecture for more information.

- Revision
  A description and explanation of significant changes after each revision, along with an overview of how the votes and views of the shareholders on the remuneration policy and reports have been considered since the most recent vote on the policy at the general meeting of shareholders.

In Belgium, the vote on remuneration is binding, meaning that directors can only receive remuneration in accordance with the organisation's approved remuneration policy. Following the general meeting's vote, the organisation should promptly disclose the policy, vote date and results on its website. This information remains publicly accessible for the duration of the policy[224]. It is possible for organisations to temporarily deviate from the remuneration policy under exceptional circumstances, provided it serves the organisation's long-term interests or viability[225].

2.3.2. Specific remuneration requirements

Quoted organisations face a number of specific requirements concerning their executive remuneration, including minimum vesting periods, deferred remuneration and termination period restrictions.

- Vesting period
  Unless otherwise stated in their articles of association or expressly approved by the general meeting, directors of quoted organisations may not acquire shares or exercise stock options or any other rights to acquire shares until at least three years after their award[226]. The 2020 Belgian Corporate Governance Code further specifies that stock options should not vest and be exercisable within less than three years. Furthermore, the organisation should not enter into derivative contracts related to such stock options or hedge the attached risks, as this is not consistent with the purpose of this incentive mechanism[227].

- Deferred remuneration
  At least a quarter of an executive's variable remuneration must be based on predetermined and objectively measurable performance criteria over a period of at least two years, and another quarter must be based on predetermined and objectively measurable criteria over a period of at least three years unless otherwise provided in the articles of association or expressly approved by the general meeting. This obligation does not apply if the variable remuneration is equal to or less than one-quarter of the annual remuneration[228].

- Termination payment
  In case of early termination, the severance pay should not exceed 12 months of the total remuneration, i.e., the total of the base- and variable remuneration, pension and any other components. If this amount is exceeded, it is always conditional on shareholder approval at the general meeting. Additionally, if the amount exceeds 18 months of remuneration, the termination payment can only be approved based on an unanimous and motivated opinion delivered by the Remuneration Committee[229].

2.3.3. Governance principles for executives

The remuneration policy for executives describes the different components of their remuneration, determining an appropriate balance between fixed and variable remuneration, and cash and deferred remuneration.

The Belgian Code on Companies and Associations does not specify a limit on the variable component of remuneration for directors of quoted organisations. However, the 2020 Belgian Corporate Governance Code introduces a cap on short-term incentives, without explicitly defining this limit. This observation explains the growing trend where variable pay is increasingly composed mainly of long-term incentives (LTI). The 2020 Belgian Corporate Governance Code also states that the board should set a minimum threshold of shares to be held by the executives[230].

2.3.4. Governance principles for non-executives

For non-executive board members, the remuneration policy should consider their roles as board members, including specific positions such as chair of the board or member of board committees, along with the associated responsibilities and time commitment. However, they should not receive any performance-related remuneration that is directly related to the organisation's results.

According to the 2020 Belgian Corporate Governance Code, non-executive board members should receive a portion of their remuneration in the form of shares. These shares are required to be held until at least one year after the non-executive board member departs from the board and a minimum of three years after the award date. It should be noted that the code prohibits the granting of stock options to non-executive board members[231].

2.3.5. Say on pay

The revised EU Shareholders Rights Directive (SRD II) introduced the right of shareholders to vote on executive remuneration packages presented by the organisation (the so-called say on pay). Shareholders have the opportunity to exercise their oversight role both ex-ante, by approving or disapproving the remuneration policy, and ex-post, by reviewing the remuneration report. The remuneration report provides an overview of the remuneration effectively paid during the previous year, allowing shareholders to retrospectively assess and scrutinise the actual remuneration outcomes. This dual oversight mechanism contributes to the organisation's transparent and accountable remuneration practices.

The remuneration policy is required to be presented at the general annual meeting at least once every four years or whenever there is a material change to the policy. In Belgium, the vote on the remuneration policy is binding, meaning that directors can only receive remuneration in accordance with the organisation's approved remuneration policy. Shareholders also vote on any variable remuneration that does not satisfy specific performance period requirements, equity-based awards with vesting periods of less than three years, severance agreements exceeding 12 or 18 months of annual remuneration, variable remuneration payable to a non-executive director and the annual remuneration report.

There has been an increasing number of remuneration-related items at general meetings since the introduction of say on pay. At the same time, there has been decreasing shareholder acceptance of remuneration-related matters during general meetings[232]. This trend confirms an increased scrutiny of organisations' pay practices, a perspective further substantiated by the growing media and public attention surrounding executive remuneration.

Corporate governance rules require organisations to revise their remuneration policy when a significant proportion of votes has been cast against the remuneration policy and/or the remuneration report[233]. Inaction could be perceived as weak governance on matters related to pay, damaging the organisation's performance. It can also have an impact on the way in which shareholders vote on other matters.

While there are no specific guidelines on how organisations should respond to shareholder dissent on the remuneration report, it is crucial to recognise that such dissent signifies a divergent view on the organisation's remuneration practices. It is worth noting that Belgian quoted organisations are required to explain how shareholder votes and feedback on both the remuneration policy and the remuneration report have been considered when presenting a revised remuneration policy for voting at the annual general meeting[234].

After shareholders were granted the right to vote on an organisation's executive remuneration programmes and express dissatisfaction with certain arrangements, the necessity for discussing executive remuneration became evident. Establishing an open and transparent dialogue with shareholders on remuneration and governance is crucial for understanding the reasons behind dissenting votes and deciding on appropriate actions. Director-shareholder engagement today covers a range of topics, including ESG issues, executive remuneration, strategy oversight and board composition, with executive remuneration close to the top of the list[235].

2.3.6. Investor considerations

Striking a balance with executive remuneration entails designing programmes that attract and motivate executives while aligning with the expectations of a wide range of stakeholders (i.e., shareholders, investors, regulators and the general public). Remuneration is subject to increased scrutiny of shareholders and investors[236].

- Transparency
  Shareholders and investors expect clear and comprehensive information on executive remuneration, including details of the connection between remuneration and the organisation's long term strategy, supported by financial and non-financial KPIs.

  Transparency on executive pay is crucial for investors to evaluate alignment with the organisation's interests, manage risks and assess performance. It fosters trust and enables informed decision making while ensuring compliance with legal and regulatory requirements.

- Governance
  Executive remuneration should be appropriately linked to performance, focusing on long-term value creation for shareholders and investors. In this context, there has been a transition from a pay for performance to a pay for sustainability philosophy[237]. Stakeholders, including shareholders, investors and the general public, are increasingly emphasising the importance of sustainability and responsible corporate behaviours in addition to traditional performance metrics.

  Organisations are increasingly implementing independent and effective Remuneration Committees to try and avoid inappropriate executive remuneration, unjustified increases in remuneration levels, a lack of deferred remuneration, the awarding of excessive discretionary bonuses and the absence of performance conditions in long-term incentive plans (LTIPs).

  Remuneration Committees also work to ensure KPIs linked to remuneration align with the organisation's long-term strategy and objectives as well as with shareholder interests. Together, these actions eliminate the opportunity for executives to deviate from the approved remuneration policy.

- Risks
  Remuneration policies should avoid arrangements that may reward failure. This could be due to a lack of risk adjustment mechanisms or the Remuneration Committee's seeming reluctance to clawback variable remuneration in practice.

  Investors favour risk adjustment mechanisms in executive remuneration as such measures mitigate the risks associated with executive behaviour, financial misstatements or misconduct. This safeguards shareholder interests, promotes accountability and maintains confidence in corporate governance and performance.

Figure 46: Key governance principles for quoted and unquoted organisations.

	QUOTED ORGANISATIONS	UNQUOTED ORGANISATIONS
REGULATORY COMPLIANCE	Subject to strict regulatory oversight, including disclosure requirements for executive and non-executive board member remuneration.	Generally subject to fewer regulatory requirements regarding the disclosure of executive and non-executive board member remuneration.
SHAREHOLDER OVERSIGHT	Shareholders have a say in executive remuneration through their say on pay votes. Board members' remuneration may be more scrutinised.	Remuneration decisions may be more internally determined, with less external shareholder influence due to concentrated ownership.
BOARD COMPOSITION	Independent directors may have a more significant role in remuneration committees, especially for executive remuneration decisions.	Board composition may include family members or representatives.
TRANSPARENCY	High level of transparency in disclosing executive remuneration.	Lower transparency requirements, with remuneration details not as publicly disclosed as in quoted organisations.
MARKET DYNAMICS	Executive remuneration is influenced by market forces, industry benchmarks and investor expectations.	Remuneration decisions may be more internally determined, with less direct influence from market dynamics.
FLEXIBILITY	Remuneration structures need to align with market norms and comply with regulatory standards.	More flexibility in designing remuneration structures to meet the needs of the organisation and its ownership structure.

3. Differing reward needs

This chapter explored the diverse needs and requirements influencing remuneration design across different types of organisations, including partnerships and quoted and unquoted organisations. From specific industry dynamics to regulatory frameworks and organisational objectives, it is clear that each type of organisation faces different challenges and considerations which shape their approach to remuneration.

For more information on how the banking and insurance industry handles remuneration governed by strict regulations, turn to chapter 12.

Special dossiers

10.
Equal pay

Key takeaways

1. New regulations mandate actionable steps towards closing the gender pay gap, holding organisations accountable for tangible progress.

2. Pay transparency is not just a passing trend; it is a legal requirement and a moral imperative for organisations.

3. Addressing the gender pay gap through pay transparency measures uncovers systemic issues and enables employees to claim their rights to equal pay.

4. The Pay Transparency Directive incorporates a comprehensive set of transparency requirements that impact the organisation's pay philosophy and affect pay decision-making processes, from recruitment onward.

5. Breaking the glass ceiling is crucial for addressing the gender pay gap, as it is one of the root causes of underrepresentation of women in leadership positions.

Addressing the gender pay gap has emerged as a pivotal aspect of workplace equity and one of the key priorities of gender policies at both the EU and national levels. Within the EU, the European Commission emphasised the importance of tackling the gender pay gap, alongside earnings and pension disparities, by making it a crucial element within its Gender Equality Strategy 2020-2025 framework[238].

In recent years, there has been increasing pressure on organisations to report environmental and social metrics in addition to financial performance. Initiatives such as the Corporate Sustainability Reporting Directive (CSRD), the Global Reporting Initiative (GRI) and the Pay Transparency Directive (PTD)[239] require organisations to disclose information that gives stakeholders a comprehensive understanding of their efforts towards promoting gender equality. This section focuses on the transformative potential of pay transparency as a catalyst for change and the impact of the glass ceiling on the gender pay gap.

Executives and HR professionals play a crucial role in building a resilient and socially responsible organisation. Executives must make critical decisions that define their sustainable strategies, weighing the advantages of compliance-driven approaches compared to prioritising workplace equality as a fundamental ethical imperative that goes beyond legal obligations. HR professionals are well positioned to show executives that organisations that prioritise investments in their workforce are better positioned to navigate changes and are more resilient in the face of challenges.

1. The EU Pay Transparency Directive

Without pay transparency, gender-based pay discrimination and biases may persist unnoticed or they are challenging to prove if they are suspected. In response to this issue, the EU's PTD[240] aims to ensure equal pay for equal work or work of equal value. It addresses the gender pay gap through pay transparency with the objective of enabling employees to claim their rights to equal pay. Member States have up to June 7, 2026, to transpose the directive into their national law.

Pay transparency is both a legal requirement and a moral imperative, not merely a trend. Addressing the gender pay gap is crucial for broader gender equality goals, and it involves the confrontation of systemic issues. Equal pay and transparency underpin sustainable business practices, enhancing social responsibility, wellbeing and talent management. Fair remuneration boosts employee motivation, reducing absenteeism and turnover, consequently improving employer financial health.

1.1. Generalities

While equal pay and the gender pay gap are related concepts, they address different aspects of gender equality. Equal pay refers to the principle that individuals who perform the same job or work of equal value should receive the same remuneration, regardless of their gender or any other protected characteristic. The gender pay gap, on the other hand, looks at the overall income disparities between men and women in the workforce, considering various factors that contribute to this gap, such as occupational choices, career progression and work patterns.

1.1.1. Scope of the directive
The PTD applies to all employers, whether public or private, regardless of their size, industry or other characteristics. It covers all employees and applicants for employment.

Figure 47: Scope of the EU Pay Transparency Directive.

ALL EMPLOYERS	ALL EMPLOYEES	OTHERS
• Public employers • Private employers	• Part-time workers • Fixed-term contracts • Employees via temporary agency • Trainees & apprentices • Etc.	• Applicants

Employees are individuals who have an employment contract or relationship as defined by law, collective agreement or prevailing practice in each Member State. The determination of whether an employment relationship exists should be based on the actual work performance and not solely on how the parties involved describe the relationship. This is essential to prevent employers from misclassifying workers to evade their obligations regarding pay transparency.

The directive introduces binding measures to improve pay transparency, complemented by provisions that clarify existing legal concepts and measures that improve enforcement mechanisms and access to justice. Among these key provisions is a clarification of the definition of pay and a refined understanding of work of equal value.

1.1.2. Definition of pay
'Pay' refers to fixed and complementary or variable components of remuneration. It includes salaries, wages and any additional benefits received by workers directly or indirectly from their employer in connection with their employment. This definition encompasses all forms of reward, whether provided in cash or in kind, and should encompass all elements of remuneration mandated by law, collective agreements and prevailing practices in each Member State.

1.1.3. Definition of work of equal value
The directive seeks to prevent job architecture from inadvertently perpetuating gender bias, which may reinforce hierarchical norms and undervalue traditionally female-dominated roles.

Employers must establish pay structures that ensure equal pay for equal work as well as for work that holds equal value. 'Work of equal value' refers to work that is determined to have equal value using non-discriminatory and objective gender-neutral criteria such as skills, effort and responsibility.

In this respect, employers are required to adopt a rigorous and impartial gender-neutral methodology, such as a job evaluation and classification system, to ascertain jobs of equivalent value. According to the specifications outlined in the directive regarding the methodology, there is a preference for the point-factor method (see chapter 6).

1.2. Pay transparency requirements

The directive establishes minimum standard requirements, granting Member States the flexibility to enforce stricter regulations through their national laws. The EU acknowledges the multifaceted nature of the gender pay gap, which is influenced by a variety of factors. Consequently, the directive incorporates a comprehensive set of transparency requirements that not only impact the organisation's pay philosophy but also affect pay decision-making processes, from recruitment onward.

1.2.1. Recruitment
Employers are required to furnish applicants with pay-related information, including the initial pay or pay range for the position, along with the criteria used to determine their pay. This information should be communicated either in the job advertisement or before the candidate's first interview. Additionally,

employers are prohibited from soliciting pay history from applicants. These obligations promote transparent and equitable pay negotiations. Furthermore, job vacancy notices and job titles should be gender-neutral and the recruitment process should be conducted without any form of discrimination.

1.2.2. Approach and philosophy to pay

Organisations are required to be transparent regarding their pay setting and progression policies by providing clear and easily accessible information to employees detailing the criteria used to determine pay, pay levels and pay progression. This information should be objective, gender-neutral and readily available to all employees within the organisation.

1.2.3. Right to information on pay levels

Employees are entitled to request information concerning their pay level, as well as the average pay levels disaggregated by gender, for categories of employees performing similar work or work of equal value. Employees should be informed annually about their right to information and the procedure for obtaining it.

Employers are required to provide the requested information within two months, as well as comprehensive explanations of pay data, upon employee request. The information should be provided in a format accessible to individuals with disabilities, taking into account their specific needs.

1.2.4. Reporting on the gender pay gap

Unlike other requirements, the obligation to report on the gender pay gap varies depending on the size of the organisation. Organisations with 100 or more employees are obliged to produce reports on the gender pay gap, with large organisations with over 250 employees reporting annually, compared to every three years for smaller organisations. Organisations with fewer than 100 employees can report on a voluntary basis. The initial reporting obligation commences in 2027 for organisations with more than 150 employees, with organisations with 100-149 employees starting in 2031.

The reporting on the pay gap encompasses the following elements:

a) the (average) gender pay gap.
b) the (average) gender pay gap in complementary or variable components.
c) the median gender pay gap.
d) the median gender pay gap in complementary or variable components.
e) the proportion of female and male workers receiving complementary or variable components.
f) the proportion of female and male workers in each quartile pay band.
g) the gender pay gap between employees based on categories that are broken down by the ordinary basic wage or salary and complementary or variable components.

Workers, representatives, labour inspectorates and equality bodies have the right to seek clarification on pay data and gender pay gap differences. In such cases, employers are obliged to provide substantial replies and remediate gender pay differences within six months.

1.2.5. Joint pay assessment

Organisations must initiate a joint assessment if they identify a pay gap of more than 5% in any category that remains unjustified by the employer based on objective and gender-neutral criteria or if the employer fails to remedy such a difference within six months of submitting the pay report. This assessment involves a comprehensive review of the pay structure in collaboration with employee representatives. It includes scrutinising pay gap reporting, analysing root causes, evaluating remediation measures and assessing their effectiveness. It should be noted that the impact of parental leave on pay decisions is taken into consideration.

1.2.6. Enforcement mechanisms and sanctions

The directive aims to remove any procedural obstacles faced by victims of discrimination when claiming their rights to equal pay. Consequently, various enforcement mechanisms and sanctions are foreseen (e.g., the right to the full recovery of back pay, the shift of burden of proof to the employer, the possibility of collective or class action, protection against retaliation and financial sanctions).

In addition, a judge may order structural or organisational measures such as reviewing pay-setting mechanisms, implementing action plans to address pay inequalities and reduce gender pay gaps, raising awareness of employees' rights to equal pay and providing mandatory training.

1.3. Steps towards pay transparency[241]

The timeline to prepare for pay transparency depends on several factors, such as the size and complexity of the organisation, the current level of pay transparency and the organisation's specific needs and goals. Engaging external experts can be beneficial for organisations lacking internal resources or seeking impartial assessments and support in challenging assumptions throughout the pay transparency journey.

Figure 48: The recommended steps in the journey towards pay transparency.

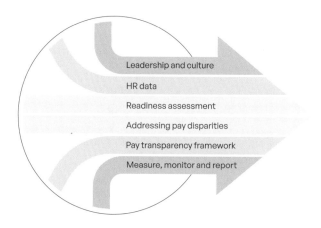

1.3.1. Leadership and culture
The pay transparency journey starts with executive support. Leadership awareness and endorsement are crucial for successful pay transparency initiatives, including the implications in terms of employer branding, reputation, risks and opportunities. Moreover, the right organisational culture is vital for implementing effective pay transparency initiatives

as it ensures alignment with organisational values, encourages open communication and promotes a commitment to fairness and equality.

1.3.2. HR data
As all subsequent steps rely on HR data and information, organisations must ensure that their data are accurate, complete and up to date. Furthermore, IT, HR and legal professionals must collaborate to ensure seamless access to this data from HR systems while adhering to local data protection and privacy laws.

1.3.3. Readiness assessment
As the next step, organisations must evaluate their current status and address any existing pay disparities. This assessment will entail both quantitative and qualitative analyses, including a review of the pay structure, HR policies and processes and HR KPIs, such as the proportion of male and female employees who received promotions or salary increases, performance ratings and training. In this context, exit interviews and employee surveys can offer valuable insights into employees' perceptions of the organisation's pay practices.

1.3.4. Addressing pay disparities
Depending on the outcome of the readiness assessment, organisations may find it necessary to review their pay structure, job evaluation and grading systems, make salary adjustments and update policies accordingly.

C-level executives must be actively involved in these exercises, recognising that any changes to salaries can significantly impact employer branding and reputation. C-level executives typically have the authority and responsibility to oversee strategic decisions related to remuneration, and their involvement ensures alignment with the organisation's overall goals and values.

In the context of reviewing pay structures and making salary adjustments, it is also crucial to involve the finance and legal departments to assess the financial implications and ensure compliance with employment regulations.

Furthermore, meticulously documenting all decisions related to pay and any remedial actions taken is essential. This documentation serves as crucial evidence to defend against potential equal pay claims and helps maintain transparency and accountability within the organisation.

1.3.5. Pay transparency framework

Once embarked on the journey to transparency, establishing a framework for pay becomes essential. This involves drafting a policy detailing how employees can exercise their right to information, outlining responsibilities and setting internal timelines, etc. Additionally, it is crucial to establish a grievance procedure to address any concerns employees may have regarding their pay and mitigate risks effectively.

Furthermore, implementing a comprehensive communication plan and providing manager training are imperative to equip frontline managers with the skills to address employee inquiries effectively. Communication efforts should be tailored to each stakeholder group as effective communication strategies can help increase support for pay transparency initiatives and mitigate resistance.

1.3.6. Measure, monitor and report

It is essential to acknowledge that closing the gender pay gap requires ongoing dedication. The pay gap is a dynamic target influenced by employees joining or leaving the organisation, strategic shifts and organisational changes (e.g., reorganisation).

As a result, continuous monitoring is crucial and should be supported by adequate budgeting and resource allocation. Reporting these findings transparently to stakeholders fosters accountability, trust and continuous improvement in pay practices within the organisation.

As organisations embrace pay transparency to promote fairness and equal pay, it becomes increasingly evident that breaking the glass ceiling is imperative to ensure equal opportunities and advancement for all individuals, regardless of gender or other demographic factors.

2. Women on Boards Directive

Breaking the glass ceiling is crucial for addressing the gender pay gap, as one of its root causes lies in the underrepresentation of women on boards and in leadership positions. The glass ceiling is a metaphorical barrier that prevents women and minorities from advancing to higher levels of leadership and success within organisations, particularly in the corporate world. It represents the invisible but pervasive barriers, such as gender bias, stereotypes and discriminatory practices, that limit the career advancement and opportunities of qualified individuals solely based on their gender or other protected characteristics. Breaking through the glass ceiling requires addressing systemic inequalities, promoting diversity and inclusion, and implementing policies and practices that create equal opportunities for all individuals to advance and succeed in their careers. The EU aims to tackle this with the EU Women on Boards Directive.

2.1. Scope of the directive

The goal of the EU Women on Boards Directive is to achieve at least 40% representation of women among non-executive directors or 33% among all directors in EU quoted organisations by 2026[242].

This directive aims to enhance gender balance and diversity within corporate boards across the European Union. Member States are required to transpose the directive's requirements into national law by December 28, 2024.

The key provisions of the directive include:

- Priority to the underrepresented gender
  The directive stipulates that, when presented with equally qualified candidates for promotion to or employment at a director level, priority can be given to the underrepresented sex in certain circumstances. However, merit remains the primary criterion in the selection process.

- Enhanced transparency

  Listed organisations are required to disclose information on gender representation on their board on their website and in their annual report. Organisations that do not reach the target will have to implement selection and appointment procedures designed to rectify the situation. Furthermore, they should disclose the efforts taken so far and their planned future measures to meet the quantitative objectives.

- Penalties

  The directive includes enforcement mechanisms. Member States should implement effective, dissuasive and proportionate penalties for organisations that fail to comply with open and transparent appointment procedures and quantitative objectives, such as fines or the nullity or annulment of the board of directors selection by a judicial body.

While there may be debates about the effectiveness and potential drawbacks of gender quotas, proponents argue that they are a necessary step toward achieving greater gender equality in leadership positions. This seems to be confirmed by figures from the OECD showing a correlation between mandated quotas and, to a lesser extent, voluntary targets with increased representation of women on boards over time.

The slow progression of women into senior leadership positions can, at least partially, be attributed to the lack or absence of succession planning in the boardroom. Despite 45% of directors recognising the need to replace at least one fellow board member[243], there are challenges in initiating the necessary conversations and dedicating efforts to long-term board succession planning. This continues to pose significant obstacles to effective board refreshment.

Figure 49: Aggregate change in the percentage of women on Boards 2017-2022 according to OECD figures[244].

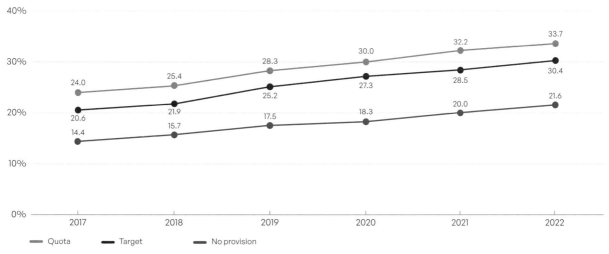

2.2. Women on boards in Belgium

In Belgian quoted organisations and public interest entities, regulations mandate that at least one third of board members should be of a different gender from the majority. If a board member represents a legal entity, the gender is determined by the permanent representative.

If the board of directors fails to meet the one-third threshold, remedial action must be taken at the subsequent general meeting. Any appointments made outside of compliance with the quota are considered void. Furthermore, if the board composition remains non-compliant after the subsequent general meeting, any financial or non-financial benefit for the directors based on their mandate is suspended until the quota requirement is fulfilled.

The composition of the board of directors of newly quoted organisations must comply with the quota of women on the board from the first day of the sixth year following the listing.

Women's representation on boards in Belgium remains a critical issue, with notable disparities observed across executive and non-executive roles. According to PwC's annual survey[245], only 13% of executive directors and a mere 5% of CEOs are women, highlighting significant underrepresentation in top leadership positions. However, there is a more balanced gender distribution among non-executive directors, with 42% being women, signalling progress in achieving gender diversity at this level of governance.

Figure 50: Gender representation of executive directors in Belgian quoted organisations.

Women	Men
13%	87%

Figure 51: Gender representation of non-executive directors in Belgian quoted organisations.

Women	Men
42%	58%

3. The future of equal pay

This chapter has shown that there has been a significant shift in corporate responsibility regarding equal pay regardless of gender. While initial reporting obligations served to shed light on disparities, the EU directives on Pay Transparency and Women on Boards mandate actionable steps towards closing the gender pay gap, holding organisations accountable for tangible progress.

This transition reflects a crucial evolution from a mere duty to report to a proactive duty to act, emphasising the requirement for organisations to implement concrete measures to address gender inequality in the workplace. As echoed by the principle 'what is reported is done', accountability in reporting translates directly into meaningful action. Through this comprehensive approach, businesses can enhance transparency while fostering a more equitable and inclusive work environment which ultimately contributes to broader societal progress.

Leveraging pay transparency can serve as a cornerstone in promoting good governance practices and positioning an organisation as a top employer. By openly communicating about pay structures, criteria for determining compensation and opportunities for advancement, organisations demonstrate their transparency and accountability, fostering trust among employees and stakeholders. Furthermore, embracing pay transparency showcases a commitment to fairness, diversity and inclusivity, aligning with modern workforce expectations and solidifying the organisation's reputation as an employer of choice that values equity and transparency in its practices.

11.
Occupational pension plans

Key takeaways

1. Branch 21 and Branch 23 pensions offer employers different ways to invest their employees' pension savings. Each has different pros and cons in terms of their return.

2. Employees have a legal right to a minimum return on their pension savings, at the expense of their employer.

3. There are interesting alternatives to common defined contribution plans for larger groups of employees.

4. Different pension plans are more appropriate for individuals of different ages and groups of different sizes.

The Belgian occupational pension landscape for employees is a complex and multifaceted domain that requires careful navigation. This chapter unravels the complexities of this landscape, focusing on various investment options including the common types of pension plans in Belgium and how they are used in practice.

1. Occupational pensions for employees in Belgium

Within the Belgian pension law framework, a legal minimum return is mandated for occupational pension plans organised for the benefit of employees. This fluctuates as it is tied to the interest rate of 10-year government bonds. Employers are responsible for covering any deficits relative to the legal minimum, either when the pension is paid out or when the employee transfers the reserves to a new pension plan.

Defined contribution (DC) plans are a common type of pension plan in Belgium. DC plans involve predetermined contributions from employers and/or employees, where the final pension benefit depends on both the contributions and investment performance. Collective defined contribution (CDC) plans and cash balance (CB) plans can be useful alternatives to DC plans. CDC plans introduce a collective investment mix and buffer to smooth out fluctuations and mitigate deficits. CB plans guarantee a pension benefit based on a defined contribution increased by a return determined in the plan rules.

When considering long-term investments, the viability of branch 21 and branch 23 products comes into question. Branch 21 products may struggle to provide attractive returns, especially when interest rates are lower than inflation. In contrast, branch 23 products offer the potential for higher returns, but also carry the risk of poor investment results.

To address potential deficits and enhance the attractiveness of pension plans, various solutions have emerged in the Belgian branch 23 market. These include life cycle solutions in DC plans, which customise investment mixes based on the employee's age and investment horizon. Additionally, comparative numerical analyses of DC, CDC and CB plans shed light on potential financial outcomes and risk profiles associated with each type of plan.

Before we look at the impact of these alternatives for smaller and larger groups, let's first review these concepts and terms.

1.1. Branch 21 and branch 23

Branch 21 and branch 23 are terms used in the Belgian insurance industry to categorise different types of life insurance products.

In branch 21 products, the insurance company guarantees a fixed interest rate on the premiums invested. Policyholders are entitled to a guaranteed minimum return on their investment as the insurance company manages the investments and takes on the investment risk. Branch 21 life insurance contracts are often considered low-risk investment options, suitable for clients seeking stability and capital preservation.

For years, the returns on branch 21 insurance products have been low, primarily due to the low returns on fixed-income products. However, the returns on fixed-income products have significantly increased since 2022, resulting in a modest rise in branch 21 returns. Even so, the increase in branch 21 returns is lower than the increase in returns for fixed-income products as insurers have long-term obligations and must meet capital buffer requirements imposed by the European Solvency II Directive.

Branch 23 products are investment-linked life insurance products that combine life insurance coverage with investment opportunities. Policyholders have the flexibility to allocate their premiums to different investment funds, such as stocks or bonds. The performance of these investment funds directly affects the value of the policy.

1.2. Legal minimum return

The legal minimum return on pensions is tied to the interest rate on 10-year Belgian government bonds, also known as linear obligations (OLO), with a duration of 10 years. This means that when the interest rate on government bonds increases or decreases, so does the legal minimum return. As a result, the legal minimum return can vary from year to year, within a fixed range of 1.75% and 3.75% according to Belgian pension law.

The legal minimum return has been set at 1.75% since 2016. However, due to recent increases in government bond yields, it is expected that it will rise to 2.5% by 2025. This minimum rate applies as long as the employee's job contract remains active. Upon leaving employment, the employee's accrued legal minimum reserve is frozen, meaning that the legal minimum return amounts to 0% for deferred vested members.

If there are any deficits relative to the legal minimum, it is the employer's responsibility to cover them. However, these deficits do not necessarily need to be settled every year. Instead, the employer only needs to cover deficits relative to the legal minimum either when the pension is paid out upon the employee's retirement or when the employee transfers the pension reserves to the pension plan of their new employer.

1.3. DC plan, CDC plan and CB plan

DC plans, CDC plans and CB plans work in different ways, offering different benefits and risks for employers and employees.

In a DC pension plan the employer and/or employee make predetermined contributions into a retirement savings plan. The final pension benefit is not guaranteed, and depends on the contributions made and the investment performance over time. DC pension plans have become very common, especially in the private sector, as they shift the responsibility and risk of retirement savings from employers to employees. However, there is still a significant risk for employers due to the Belgian legal minimum return.

Each member of a DC plan has an individual account. If an employee retires or transfers their accrued pension reserves to a new employer's pension plan after a period of favourable investment returns, they will have a higher pension. Conversely, if they retire after a financial crash, they will have a lower pension due to negative returns. Any surplus above the legal minimum can quickly disappear and, if there is a deficit at retirement or upon transfer of the pension reserves to another pension plan, the employer must cover that deficit. There is no solidarity between the plan members, meaning one member's returns cannot be used to compensate for another member's deficits.

CDC plans allow for a portion of the achieved investment returns to be set aside as a collective buffer. If the return exceeds a certain level determined in the pension plan rules, the excess is used to create a 'free reserve'. This reserve cannot be used for normal premium payments, but it can be used by the employer to cover deficits, provide extra returns to both active and deferred vested members or grant additional pension premiums only to active members.

Regarding the legal minimum, there is an important distinction between granting an additional pension premium or an additional return. Additional pension premiums result in an increase in the legal minimum as this is determined by adding up all normal and additional pension premiums. As the legal minimum increases, the likelihood of potential deficits also increases. While granting additional returns helps mitigate the risk of deficits relative to the legal minimum. The legal minimum is not increased due to the additional returns, while the value of the pension contracts increases.

In both DC and CDC plans, any deficit relative to the legal minimum must be covered by the employer when the pension is paid upon the individual's retirement or when the pension reserves are transferred to a new pension plan. Fluctuations along the way do not need to be immediately compensated.

In a CB plan, the employer commits to a defined contribution pension increased by a return determined in the pension plan rules. The employer also guarantees the pension benefit at retirement, unlike in a DC plan. This guaranteed benefit is expressed as the capitalisation of the pension contributions at a return determined in the plan rules, known as the cash balance return (CB return). Examples of the CB return include a fixed interest rate or the performance of a public index.

If the achieved return in a year exceeds the contractually determined cash balance return, the surplus serves as a buffer. This collective buffer can be used by the employer for the purposes mentioned in the CDC plans, as well as for normal premium payments. In other words, the employer can benefit from a discount on normal premiums, called a premium holiday, which is a significant advantage for employers compared to CDC plans. However, CB plans require that any deficits relative to the contractually guaranteed CB return must be immediately covered with additional payments. This can burden employers with volatile cash flows, consisting of additional deposits in years with poor investment results and premium holidays in years with favourable investment results.

2. Long-term investments

In many cases, the return on branch 21 contracts is expected to be lower than the legal minimum return in the coming years. Therefore, deficits are anticipated to arise or increase in many branch 21 contracts.

Considering the 0% legal minimum return for deferred vested members, the extent of these deficits largely depends on the duration of active membership in the organisation's pension plan. Organisations that experience high employee turnover will typically have limited deficits in branch 21 contracts. However, organisations with low employee turnover can see deficits in branch 21 contracts accumulate significantly.

When interest rates in branch 21 products are lower than inflation, the question arises whether long-term investment in branch 21 is still viable. This investment becomes even more questionable when employers are unable to offer employees protection against inflation as the purchasing power of the investment may significantly erode over a long investment period.

In contrast to branch 21 investments, it is generally expected that fluctuations in branch 23 investments will level out significantly over time if the investment horizon is long enough. This argument discourages long-term investment in branch 21. However, the immediate concern for branch 23 insurance products is the potential financial consequences of poor or even negative investment results.

With this in mind, the rest of this chapter will explore the branch 23 insurance market that aims to mitigate the need for additional employer deposits to address funding deficits. We start by looking at life cycle DC plan solutions, before turning to a comparative numerical analysis of DC, CDC and CB plans. Please note that a few solutions will be compared based on numerical data, so it does not encompass a comprehensive analysis of all solutions currently available in the Belgian market.

3. Life cycle solutions

When it comes to DC plans, there is no solidarity between members, meaning that the returns of one member cannot be used to compensate for the deficits of another member. However, it is possible to customise the investment mix based on the age or investment horizon of each member. Younger members typically start with a higher risk profile, which gradually decreases as they approach retirement age. This is achieved by adjusting the ratio between stocks and bonds in the investment mix over time, resulting in a gradual reduction of risk.

In recent years, several insurers have promoted the life cycle approach, using 'target volatility funds' as the underlying investment to take into account the legal minimum return. This approach both considers the strategic asset allocation and aims to control the target volatility, with the total volatility decreasing as the member gets closer to retirement age.

In other words, when the retirement horizon is distant, the life cycle approach uses dynamic investing as it smoothens potential fluctuations within an envisaged upward trend. However, a more cautious approach is adopted as retirement approaches. During the final years, it becomes crucial to mitigate the risk of significant downturns, as there may be accumulated surpluses that could be depleted with insufficient time to recover losses, given the shorter time horizon.

On an individual level and for small groups of employees, life cycle solutions can be interesting for managing risk. When dealing with larger groups of employees (that number at least in double digits), it is useful to assess whether the individual life cycle approach effectively takes advantage of potential economies of scale, particularly in light of the average investment duration of the group of plan members. In contrast to the shrinking individual investment horizon for one plan member, the collective investment horizon should remain relatively stable as long as the older departing plan members are replaced by sufficient incoming younger employees.

4. Optimising group pension plans

This section uses simulations to assess the potential financial outcomes of investments in branch 23 products based on the assumptions mentioned below. The simulations cover a DC plan (without life cycle), a CDC plan and two different types of CB plans.

For each simulation, we start by randomly generating 1,000 series (scenarios) of annual return based on an expected net return of 3% and an assumed volatility of 8%. In these models, the returns are generated year after year using independent normal distributions.

We assume an annual staff turnover rate, including retirements, of 10%.

For each series, we calculate the pension reserves and the legal minimum reserves (set at 1.75%) over a 40-year period. We assume that the normal employer's premium, excluding any additional premiums to cover deficits relative to the legal minimum, for the entire group of employees amounts to 100 per year. Therefore, the total sum of normal employer's premiums over the 40-year period amounts to 4,000.

For each 40-year series, we project from year to year the pension reserves and the legal minimum reserves (i.e., 1.75%). At the point when the legal minimum must be effectively fully funded (i.e., at retirement or the transfer of reserves to the next employer's pension plan), we verify whether the projected pension reserves, together with the assets in the buffer, are at least equal to the legal minimum. For each series, we quantify all deficits relative to the legal minimum over the entire 40-year period.

It is worth noting that when generating multiple sets of 1,000 series, the results may vary slightly each time due to the random nature of the series. However, since we have generated a sufficient number of series, the results are very similar and the differences are negligible.

4.1. DC versus CDC plans

For the CDC plan, we assume that any returns exceeding 4% are fully allocated to the collective buffer. For example, if the return in a given year is 5%, then 1% is added to the collective buffer. This collective buffer is specifically utilised to address deficits relative to the legal minimum.

In practice, the question arises as to whether employees choose to keep their accrued pension reserves within the pension plan after leaving the organisation or opt to transfer the accrued pension reserves to the new employer's pension plan. To illustrate the impact of this, we present three models. The first model assumes that all members' reserves are withdrawn from the pension plan upon leaving the organisation, this could be because they were transferred to the new employer's pension plan or they were paid out at retirement. The second model assumes that reserves remain in the pension plan for all members for a period of 10 years after the termination of their employment contract. The third model assumes that reserves remain in the pension plan for 20 years after the termination of their employment contract.

In figure 52, we examine the total sum of additional premiums that must be paid to meet the legal minimum over the entire 40-year period. This sum can be compared to the total sum of normal DC or CDC premiums, which amounts to 4,000 in this simulation (a 40-year series with a normal premium of 100 per year).

Figure 52: The sum of additional premiums that should be paid to meet the legal minimum for a DC and CDC plan.

SUM OF ADDITIONAL PAYMENTS OVER THE 40-YEAR PERIOD	FREQUENCY DC PLAN			FREQUENCY CDC PLAN		
	0 years after leaving the organisation	10 years after leaving the organisation	20 years after leaving the organisation	0 years after leaving the organisation	10 years after leaving the organisation	20 years after leaving the organisation
0	2.6%	50.8%	81.4%	28.1%	94.7%	99%
0 – 100	57.5%	35.2%	14.4%	58.7%	2.9%	0.25%
100 – 200	20.8%	7.6%	2%	7.3%	1.2%	0.25%
200 – 300	10.9%	3.4%	1%	3.2%	0.7%	0.25%
300 – 400	5.5%	1.4%	0.9%	1.3%	0.3%	0.25%
> 400	2.7%	1.6%	0.3%	1.4%	0.2%	0%

How should we interpret the results in figure 52?
Based on the assumption that reserves are withdrawn from the pension plan upon leaving the organisation, approximately 3% of the scenarios in a DC scheme do not require any additional deposits throughout the entire 40-year period to meet the legal minimum. However, if the reserves remain invested in the group insurance scheme for 10 or 20 years after the termination of the employment contract, the percentage increases to 51% and 81% respectively. This is logical because the legal minimum return is fixed at 0% instead of 1.75% after the termination of the employment contract. As a result, the bar is not raised during the 10 or 20 years while the reserves remain invested, and any years with negative returns have a high probability of being offset by years with positive returns. There is a 60% probability that the sum of deficits is lower than 100 (rows 1 and 2), assuming the immediate transfer of reserves. This probability increases to 86% and 96% respectively when the reserves are transferred 10 or 20 years after the termination of the employment contract.

For a CDC scheme where the return is capped at 4% per annum, the probability of never needing to make additional payments increases to 28%, 95% and 99% respectively (immediately after the termination of the employment contract, 10 years after and 20 years after). This indicates a significantly reduced likelihood of having to make up deficits compared to a DC scheme. This is not surprising since we assume that all returns above 4% are deposited into the buffer, which is only used to address deficits.

In figure 53, we examine the highest additional payment that must be made in a single year over the entire 40-year period to meet the legal minimum. This represents the 'worst year' scenario.

What conclusions can we draw from the assumption that reserves will remain in the group insurance scheme for 0, 10 or 20 years after the termination of the employment contract?

Regarding the DC plan, approximately 3%, 51% and 81% of the scenarios do not require any additional payments to meet the legal minimum. In about 32%, 74% and 92% of the scenarios, the highest additional payment never exceeds 10 over the entire 40-year period.

In the case of the CDC plan, approximately 28%, 95% and 99% of the scenarios do not necessitate additional deposits to meet the legal minimum. Furthermore, in about 72%, 96% and over 99% of the scenarios, the highest additional payment never exceeds 10 over the entire 40-year period. These results demonstrate a significantly reduced likelihood of requiring additional payments compared to the DC plan.

Based on the assumptions outlined above, these stochastic simulations demonstrate that the probability of needing additional payments to supplement deficits can be significantly reduced in CDC plans.

It is not surprising that we observe some instances of (very) negative results in the 1,000 series, as the returns in these models are generated randomly each year using independent normal distributions. These highly negative results typically occur in scenarios where long series of consecutive years of poor returns are experienced. However, it is crucial to provide some nuance to these findings. In practice, very negative years, such as during an economic crisis, are often followed by a highly favourable economic recovery. These compensating effects are not reflected in the results presented in figures 52 and 53.

Figure 53: The worst year scenario showing the highest additional payment that needs to be made in a single year for a DC or CDC plan.

HIGHEST ADDITIONAL PAYMENT IN ONE SINGLE YEAR OVER THE 40-YEAR PERIOD	FREQUENCY DC PLAN			FREQUENCY CDC PLAN		
	0 years after leaving the organisation	10 years after leaving the organisation	20 years after leaving the organisation	0 years after leaving the organisation	10 years after leaving the organisation	20 years after leaving the organisation
0	2.6%	50.8%	81.4%	28.1%	94.7%	99%
0 – 10	29.3%	23.2%	10.6%	43.4%	0.9%	0.2%
10 – 20	35.4%	13.9%	4.3%	9.8%	0.9%	0.2%
20 – 30	23.8%	8.1%	1.9%	8.4%	1.6%	0.2%
30 – 40	7.3%	2.9%	1.3%	7%	0.9%	0.2%
> 40	1.6%	1.1%	0.5%	3.3%	1%	0.2%

Regarding the CDC plan, we assume that any returns exceeding the target yield of 4% are entirely allocated to the buffer and that the buffer is solely utilised to address deficits. It should be noted that the more returns are allocated to the buffer, the lower the attractiveness of the pension plan becomes for employees as it reduces their potential returns. However, it can be determined that if the buffer is more than adequately filled over time, additional returns will be allocated to all members, including both employees and deferred vested members. This approach allows for a balance which provides protection for the employer while also offering members the opportunity for attractive returns.

Several Belgian insurers have developed and introduced the CDC concept in recent years. Within the CDC product range, there are various methods for buffering and allocating yields to members. The level of the target yield can be chosen, and it is also possible to allocate returns that exceed the target yield to be divided between the buffer and the members. The specific possibilities should be considered within the product range limitations of each respective insurer.

4.2. CB plan (with 0% CB return)

For this simulation, we again randomly generated 1,000 series of returns, based on the assumptions mentioned above.

We assume that the CB return is contractually set at 0%. To make the plan attractive to employees, 50% of the exceeding return is granted as an additional employer premium to employees in the years when the investment return of over 1.75% is achieved. For example, if the return in a certain year is 5%, then 1.625% (i.e., (5%-1.75%) x 0.5) is granted to employees as an additional employer's premium. No additional premiums are granted to deferred vested members. The remaining part of the excess return is deposited in the buffer, which is only used to cover any deficits relative to the legal minimum and any CB deficits, based on the assumptions above. The buffer is not used for normal premium payments (premium holidays). Any surplus in the buffer is retained.

When employees leave the organisation, we assume they choose to transfer their pension reserves immediately to their new employer's pension plan. This means that after termination of their employment contract, they no longer benefit from any investment return. The CB return is set at 0% and the legal minimum is frozen.

In figure 54, we analyse the highest additional premium that needs to be paid in a single year over a 40-year period to achieve both the fully funded CB return every year for all members and the legal minimum for employees who leave the organisation. This represents the 'worst year' scenario.

Figure 54: The worst year scenario showing the highest additional payment that needs to be made in a single year for a CB plan with 0% CB return.

HIGHEST ADDITIONAL PAYMENT IN ONE SINGLE YEAR OVER THE 40-YEAR PERIOD	NUMBER OF OBSERVATIONS (1,000 IN TOTAL)
0	62
1-50	287
51-100	292
101-150	239
151-200	98
201-250	17
250-300	5

How should we interpret figure 54?
In approximately 6% of scenarios, no additional payments are required to meet the legal minimum and CB minimum. In about 35% of scenarios, the highest additional payment never exceeds 50 over the entire 40-year period. In about 64% of scenarios, the highest additional payment never exceeds 100 over the entire 40-year period. In 88% of scenarios, the highest payment never exceeds 150 over the entire 40-year period. In 98% of scenarios, the highest payment never exceeds 200 over the entire 40-year period. In 99.5% of scenarios, the highest payment never exceeds 250 over the entire 40-year period. These additional premiums can be compared to normal pension premiums of 100 per year.

The likelihood of having to make additional premium payments to cover deficits in certain years is relatively high. This is partly due to the sum of the paid pension premiums, capitalised at 0% (the assumed CB-return), must be fully funded in all years for all plan members. From the employer's perspective, this represents a significant disadvantage of CB plans in comparison to DC or CDC plans. Furthermore, when the investment return exceeds the CB-return, 50% of the surplus is allocated to the employees, while the remaining 50% is used as a buffer for the employer.

On the other hand, years with lower returns solely burden the employer, who must cover any deficits using the buffer (if sufficient) or through making additional payments. Lastly, this example assumes that 50% of the surplus is allocated to active plan members in the form of additional pension contributions (rather than as additional returns), which, as mentioned above, increases the likelihood of deficits relative to the legal minimum.

In figure 54, we only consider the risk that the employer must make additional contributions in certain years. If we also consider the years with favourable returns in which the buffer is filled, the overall picture becomes more attractive. When we consider the sum of all surpluses and deficits over the 40-year period, we find an overall deficit in 16% of the scenarios. In other words, based on the aforementioned assumptions, the risk of an overall deficit is not negligible.

4.3. CB plan (linked to public index)

According to Belgian pension law, the CB return can be tied to the performance of a public index or different public indexes. Public indexes, also known as market indexes or stock market indexes, represent the performance of specific groups of stocks or other assets in financial markets. Examples of well-known public indexes include the S&P 500, Dow Jones Industrial Average and FTSE 100. These indexes encompass a wide range of stocks, bonds and other assets listed on major exchanges. Index funds follow and reflect a particular market index, but do not try to beat it. CB plans linked to public indexes have recently been developed by a few insurers in Belgium, and the initial rollout of these plans is currently underway.

The employer's risk of needing to make mandatory additional deposits can be significantly reduced by linking the CB return to an index, regardless of whether the index's performance is negative or positive.

Assuming that the CB plan is invested in an underlying index fund that replicates the index's performance to which the CB return is linked, there should be no risk of a CB deficit occurring. However, it is important to consider potential tracking errors, which are deviations between the index and the index fund. Factors such as transaction costs, management fees and imperfect replication can result in the fund's returns not perfectly matching the index's returns. This is why it is crucial to assess the fund's historical tracking error, expense ratio and other factors that may impact its ability to closely track the index when selecting an index fund.

The employer's ability to effectively reduce the risk of having to pay additional premiums to cover CB deficits is a significant advantage compared to the CB plan with a 0% CB return discussed in the previous section. However, any deficits relative to the legal minimum return must still be addressed when the pension is paid out at retirement or when the employees transfer their pension reserves to their new employer's pension plan.

To minimise the potential need for mandatory additional contributions due to deficits relative to the legal minimum return, a portion of the investment returns can be used to establish a collective buffer. An option is to allocate the entire difference between the achieved investment return and the legal minimum return to the buffer in years where the achieved return exceeds the percentage of the legal minimum return (currently 1.75%).

Any funding deficits upon retirement or the transfer of reserves to the new employer's pension plan are covered from the collective buffer. If the buffer is insufficient, the employer must make additional deposits. Such additional deposits are reimbursed to the employer as soon as funds become available in the buffer again.

Once the buffer reaches a sufficient level to cover potential deficits, the attractiveness of the plan can be enhanced by granting an additional return to both active members and deferred vested members or by granting additional pension premiums only to active members. In this simulation, we chose to allocate an additional return to both active members and deferred vested members in order to minimise the likelihood of funding deficits. This approach represents a significant difference from the CB plan with a 0% CB return (described above), where we assumed that surpluses would be used to allocate additional premiums only to active members. As previously mentioned, allocating additional returns to all plan members is more advantageous in avoiding any deficits relative to the legal minimum.

Once again, we randomly generated 1,000 series of returns, based on the assumptions mentioned above. We assume that the index-linked CB return is equal to the yields generated in the underlying index fund. Any difference between the achieved investment return and the legal minimum return is allocated to a collective buffer in years where the achieved return exceeds the legal minimum return (i.e., 1.75%). Once the buffer exceeds 5% of the total sum of pension assets, 50% of the excess is allocated to both active members and deferred members as an additional return. The remaining excess returns are used by the employer for premium holidays.

We assume that members choose to immediately transfer their pension reserves to their new employer's pension plan when they leave the organisation.

In figure 55, we show the highest additional premium that needs to be paid in a single year over a 40-year period to achieve both the CB return (which must be fully funded every year for all members) and the legal minimum return (only for employees who leave the organisation). This represents the 'worst year' scenario.

Figure 55: The worst year scenario showing the highest additional payment that needs to be made in a single year for a CB plan linked to a public index.

MAXIMUM ADDITIONAL PAYMENT IN ONE SINGLE YEAR OVER THE 40-YEAR PERIOD	NUMBER OF OBSERVATIONS (1,000 IN TOTAL)
0	136
1-10	187
10-20	79
20-30	137
30-40	264
40-50	163
50-60	34

We observe that the highest additional premium in the worst year (out of the 40 years) of the worst scenario (out of the 1,000 scenarios) is lower than 60 (compared to a normal annual premium of 100). This is significantly lower than the highest additional payment of 300 from the CB plan with 0% CB return described above (see figure 54).

In figure 56, we show the sum of all additional premiums that need to be paid over the entire 40-year period to meet the legal minimum. We also show the sum of all premium holidays that the employer benefits from during this period. These sums can be compared to the total sum of all normal DC/CDC premiums, which amounts to 4,000 (i.e., a series of 40 years with a normal premium of 100 per year).

Figure 56: The sum of all additional premiums and premium holidays that need to be paid over the entire 40-year period for a CB plan linked to a public index.

	SUM OF ALL ADDITIONAL PAYMENTS OVER THE 40-YEAR PERIOD	SUM OF PREMIUM HOLIDAYS OVER THE 40-YEAR PERIOD
MINIMUM	0	19.9
MEDIAN	69.83	380.83
99.5TH PERCENTILE	612.70	1,195.61

We observe that the sum of the expected premium holidays is considerably higher than the sum of the expected additional payments over the 40-year period. This CB approach appears to be attractive for employers aiming for stable cash flows, with relatively minimal additional contributions in challenging years, and substantial savings, through substantial premium holidays in prosperous years. Moreover, this CB concept enables employers to provide the potential of appealing returns to plan members.

We repeated this exercise with a second randomly generated series of 1,000 returns, but with one difference. This time we assume that 80% of the excess returns, instead of the previous 50%, are allocated to plan members in the form of an additional return.

Figure 57: The worst year scenario showing the highest additional payment to be made in a single year for a CB plan linked to a public index.

MAXIMUM ADDITIONAL PAYMENT IN ONE SINGLE YEAR OVER THE 40-YEAR PERIOD	NUMBER OF OBSERVATIONS (1,000 IN TOTAL)
0	228
1-10	322
10-20	70
20-30	83
30-40	157
40-50	120
50-60	20

Figure 58: The sum of all additional premiums and premium holidays that need to be paid over the entire 40-year period for a CB plan linked to a public index.

	SUM OF ADDITIONAL PAYMENTS OVER THE 40-YEAR PERIOD	SUM OF PREMIUM HOLIDAYS OVER THE 40-YEAR PERIOD
MINIMUM	0	13.33
MEDIAN	8.36	202.63
99.5TH PERCENTILE	551.76	626.15

By allocating 80% instead of 50% of the excess returns to all plan members, the likelihood of the employer having to make additional payments decreases. Additionally, we observe a decrease in both the total sum of additional payments over the 40-year period and the sum of expected premium holidays. This is not surprising, considering the redistribution of a larger portion of the achieved returns among all plan members and the smaller portion allocated to the employer.

As previously mentioned, these results assume that members choose to immediately transfer their pension reserves to their new employer's pension plan upon leaving the organisation. However, in practice, it is expected that many deferred vested members will opt to keep their pension reserves in the plan. This is because they can continue to benefit from promising returns linked to the index, while also having the security of a capital guarantee (i.e., the frozen legal minimum guarantee) as a bottom protection.

If we assume that the reserves remain invested for 10 or 20 years after the termination of the employment contract, the results significantly improve. This is because the legal minimum return remains constant at 0% after resignation, while the reserves continue to be invested for a longer period. Additionally, any years with negative returns have a high probability of being offset by years with positive returns (see the analysis on DC versus CDC plans above).

5. Choosing the right pension plan

With a CDC plan or CB plan, there is a single collective investment mix for all members, aiming to smooth out fluctuations through the use of a collective buffer. To minimise the risk of additional payments by the employer, the employer may consider selecting an investment mix with a target net return close to the legal minimum return (1.75% since 2016 and probably 2.5% in 2025) and with minimal volatility. From the perspective of the plan members, however, a branch 23 pension plan with a relatively modest target net return is not more attractive than a branch 21 pension plan.

In a CB plan, the employer can benefit from favourable returns by utilising the buffer for normal premium payments. The drawback is that CB deficits must be addressed every year, unlike deficits relative to the legal minimum, which only need to be addressed when the employee leaves the organisation or retires. This drawback can be avoided by linking the CB return to the evolution of an index or a combination of indexes. It is also possible to replicate this index blend in the underlying investments. To minimise tracking errors, it is advisable to invest in low-cost index funds with a history of low tracking errors that closely replicate the index performance.

In the context of lifecycle solutions, the philosophy is entirely different. Instead of a single collective investment mix for all members, the investment mix is personalised based on the age and investment horizon of each member. This allows for a higher risk profile for younger members, gradually reducing to a lower risk profile in the years leading up to retirement. This approach aims to avoid significant setbacks towards the end of their career. Each member has an individual account that remains separate from others, ensuring that the returns of one member cannot be used to compensate for deficits of another member.

The disadvantage of individual life cycle solutions is that the expected return decreases as the employee gets older and therefore invests more defensively. Given the possibilities in CDC and CB plans, we believe that collective investing for larger groups of plan members can be efficient because the investment mix can be aligned with the weighted average investment duration for the entire group of plan members, allowing more dynamic investing for plan members approaching retirement age. Volatility of investment returns in branch 23 can be smoothed out across the entire group and over a longer period through the active use of a collective buffer.

In branch 23 life insurance products, it is important to consider not only the loadings on premiums but also the loadings of the underlying investment funds. Higher charges result in lower net returns. Negotiating the costs of investment funds is usually feasible for large premium volumes, but it can be more challenging for small groups with limited premium volumes. Passive funds, such as index funds that track indexes, generally have lower costs, but not all insurers offer passive funds in branch 23. It is essential to explore and negotiate the options within the product range of the insurer.

Understanding the demographics of the workforce is crucial when determining the most suitable pension plan. Factors, such as the number of employees, age distribution, salary levels and expected turnover, can help to design an appropriate plan and select the right investment mix.

Additional important considerations include the risk appetite for investments, the employer's desire to provide additional premiums to active plan members or additional returns to all plan members and the employer's ambition to pursue premium holidays. Taking into account the legal minimum return that the employer is obligated to meet, the focus lies on the employer's risk tolerance. Some employers may prefer a conservative investment approach with lower risk, while others may be comfortable with higher-risk investments that offer the potential for higher returns. Much of this decision making is closely tied to the employer's financial capabilities to address potential funding deficits during challenging years. In this regard, it is worth noting that both CDC plans and certain types of CB plans offer the opportunity to significantly mitigate the risk of funding deficits during challenging years.

12.
Remuneration in the banking and insurance industry

Key takeaways

1. Stricter regulations have been implemented after the financial crisis to mitigate systemic risks, improve governance and restore public trust in the financial system.

2. The remuneration of 'Identified Staff' or 'Material Risk Takers' in the banking and insurance industry is subject to specific restrictions, particularly regarding the structure of their pay and variable components.

3. These rules encompass transparency, effective governance and robust risk management requirements to ensure sound remuneration based on performance.

4. Implementing these regulations presents practical challenges, especially in a group context.

The 2008 financial crisis exposed significant weaknesses in the banking industry, including excessive risk-taking, inadequate risk management practices and a lack of accountability among executives. Executive remuneration structures at many banks were criticised for incentivising short-term profit-seeking behaviour without sufficient regard for long-term financial stability.

Similarly, the insurance industry faced heightened regulatory scrutiny, although its role in the financial crisis was generally less direct compared to banks. However, regulators recognised that insurance companies also play a significant role in the financial system and could pose systemic risks if not properly regulated.

In response, stricter regulations were introduced to align incentives with long-term stability and prudent risk management. These measures aim to mitigate systemic risks, enhance governance, and restore public trust in the financial system.

1. General requirements

The remuneration requirements for the banking industry in the European Union are primarily sourced from the Capital Requirements Directive IV (CRD IV)[246] and its subsequent iteration, the Capital Requirements Directive V (CRD V)[247]. These directives, along with the Capital Requirements Regulation (CRR), constitute the regulatory framework known as CRD IV/CRR. These requirements on the remuneration policy are transposed in the Belgian Law of 25 April 2014 on the legal status and supervision of credit institutions (the Belgian Banking Law) on articles 67 – 71 and further described in Annex II.

The main regulatory framework governing the insurance industry in the EU is the Solvency II Directive[248] and Delegated Regulation 2015/35, also known as the Solvency II Delegated Regulation which provides more detailed rules on various aspects of the directive[249]. These requirements on the remuneration policy are transposed in the Belgian Law of 13 March 2016 on the legal status and supervision of insurance or re-insurance companies (the Belgian Solvency II Law)[250].

Both require remuneration policies and practices to promote and be consistent with sound and effective risk management. In other words, their remuneration policies should not encourage risk-taking that exceeds the risk tolerance limits of the undertaking. The CRD V also requires banking undertakings to have gender-neutral remuneration policies and practices. This requirement is part of broader efforts to address gender imbalances and promote diversity and inclusion within the financial industry.

The regulations cover all forms of payments or benefits, whether financial or non-financial, that are made directly or indirectly (but on behalf of the organisation) to staff of a bank or insurance organisation. It covers fixed remuneration, as well as variable and complementary payments. The regulations distinguish between fixed and variable remuneration payments where fixed remuneration is all payments and benefits received without any consideration of performance criteria, and variable remuneration covers all additional pay-outs and benefits that are dependent on performance or other contractual criteria.

The CRD IV (V) provides for general requirements that apply to all staff such as the prohibition of guaranteed variable remuneration except for the first year of employment, golden parachutes without performance risk adjustment, and personal hedging strategies or insurance[251].

Credit institutions and investment firms may apply the provisions of Belgian banking law in different ways according to their size, internal organisation and the nature, scope and complexity of their activities. Complex financial institutions typically implement sophisticated remuneration policies accompanied by advanced risk measurement methods. Conversely, smaller and less complex financial institutions may adopt simpler remuneration policies and methods.

2. Specific requirements

The banking and insurance industries have specific remuneration requirements for their 'identified staff' or 'material risk-takers', staff whose professional activities have a material impact on the undertaking's risk profile[252]. This assessment is based on analysing job functions, remuneration levels and responsibilities. The organisation should appropriately document the process used to select their identified staff.

Banking regulations specify that identified staff include executive members of the institution's corporate body, senior management responsible for daily management or in charge of a significant business line or regional area, staff responsible for independent control functions and other risk takers whose total remuneration takes them into the same income bracket as senior management. Additionally, the National Bank of Belgium considers that any employees with authorisation to conduct risky transactions within trade departments must be categorised as identified staff[253].

Remuneration requirements on the pay-out of instruments, deferral and pension requirements do not apply to non-large institutions or staff members whose annual variable remuneration does not exceed € 50,000 and does not represent more than one third of their total annual remuneration under the CRD V.

2.1. Mix of remuneration components

Identified staff should have carefully balanced remuneration to prevent them from becoming overly dependent on the variable components.

For the banking industry, the remuneration policy should enable the undertaking to operate a fully flexible bonus policy, including the possibility of paying no variable component in case of negative performance[254].

European regulations stipulate that variable remuneration cannot exceed 100% of the total fixed remuneration (or 200% with shareholder approval). Belgian banking law is even stricter, limiting the variable remuneration to 50% of the fixed remuneration or € 50,000, without exceeding the fixed remuneration. Additionally, at least 50% of the variable remuneration should be a balance of shares or equivalent ownership interests or share-linked instruments and other instruments that reflect the credit quality of the institution as a going concern. CRD V extends the possibility to share-linked instruments to both quoted and unquoted institutions[255].

For insurance undertakings, the guidelines issued by the European Insurance and Occupational Pensions Authority (EIOPA) use the principle of proportionality to determine the balance of fixed and variable remuneration for identified staff. EIOPA has stricter requirements for "identified staff receiving significant variable remuneration" i.e., identified staff whose annual variable remuneration exceeds € 50,000 and/or more than a third of their total annual remuneration is variable. Consequently, when the reference ratio of 1:1 (or 1:0.5 for employees responsible for the independent control functions) is exceeded, the organisation needs to justify why it does not comply with this ratio. Attention is also paid to very low fixed remuneration[256].

2.2. Pay for performance

When variable remuneration is performance-related, the total amount of variable remuneration is based on a combination of the assessment of the performance of the employee, business unit and overall organisation. This should take into account the risks and performance of the individual employee as well as the business unit.

The performance measurement should combine quantitative (financial) and qualitative (non-financial) criteria, where the quantitative measures occur over a period long enough to properly capture the risk of the staff member's actions and incorporate risk adjustment and economic efficiency measures, while the qualitative measures include the achievement of strategic targets, customer satisfaction levels and adherence to risk management policy.

2.3. Deferred remuneration

Regardless of the form in which it is paid, a substantial portion of the variable remuneration for identified staff is a flexible, deferred component that takes into account the nature and time horizon of the organisation's business. The deferral period is at least three years, and is aligned with the nature of the business, its risks and the activities of the staff in question.

For the banking industry, at least 40% of variable remuneration should be deferred for at least 4-5 years, and not less than 5 years for members of the management body and senior management of significant institutions. When the variable remuneration is a particularly high amount, as determined by the institution, at least 60% is deferred. In no case should this amount exceed € 200,000[257].

The institution should also implement a retention policy to obtain the necessary risk alignment for different instruments. Belgian banking law states that the owner of the instrument is obliged to keep it for a period of at least one year[258].

For the insurance industry, deferring 40% of the variable remuneration for a minimum of three years is required for "*identified staff receiving significant variable remuneration*". In cases where an individual's fixed-to-variable ratio exceeds 1:1, a higher deferral rate should be applied. Any deviation from this requirement should be justified by the insurance organisation[259].

2.4. KPIs

When assessing an employee's performance, a balance of financial and non-financial criteria should be taken into account, where the non-financial criteria contribute to the creation of value for the organisation, such as compliance with regulations, the efficiency of customer service management or achieving strategic environmental, social and governance (ESG) goals.

The financial and non-financial criteria should be transparent, with precise descriptions of the fixed and variable remuneration components, clear definitions and criteria for performance measurements and risk adjustments and comprehensive documentation of the decision-making process[260].

2.5. Downwards risk adjustment

When performance is measured as the basis for variable remuneration, there should be mechanisms that enable a downwards adjustment to cover potential exposure to current and future risks, taking the organisation's risk profile and cost of capital into account.

Mechanisms such as malus, clawback and in-year adjustments ensure that variable remuneration reflects the current risks as they crystallise in the future for unvested, awarded/vested (but not paid) and paid variable pay (without disregarding relevant contract and labour law).

Banking regulations and EIOPA Guidelines give details of how downwards risk adjustment should work in practice[261].

Figure 59: Malus and clawback mechanisms.

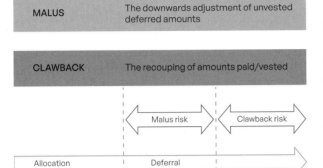

2.6. Termination payments

As in other industries, termination payments in the banking and insurance industries should be related to the achieved performance over the whole period of activity and designed in a way that does not reward failure. Banking regulations and EIOPA guidelines clarify what does and does not qualify as a termination payment. They require documenting the reasons for such payments, the appropriateness of the amount awarded and the criteria used to determine the amount, including a link to achieved performance and the avoidance of rewarding failure[262].

2.7. Control functions

To avoid potential conflicts of interest, the variable remuneration received by employees engaged in control functions in the insurance industry should be independent from the performance of the operational units and areas they oversee.

2.8. Anti avoidance rules

Identified staff should abstain from trading or carrying out operations that undermine any of the dispositions included in Annex II of the Belgian banking law in any way. In particular, this is with respect to operations that may neutralise the risks resulting from the modalities of their variable remunerations. In turn, organisations refrain from attributing or paying variable remuneration through any vehicle or method that facilitates the non-compliance with the banking law or EU regulations[263].

2.9. Practical challenges

The banking and insurance industry are facing a number of practical challenges in the implementation of the regulations for identified staff.

2.9.1. Remuneration policy
For their remuneration policy, organisations need to ensure that employees have appropriate knowledge of both remuneration and risk, as well as implementing gender neutral remuneration policies and practices, which has a potential impact on HR processes.

2.9.2. Identified staff
It is not straightforward for an organisation to identify and quantify the risks facing its business, determine to which extent a material business unit exists within their structure or identify the employees who have the capacity to materially contribute to these risks exceeding the (prescribed) thresholds.

2.9.3. Ex-post risk adjustment
The organisation needs to develop a framework that calculates both the amount subject to adjustment and the amount of the adjustment in a consistent and equitable manner that is linked to the impact of the crystallised risk. The framework needs to enable robust and consistent application of malus or clawback mechanisms, including handling the legal and practical implications.

2.9.4. Group context

Banking and insurance organisations operating across national borders face significant challenges to comply with different regulatory frameworks. The Belgian National Bank stipulates that Belgian regulations extend to foreign subsidiaries if those subsidiaries employ personnel whose professional roles significantly influence the group's risk profile. Conversely, adherence to Belgian regulations should not be circumvented by compensating staff of a Belgian subsidiary through a foreign entity within the group without any actual services being rendered to that entity in return[264].

Further, harmonising remuneration policies and practices across these diverse entities can be challenging due to differences in local laws, cultures, and business practices. For instance, regulations concerning the balance between fixed and variable vary from one country to another. And some countries, such as Belgium, are stricter than the EU regulations.

Afterword

As the previous pages have shown, reward remains a fascinating and multifaceted subject that has the power to motivate employees and help organisations to attract and retain the talent they need to achieve their ambitions. Additionally, as reward tends to represent a significant investment in people, it is unsurprising that organisations want and need to see a good return on this cost.

But, as we saw in our take on a well-known fable from the beginning of chapter 1, it is not always straightforward to match the work that needs to be done to the expected reward. Just like the hare at the start of his race, organisations used to only believe that external motivation was the only reward needed. And so, reward became a financial transaction when dealing with employees: labour in exchange for a base salary.

Over time, organisations started to realise the importance of internal motivation as they began to understand the tortoise's perspective of reward. Consequently, reward evolved from being a financial reward to total reward, which incorporates short- and long-term financial and non-financial components, including recognition. We have seen some organisations using a holistic approach to take reward even further by offering total wellbeing to their employees.

In addition to increasing employee motivation and improving employee retention, reward can also be used to mitigate some of the negative impacts caused by the megatrends that our society is now facing. To repeat a few examples that we saw in chapter 3, organisations can create personalised learning paths to upskill and reskill employees to reduce potential skill gaps, customise reward options to recognise and incentivise employees while fostering a sense of purpose and commitment and prioritise employee wellbeing with healthcare benefits and flexible work arrangements. At the end of the day, we need to remember that a career is a marathon, not a sprint, and organisations need to use reward to support employees as they deal with the pressures and challenges that lie ahead of them as they adapt to meet the organisation's changing needs.

However, reward isn't a one-size-fits-all solution and organisations can't simply copy an existing reward system. Instead, each reward system needs to be adapted to the specific organisation, including its industry, maturity level, structure and location. And this was our focus in part 2, which covered the scope of the reward system, job architecture and benchmarking, the mix of the reward components, understanding the drive behind the change and the impact of the organisation's structure on the reward system. By following this comprehensive roadmap, organisations can develop and implement a reward system that fits their unique situation while incentivising and motivating their employees.

We ended our investigation into reward by taking a deep dive with our special dossiers into specific aspects of reward that deserve additional focus in order to promote inclusivity and diversity in the workplace and financial security for all employees.

Together with the contributors to this book, we believe it is important for organisations to create truly great places to work, promote feelings of belonging and not tolerate discrimination of any kind. We hope that this text demonstrates our beliefs and encourages you to develop and implement reward systems that achieve this in your organisation.

Axel and Bart

Acknowledgments

Traditionally, when there is a shortage of talent in the market, organisations are expected to offer more competitive remuneration and benefits packages. However, providing higher salaries and larger benefit packages, sometimes at the cost of eroding profitability, is not sustainable in the long run. This book provides practical guidance for attracting and retaining talents with compelling reward. Describing the tools and strategies for these purposes required time for reflection on the foundations of reward models. It required time to craft our vision on the past and future of reward.

Without the unwavering support of our families, neither of us would be able to fulfil our professional responsibilities, let alone find and dedicate the time required to compile this book. We are immensely grateful to them for their understanding and patience during the moments when we were unavailable, driven by our shared eagerness to bundle our reward experience and expertise together in this book.

We would like to express our deep appreciation to our contributors, whose invaluable contributions were instrumental in the successful completion of this project. Their extensive knowledge and expertise in various fields enabled us to create a comprehensive guide on reward. We extend our sincere thanks to each and every one of them, whose names can be found at the beginning of this book. We feel incredibly fortunate and proud to be surrounded by such a talented group of people.

We extend our sincere gratitude to Line De Decker, whose insightful and inspiring foreword has put the reward topic in a broader and day-to-day HR context. Thank you, Line, for generously sharing your expertise and lending your esteemed credibility to this book.

We would also like to extend a special acknowledgment to Christine Mes. While we had a clear vision for the direction of this story and our contributors provided valuable content, Christine played an indispensable role in transforming our initial ideas into the polished book that we are proud to present to you today. In a project involving multiple writers, having an experienced wordsmith like Christine was crucial in ensuring the manuscript was cohesive and engaging for readers. We are immensely grateful for her contribution in making this publication consistent and highly readable. Thank you, Christine, for your invaluable work. It has been a pleasure working with you.

Creating a book requires effort to track down the authors, collaborate with the publisher, carefully evaluate the aesthetics, and ultimately guarantee the creation of a print ready manuscript and finally the launch of a tangible book. For these efforts, we thank Elodie Scarniet, Leni Smits, Saskia Rademakers and Sofie Vanderhasselt.

Our last thanks are for Sandra De Weerd. Originally, she planned to only be a contributor to certain chapters of this book before she became part of the coordinating team, demonstrating how rewarding intrinsic motivation can be.

Compiling this book on reward has been a real pleasure for us. We hope that you, as a reader, have enjoyed the discovery of the reward drivers and reward pillars, and that they will serve as a pole star when you consider (re-)designing your organisation's reward framework. Going forward, we should remember the words of the Brazilian author Paulo Coelho: "*The reward of our work is not what we get, but what we have become.*"

Glossary

AI	Artificial intelligence
CB	Cash balance
CB return	Cash balance return
CBA	Collective bargaining agreement
CBA90	Collective bargaining agreement 90
CDC	Collective defined contribution
CPI	Consumer price index
CRD IV	Capital Requirements Directive IV
CRD V	Capital Requirements Directive V
CRR	Capital Requirements Regulation
CSRD	Corporate Sustainability Reporting Directive
DC	Defined contribution
EAP	Employee assistance programme
ECB	European Central Bank
ecoDa	European Confederation of Directors' Association
EIOPA	European Insurance and Occupational Pensions Authority
EOM	Employee of the month
ESG	Environmental, social and governance
ESPP	Employee stock purchase plan
EV	Electric vehicle
EVP	Employee value proposition
EX	Employee experience
FMV	Fair market value
GRI	Global Reporting Initiative

HICP	Harmonised index of consumer prices
HRM	Human resources management
IASB	International Accounting Standards Board
IFRS2	International Financial Reporting Standard 2
IPO	Initial public offering
IRR	Internal rate of return
KPI	Key performance indicator
LTI	Long-term incentives
LTIP	Long-term incentive plan
M&A	Mergers and acquisitions
MIP	Management incentive plan
MoM	Multiple of money
OLO	Linear obligation
PE	Private equity
PEIS	Partner evaluation and income systems
PTD	Pay Transparency Directive
PVP	People value proposition
RSU	Restricted stock unit
SAR	Stock appreciation right
SRD II	Shareholders Rights Directive
STI	Short-term incentive
STIP	Short-term incentive plan
WFA	Working from anywhere
WFH	Working from home

Endnotes

1. M. Armstrong, *Armstrong's handbook of reward management practice: Improving performance through reward*, 2010, Kogan Page Publishers.
2. D. Podmoroff, *365 ways to motivate and reward your employees every day--with little or no Money*, 2005, Atlantic Publishing Company.
3. M. Armstrong, *Armstrong's handbook of reward management practice: Improving performance through reward*, 2010, Kogan Page Publishers.
4. J. Cameron, and W.D. Pierce, *Rewards and intrinsic motivation: Resolving the controversy*. 2002, Bloomsbury Publishing USA.
5. Idem
6. C.P. Cerasoli, J.M. Nicklin and M.T. Ford, *Intrinsic motivation and extrinsic incentives jointly predict performance: a 40-year meta-analysis*, 2014, Psychological bulletin, 140(4), 980.
    G.D. Jenkins Jr, A. Mitra, N. Grupta and J.D. Shaw, *Are financial incentives related to performance? A meta-analytic review of empirical research*, 1988, Journal of applied psychology, 83(5), 777.
7. PwC Netherlands, *What does young talent want? - Workforce Preference Study 2023*, 2023, PwC website, https://www.pwc.nl/nl/actueel-publicaties/assets/pdfs/workforce-preference-study-2023.pdf, date accessed February 12, 2024.
8. Idem
9. G. Valkeneers, S. Mestdagh and T. Benijts, *Gedrag in organisaties: de basis (Behaviour in organisations: the basics)*, 2011, Acco, Leuven.
10. F.W. Taylor, *The principles of scientific management*, 1911, NuVision Publications, LLC.
11. J.R. French, *Experiments in field settings*, 1953, in L. Festinger and D. Katz (eds.), Research methods in the behavioural sciences, Dryden Press.
12. The researchers increased the lighting for one group of employees and decreased or left it unchanged for another group. Surprisingly, both groups improved their productivity. This outcome led to the realisation that it wasn't the changes in physical conditions (like lighting) that were affecting productivity, but rather the attention given to the employees by the researchers. This phenomenon became known as the Hawthorne Effect.
13. A. H. Maslow, *A theory of human motivation*, 1943, Psychological Review, 50 (4), 370–396.
14. C. Alderfer, *An empirical test of a new theory of human needs*, 1969, Organisational Behaviour and Human Performance, 4, 142-175.
15. F. Herzberg, B. Mausner and B.B. Snyderman, *The motivation to work*, 1959, John Wiley & Sons.
16. G. Valkeneers, S. Mestdagh and T. Benijts, *Gedrag in organisaties, een psychologische benadering, (Behaviour in organisations, a psychological approach)*, 2021, LannooCampus, 96-98.
17. D. McGregor, *The Human Side of Enterprise*, 1960, McGraw-Hill.
18. E.L. Deci and R.M. Ryan, *Intrinsic motivation and self-determination in human behavior*, 2013, Springer Science & Business Media.
19. R.M. Ryan, V. Mims and R. Koestner, *Relation of reward contingency and interpersonal context to intrinsic motivation: A review and test using cognitive evaluation theory*, 1983, Journal of personality and Social Psychology, 45(4), 737-738.
20. E.A. Locke and G.P. Latham, *New directions in goal-setting theory*, 2006, Current directions in Psychological Science, 15(5), 265-268.
21. Idem
22. S.P. Robbins and T.A. Judge, *Gedrag in organisaties (tiende editie), (Behaviour in organisations (tenth edition))*, 2011, Pearson Benelux B.V.
23. J.S. Adams, *Towards an understanding of inequity*, 1963, The Journal of Abnormal and Social Psychology, 67(5), 422.
24. S.P. Robbins and T.A. Judge, *Gedrag in organisaties (tiende editie), (Behaviour in organisations (tenth edition))*, 2011, Pearson Benelux B.V.
25. J.S. Adams, *Equity theory*, 2015, in J. B. Miner, Organizational Behaviour 1, Routledge, 134-158.
26. V. Vroom, L. Porter and E. Lawler, *Expectancy theories*, 2015, in J. B. Miner, Organizational Behaviour 1, Routledge, 94-113.
27. R. De Cooman and A. Forrier, *Expectancy theory*, 2019, in W. de Lange, P. De Prins and B. Van der Heijden (eds), Canon van HRM. 50 Theorieën over een vakgebied in ontwikkeling, (Canon of HRM, 50 theories about a developing field), Vakmedianet.
28. E.L. Deci, *Effects of Externally Mediated Rewards on Intrinsic Motivation*, 1971, Journal of Personality and Social Psychology 18, 114.
29. E.L. Deci and R.M. Ryan, *Intrinsic motivation and self-determination in human behavior*, 1985, New York, NY: Plenum.
    E.L. Deci and R.M. Ryan, *The "what" and "why" of goal pursuits: Human needs and the self-determination of behavior*, 2000, Psychological Inquiry, 11, 227-268.
    R.M. Ryan and E.L. Deci, *Self-determination theory and the facilitation of intrinsic motivation, social development, and well-being*, 2000, American Psychologist, 55, 68-78.
30. A. Vanden Broeck, M. Vansteenkiste, H. De Witte, W. Lens and M. Andriessen, *De zelfdeterminatietheorie: kwalitatief goed motiveren op de werkvloer (The self-determination theory: high-quality motivation in the workplace)*, 2009, in Gedrag en Organisatie (Behaviour and Organisation), 22 (4), 316-335.
31. F. Manders and P. Biesman, *HRM voor managers (HRM for managers)*, 2013, Boom Lemma Uitgevers.
32. Ü. Alniaçik and E. Alniaçik, *Identifying dimensions of attractiveness in employer branding: Effects of age, gender, and current employment status*, 2012, Procedia - Social and Behavioral Sciences, 58, 1336-1343.
33. Korn Ferry, *Future of work - The global talent crunch*, 2018, Korn Ferry website, https://www.kornferry.com/content/dam/kornferry/docs/article-migration/FOWTalentCrunchFinal_Spring2018.pdf, date accessed January 22, 2024.
34. EUROSTAT, *EU's employment rate peaks at 75% in 2022*, 2023, EuroStat, https://ec.europa.eu/eurostat/web/products-eurostat-news/w/ddn-20230427-2, date accessed January 31, 2024.
35. Idem
36. L. S. Essien, M. D. Levinstein and G. Owens, *Unemployment rate returned to its prepandemic level in 2022*, 2023, Monthly Labor Review, U.S. Bureau of Labor Statistics, https://doi.org/10.21916/mlr.2023.15, date accessed February 12, 2024.
37. PwC, *PwC's 26th Annual Global CEO survey*, 2023, https://www.pwc.com/gx/en/issues/c-suite-insights/ceo-survey.html, date accessed January 12, 2024.
38. I. Fulmer and J. Li, *Compensation, Benefits and Total Rewards: A Bird's-Eye (Re)View*, 2022, Annual Review of Organisational Psychology and Organisational Behavior.
39. F. Lievens, *Human Resource Management - Back to basics*, 2016, Lannoo Campus.
40. A. Landry, A. Schweyer and A. Whillans, *Winning the War for Talent: Modern Motivational Methods for Attracting and Retaining Employees*, 2018, https://www.hbs.edu/ris/Publication%20Files/Accepted_CBR_dbad8715-3e85-4151-88ed-add7e2305a9b.pdf, date accessed February 12, 2024.
41. S. Werner and D. Balkin, *Strategic benefits: how employee benefits can create a sustainable competitive edge*, 2021, Journal of Total Rewards - Q1 2021. Also available at https://www.researchgate.net/profile/Steve-Werner-3/publication/351117557_Strategic_Benefits_How_Employee_Benefits_Can_Create_a_Sustainable_Competitive_Edge/links/608861e1907dcf667bcac26f/Strategic-Benefits-How-Employee-Benefits-Can-Create-a-Sustainable-Competitive-Edge.pdf, date accessed February 12, 2024.

42 Ü. Alniaçik and E. Alniaçik, *Identifying dimensions of attractiveness in employer branding: Effects of age, gender, and current employment status*, 2012, Procedia - Social and Behavioral Sciences, 58, 1336-1343. Also available at https://www.sciencedirect.com/science/article/pii/S187704281204579X, date accessed April 18, 2024.

43 D.M. Cable and D.B. Turban, *Establishing the dimensions, sources and value of job seekers' employer knowledge during recruitment*, 2001, Research in Personnel and Human Resources Management, Vol. 20, Emerald Group Publishing Limited, Leeds, 115-163.

44 *Principles of management*, 2015, University of Minnesota libraries publishing, https://2012books.lardbucket.org/books/management-principles-v1.1/, date accessed February 12, 2024.

45 Ü. Alniaçik and E. Alniaçik, *Identifying dimensions of attractiveness in employer branding: Effects of age, gender, and current employment status*, 2012, Procedia - Social and Behavioral Sciences, 58, 1336-1343. Also available at https://www.sciencedirect.com/science/article/pii/S187704281204579X, date accessed April 18, 2024.

46 B. Monteiro, V. Santos, I. Reis et al., *Employer Branding Applied to SMEs: A Pioneering Model Proposal for Attracting and Retaining Talent*, 2020, Information, volume 11, issue 12, 574.

47 Idem

48 PwC, *Workforce Preference Study (WFPS) 2020*, EMEA Focus, 2020, https://www.pwc.be/en/news-publications/2021/workforce-preference-study-2020-emea-focus.html, date accessed January 26, 2024.

49 M. Armstrong and D. Brown, *Armstrong's Handbook of Reward Management Practice: Improving performance through reward,* 2019, New York, Kogan Page.

50 F. Lievens, *Human Resource Management: Back to Basics,* 2011, Uitgeverij Lannoo Campus.

51 F. Manders and P. Biesman, *HRM voor managers (HRM for Managers)*, 2013, Boom Lemma Uitgevers.

52 P. Hemmings, *Compensation Systems*, *Job Performance and how to ask for a pay raise*, 2016, Xlibris US.

53 M. Armstrong and D. Brown, *Armstrong's Handbook of Reward Management Practice: Improving performance through reward,* 2019, New York, Kogan Page.

54 E. Kang and H. Lee, *Employee compensation strategy as sustainable competitive advantage for HR education practitioners*, 2021, https://www.mdpi.com/2071-1050/13/3/1049, date accessed January 3, 2024.

55 F. Manders and P. Biesman, *HRM voor managers (HRM for Managers)*, 2013, Boom Lemma Uitgevers.
P. Hemmings, *Compensation Systems*, *Job Performance and how to ask for a pay raise*, 2016, Xlibris US.
E. Kang and H. Lee, *Employee compensation strategy as sustainable competitive advantage for HR education practitioners*, 2021, https://www.mdpi.com/2071-1050/13/3/1049, date accessed January 3, 2024.

56 E. Dierdorff and E. Surface, *If you pay for skills, will they learn? Skill change and maintenance under a skill-based pay system*, 2008, https://journals.sagepub.com/doi/epdf/10.1177/0149206307312507, date accessed January 3, 2024.

57 C. Lee, K.S. Law and P. Bobko, *The importance of justice perceptions on pay effectiveness: A two-year study of a skill-based plan*, 1999, https://journals.sagepub.com/doi/epdf/10.1177/014920639902500604, date accessed January 3, 2024.

58 F. Lievens, *Human Resource Management: Back to Basics,* 2011, Uitgeverij Lannoo Campus.

59 CIPD, *Show the money: The behavioural science of reward,* 2015, https://www.cipd.org/uk/knowledge/evidence-reviews/reward-decisions/?_gl=1*gczrmx*_ga*MTA3NTM0NDkwOS4xNzAxNzkxNjly*_ga_D9HN5GYHYY*MTcwNDM4NDM5My42LjEuMTcwNDM4NDQ1OC42MC4wLjA, date accessed January 3, 2024.

60 Idem

61 M. Armstrong and D. Brown, *Armstrong's Handbook of Reward Management Practice: Improving performance through reward,* 2019, New York, Kogan Page.

62 F. Manders and P. Biesman, *HRM voor managers (HRM for Managers)*, 2013, Boom Lemma Uitgevers.

63 J. Delfgaauw et al, *Team Incentives, Social Cohesion and Performance: A Natural Field experiment*, 2020, https://www.econstor.eu/bitstream/10419/223940/1/dp13498.pdf, date accessed January 3, 2024.

64 B. Waber, J. Magnolfi and G. Lindsay, *Workplaces that move people*, 2014, https://hbr.org/2014/10/workplaces-that-move-people, date accessed January 3, 2024.

65 J. Delfgaauw et al, *Team Incentives, Social Cohesion and Performance: A Natural Field experiment*, 2020, https://www.econstor.eu/bitstream/10419/223940/1/dp13498.pdf, date accessed January 3, 2024.

66 M. Bolch, *Rewarding the team*, 2007, SHRM.org, https://www.shrm.org/topics-tools/news/hr-magazine/rewarding-team, date accessed January 3, 2024.

67 CIPD, *Show the money: The behavioural science of reward*, 2015, https://www.cipd.org/uk/knowledge/evidence-reviews/reward-decisions/?_gl=1*gczrmx*_ga*MTA3NTM0NDkwOS4xNzAxNzkxNjly*_ga_D9HN5GYHYY*MTcwNDM4NDM5My42LjEuMTcwNDM4NDQ1OC42MC4wLjA, date accessed January 3, 2024.

68 E. Lawler, *Creating effective pay systems for teams*, 1998, https://ceo.usc.edu/wp-content/uploads/1998/01/1998-01-g98_1-Pay_Teams.pdf, date accessed January 3, 2024.

69 C. Garvey, *Focus on compensation - Steer teams with the right pay*, 2002, SHRM.org, https://www.shrm.org/topics-tools/news/hr-magazine/focus-compensation-steer-teams-right-pay, date accessed January 3, 2024.
J. Delfgaauw et al, *Team Incentives, Social Cohesion and Performance: A Natural Field experiment*, 2020, https://www.econstor.eu/bitstream/10419/223940/1/dp13498.pdf, date accessed January 3, 2024.

70 E. Lawler, *Creating effective pay systems for teams*, 1998, https://ceo.usc.edu/wp-content/uploads/1998/01/1998-01-g98_1-Pay_Teams.pdf, date accessed January 3, 2024.

71 M. Bolch, *Rewarding the team*, 2007, SHRM.org, https://www.shrm.org/topics-tools/news/hr-magazine/rewarding-team, date accessed January 3, 2024.

72 E. Lawler, *Creating effective pay systems for teams*, 1998, https://ceo.usc.edu/wp-content/uploads/1998/01/1998-01-g98_1-Pay_Teams.pdf, date accessed January 3, 2024.

73 M. Bolch, *Rewarding the team*, 2007, SHRM.org, https://www.shrm.org/topics-tools/news/hr-magazine/rewarding-team, date accessed January 3, 2024.

74 F. Lievens, *Human Resource Management: Back to Basics*, 2011, Uitgeverij Lannoo Campus.

75 Idem

76 CIPD, *Show the money: The behavioural science of reward*, 2015, https://www.cipd.org/uk/knowledge/evidence-reviews/reward-decisions/?_gl=1*gczrmx*_ga*MTA3NTM0NDkwOS4xNzAxNzkxNjly*_ga_D9HN5GYHYY*MTcwNDM4NDM5My42LjEuMTcwNDM4NDQ1OC42MC4wLjA, date accessed January 3, 2024.

77 C. Garvey, *Focus on compensation - Steer teams with the right pay*, 2002, SHRM.org, https://www.shrm.org/topics-tools/news/hr-magazine/focus-compensation-steer-teams-right-pay, date accessed January 3, 2024.
J. Delfgaauw et al, *Team Incentives, Social Cohesion and Performance: A Natural Field experiment*, 2020, https://www.econstor.eu/bitstream/10419/223940/1/dp13498.pdf, date accessed January 3, 2024.

78   CIPD, *Show the money: The behavioural science of reward*, 2015, https://www.cipd.org/uk/knowledge/evidence-reviews/reward-decisions/?_gl=1*gczrmx*_ga*MTA3NTM0NDkwOS4xNzAxNzkxNjly*_ga_D9HN5GYHYY*MTcwNDM4NDM5My42LjEuMTcwNDM4NDQ1OC42MC4wLjA, date accessed January 3, 2024.

79   C. Garvey, *Focus on compensation - Steer teams with the right pay*, 2002, SHRM.org, https://www.shrm.org/topics-tools/news/hr-magazine/focus-compensation-steer-teams-right-pay, date accessed January 3, 2024.
       CIPD, *Show me the money! The behavioural science of reward*, 2015, https://www.cipd.org/uk/knowledge/evidence-reviews/reward-decisions/?_gl=1*gczrmx*_ga*MTA3NTM0NDkwOS4xNzAxNzkxNjly*_ga_D9HN5GYHYY*MTcwNDM4NDM5My42LjEuMTcwNDM4NDQ1OC42MC4wLjA, date accessed January 3, 2024.

80   CIPD, *Show the money: The behavioural science of reward*, 2015, https://www.cipd.org/uk/knowledge/evidence-reviews/reward-decisions/?_gl=1*gczrmx*_ga*MTA3NTM0NDkwOS4xNzAxNzkxNjly*_ga_D9HN5GYHYY*MTcwNDM4NDM5My42LjEuMTcwNDM4NDQ1OC42MC4wLjA, date accessed January 3, 2024.

81   Idem

82   Wolters Kluwer, *Geef eens een sociaal voordeel aan uw personeel, (Give a social benefit to your employees)*, 2024, Wolters Kluwer, https://www.kluwereasyweb.be/documents/voorbeeld-artikels-brokers/20120205-sociaal-voordeel.xml?lang=nl, date accessed January 5, 2024.
       Wolters Kluwer, *Fiscale wenken*, 2024.

83   OECD, *Taxing Wages 2023*, 2023, OECD Publishing, https://doi.org/10.1787/8c99fa4d-en, date accessed January 5, 2024.

84   S.F. Brosnan and F.B. De Waal, *Monkeys reject unequal pay*, 2003, Nature, 425(6955), 297-299.

85   PwC, *Megatrends: Five global shifts reshaping the world we live in*, 2022, PwC, https://www./gx/en/issues/megatrends.html, date accessed February 1, 2024.

86   PwC, *PwC's 26th Annual Global CEO Survey*, 2023, https://www.pwc.be/en/news-publications/2023/26th-ceo-survey.html, date accessed March 25, 2024.

87   PwC, *Megatrends: Five global shifts reshaping the world we live in*, 2022, PwC, https://www.pwc.com/gx/en/issues/assets/pdf/pwc-megatrends-october-2022.pdf, date accessed March 20, 2024.

88   Figure 11 is a graph covered by copyright of the European Central Bank, Frankfurt am Main, Germany (ECB), taken from the ECB's Occasional Paper Series: Understanding low wage growth in the euro area and European countries, 2019, Occasional Paper Series, No232, p60, Figure A. Some shapes and shades of colours of said graph have been changed. Also available free of charge at https://www.ecb.europa.eu/pub/pdf/scpops/ecb.op232~4b89088255.en.pdf?1ccf533dc92317c07a71721418088bd4, date accessed February 12, 2024.

89   ECB, *Occasional Paper Serie: Understanding low wage growth in the euro area and European countries*, 2019, Occasional Paper Series, No232, p57. Also available at https://www.ecb.europa.eu/pub/pdf/scpops/ecb.op232~4b89088255.en.pdf?1ccf533dc92317c07a71721418088bd4, date accessed February 12, 2024.

90   Idem

91   ECB, *Occasional Paper Serie: Understanding low wage growth in the euro area and European countries*, 2019, Occasional Paper Series, No232, p57. Also available at https://www.ecb.europa.eu/pub/pdf/scpops/ecb.op232~4b89088255.en.pdf?1ccf533dc92317c07a71721418088bd4, date accessed February 12, 2024.
       K. Bodnár, *Labour supply and employment growth*, 2018, ECB Economic Bulletin, Issue 1/2018.

92   Idem

93   PwC, *Workforce Preference Study (WFPS) 2020: EMEA focus*, 2020, PwC, https://www.pwc.be/en/news-publications/2021/workforce-preference-study-2020-emea-focus.html, date accessed February 1, 2024.

94   PwC, *Megatrends: Five global shifts reshaping the world we live in*, 2022, PwC, https://www.pwc.com/gx/en/issues/megatrends.html, date accessed February 1, 2024.

95   R. L. Heneman, *Strategic Reward Management: Design, Implementation, and Evaluation*, 2002, IAP Inc.

96   X. Baeten and B. Verwaeren, *Flexible rewards from a strategic rewards perspective*, 2012, Compensation & Benefits Review, 44(1), 40-49.

97   Figure 16 is based on figures from OECD. Stat on average annual wages, https://data-explorer.oecd.org/vis?df[ds]=dsDisseminateFinalDMZ&df[id]=DSD_EARNINGS%40AV_AN_WAGE&df[ag]=OECD.ELS.SAE&df[vs]=1.0&pd=2000%2C&dq=......&ly[rw]=REF_AREA%2CPRICE_BASE%2CUNIT_MEASURE&ly[cl]=TIME_PERIOD&to[TIME_PERIOD]=false&vw=tb, date accessed February 26, 2024.

98   ECB, *Wage indexation mechanisms in euro area countries*, May 2008, ECB, https://www.ecb.europa.eu/pub/pdf/other/mb200805_focus05.en.pdf, date accessed February 26, 2024.

99   Figures from January 2024. *Consumer price index - Inflation forecasts*, 2024, Federal Planning Bureau, https://www.plan.be/databases/17-en-consumer_price_index_inflation_forecasts, date accessed February 2, 2024.

100   P. Du Caju, E. Gauthier, D. Momferatou, M. Ward-Warmedinger, *Institutional features of wage bargaining in 23 European countries and the US and Japan*, December 2008, Wage dynamics network, Working paper series N° 974.

101   For more information and details on Belgian CLAs refer to *Conventions collectives de travail, (collective bargaining agreements)*, Service Public Federal Emploi Travail et Concertation sociale, https://emploi.belgique.be/fr/themes/commissions-paritaires-et-conventions-collectives-de-travail-cct/conventions-collectives-de, date accessed February 9, 2024.

102   P. Du Caju., E. Gautier, D. Momferatou and M. Ward-Warmedinger, *Institutional features of wage bargaining in 23 European countries, the US and Japan*, December 2008, European Central Bank, Working paper series, N° 974, European Central Bank, page 5. Also accessible on https://www.ecb.europa.eu/pub/pdf/scpwps/ecbwp974.pdf, date accessed February 9, 2024.

103   For more information, refer to P. Du Caju., E. Gautier, D. Momferatou and M. Ward-Warmedinger, *Institutional features of wage bargaining in 23 European countries*, December 2008, the US and Japan, European Central Bank, Working paper series, N° 974, European Central Bank, page 5. Also accessible on https://www.ecb.europa.eu/pub/pdf/scpwps/ecbwp974.pdf, date accessed February 9, 2024.

104   *Proposition of law related to the execution of the interprofessional agreement 2007-2008*, Doc., Ch., 2007-2008, n° 594/1, 5, https://www.lachambre.be/kvvcr/showpage.cfm?section=/flwb&language=fr&cfm=/site/wwwcfm/flwb/flwbn.cfm?lang=F&legislat=52&dossierID=0594 , date accessed February 9, 2024.

105   Acerta, *Un employé sur quatre a reçu un bonus cette année, (One out of four employees received a bonus this year)*, 5 December 2023, https://www.acerta.be/fr/insights/dans-la-presse/un-employe-sur-quatre-a-recu-un-bonus-cette-annee, date accessed February 9, 2024.

106   For more information on this regime, refer to PwC, *Worldwide tax summaries*, 2024, https://taxsummaries.pwc.com/luxembourg/individual/income-determination, date accessed February 9, 2024.

107   *Proposition of program law*, Doc., Ch., 2017-2018, n° 2746/1, 13, https://www.lachambre.be/kvvcr/showpage.cfm?section=/flwb&language=fr&cfm=/site/wwwcfm/flwb/flwbn.cfm?lang=F&legislat=54&dossierID=2746 , date accessed February 9, 2024.

108   Acerta, *Un employé sur quatre a reçu un bonus cette année, (One out of four employees received a bonus this year)*, 5 December 2023, https://www.acerta.be/fr/insights/dans-la-presse/un-employe-sur-quatre-a-recu-un-bonus-cette-annee, date accessed February 9, 2024.

109 Note that not all broad based components may be eligible to be made (partially) flexible.

110 Every year PwC Belgium conducts a survey on the executive remuneration design in Belgian quoted organisations based on the published remuneration policy and remuneration report. The data disclosed in this publication is based on remuneration data for the period January 1, 2022 to December 31, 2022. Reference is also made to: PwC, *2024 Corporate Governance and Executive Pay Report - Trends and regulations impacting listed Belgian companies*, 2024, https://www.pwc.be/en/news-publications/2024/pwc-corporate-governance-and-executive-pay-report-2024.html?utm_source=linkedin&utm_medium=cpc&utm_campaign=tls_corporate_governance_report_2024&utm_term=lead_gen&utm_content=, date accessed February 10, 2024.

111 Principle 7 of the 2020 Belgian Code on Corporate Governance.

112 For detailed comments on the remuneration of quoted organisations, see chapter 9.

113 For more information on the disclosure requirements for quoted organisations, see chapter 9.

114 The CEO pay ratio compares the total remuneration of an organisation's CEO to the median annual total remuneration of its employees, providing insight into internal pay disparities.

115 PwC, *2024 Corporate Governance and Executive Pay Report - Trends and regulations impacting listed Belgian companies*, 2024, https://www.pwc.be/en/news-publications/2024/pwc-corporate-governance-and-executive-pay-report-2024.html?utm_source=linkedin&utm_medium=cpc&utm_campaign=tls_corporate_governance_report_2024&utm_term=lead_gen&utm_content=, date accessed February 10, 2024.

116 idem

117 PwC and the Diligent Institute, *2022 PwC Corporate Governance and Executive Pay Report – Navigating uncertainty: ESG as a compass for success*, 2022, https://www.pwc.be/en/fy23/documents/corporate-governance-report-2022-executive-pay-report-navigatingnuncertainty-ESG-as-a-compas.pdf, date accessed February 10, 2024.

118 PwC, *2024 Corporate Governance and Executive Pay Report - Trends and regulations impacting listed Belgian companies*, 2024, https://www.pwc.be/en/news-publications/2024/pwc-corporate-governance-and-executive-pay-report-2024.html?utm_source=linkedin&utm_medium=cpc&utm_campaign=tls_corporate_governance_report_2024&utm_term=lead_gen&utm_content=, date accessed February 10, 2024.

119 idem

120 Principle 7.7. of the 2020 Belgian Code on Corporate Governance.

121 PwC, *2024 Corporate Governance and Executive Pay Report - Trends and regulations impacting listed Belgian companies*, 2024, https://www.pwc.be/en/news-publications/2024/pwc-corporate-governance-and-executive-pay-report-2024.html?utm_source=linkedin&utm_medium=cpc&utm_campaign=tls_corporate_governance_report_2024&utm_term=lead_gen&utm_content=, date accessed February 10, 2024.

122 idem

123 For detailed comments on the remuneration requirement for directors of quoted organisations, see chapter 9.

124 PwC, *2024 Corporate Governance and Executive Pay Report - Trends and regulations impacting listed Belgian companies*, 2024, https://www.pwc.be/en/news-publications/2024/pwc-corporate-governance-and-executive-pay-report-2024.html?utm_source=linkedin&utm_medium=cpc&utm_campaign=tls_corporate_governance_report_2024&utm_term=lead_gen&utm_content=, date accessed February 10, 2024.

125 PwC, *ESG oversight: The corporate director's guide*, 2022, https://www.pwc.com/us/en/services/governance-insights-center/pwc-esg-oversight-the-corporate-director-guide.pdf, date accessed February 9, 2024.
PwC, *Purpose driven leadership: the evolving role of ESG metrics in executive compensation plans*, 2022, https://www.pwc.com/us/en/governance-insights-center/publications/assets/pwc-esg-metrics-in-executive-compensation-plans.pdf, date accessed February 9, 2024.

126 PwC, London Business School and Centre for Corporate Governance, *Paying well by paying for good*, 2021, https://www.pwc.co.uk/human-resource-services/assets/pdfs/environmental-social-governance-exec-pay-report.pdf, date accessed January 31, 2024.

127 OECD, *G20/OECD Principles of Corporate Governance 2023*, 2023, OECD Publishing, Paris, https://doi.org/10.1787/ed750b30-en, date accessed February 12, 2024. Also see European Sustainability Reporting Standards or ESRS 2 General disclosures, Disclosure Requirement GOV-3 - Integration of sustainability-related performance in incentive schemes (Commission Delegated Regulation (EU) 2023/2772 of 31 July 2023 supplementing Directive 2013/34/EU of the European Parliament and of the Council as regards sustainability reporting standards).

128 PwC, *2024 Corporate Governance and Executive Pay Report - Trends and regulations impacting listed Belgian companies*, 2024, https://www.pwc.be/en/news-publications/2024/pwc-corporate-governance-and-executive-pay-report-2024.html?utm_source=linkedin&utm_medium=cpc&utm_campaign=tls_corporate_governance_report_2024&utm_term=lead_gen&utm_content=, date accessed February 10, 2024.

129 PwC, London Business School and Centre for Corporate Governance, *Paying well by paying for good*, 2021, https://www.pwc.co.uk/human-resource-services/assets/pdfs/environmental-social-governance-exec-pay-report.pdf, date accessed January 31, 2024.

130 idem

131 PwC, *Purpose driven leadership: the evolving role of ESG metrics in executive compensation plans*, 2022, https://www.pwc.com/us/en/governance-insights-center/publications/assets/pwc-esg-metrics-in-executive-compensation-plans.pdf, date accessed February 9, 2024.
Glass Lewis, *ESG Policy. An overview of Glass Lewis' ESG Thematic Voting Policy*, 2023, https://7114621.fs1.hubspotusercontent-na1.net/hubfs/7114621/2023%20Reports/2023-ESG-Thematic-Voting-Policy-GL.pdf?hsCtaTracking=e3b33630-9331-4ee2-b6954f557d44be0b%7C9a2bfcd1-8cb9-4b2c-9b63-9f9f1f5599f6, date accessed January 31, 2024.

132 PwC and the Diligent Institute, *2022 PwC Corporate Governance and Executive Pay Report – Navigating uncertainty: ESG as a compass for success*, 2022, https://www.pwc.be/en/fy23/documents/corporate-governance-report-2022-executive-pay-report-navigatingnuncertainty-ESG-as-a-compas.pdf, date accessed February 10, 2024.

133 PwC, *Purpose driven leadership: the evolving role of ESG metrics in executive compensation plans*, 2022, https://www.pwc.com/us/en/governance-insights-center/publications/assets/pwc-esg-metrics-in-executive-compensation-plans.pdf, date accessed February 9, 2024.

134 PwC and the Diligent Institute, *2022 PwC Corporate Governance and Executive Pay Report – Navigating uncertainty: ESG as a compass for success*, 2022, https://www.pwc.be/en/fy23/documents/corporate-governance-report-2022-executive-pay-report-navigatingnuncertainty-ESG-as-a-compas.pdf, date accessed February 10, 2024.

135 PwC, *Purpose driven leadership: the evolving role of ESG metrics in executive compensation plans*, 2022, https://www.pwc.com/us/en/governance-insights-center/publications/assets/pwc-esg-metrics-in-executive-compensation-plans.pdf, date accessed February 9, 2024.

136 Governance Insights Center, *PwC's 2023 Annual Corporate Direc-tors Survey. Today's boardroom: confronting the change imperative,* 2023, https://www.pwc.com/us/en/services/governance-insights-center/library/assets/pwc-gic-acds-2023.pdf, date accessed February 9, 2024.

137 PwC and the Diligent Institute, *2022 PwC Corporate Governance and Executive Pay Report – Navigating uncertainty: ESG as a compass for success,* 2022, https://www.pwc.be/en/fy23/documents/corporate-governance-report-2022-executive-pay-report-navigatingnuncertainty-ESG-as-a-compas.pdf, date accessed February 10, 2024.

138 idem

139 PwC, *2024 Corporate Governance and Executive Pay Report - Trends and regulations impacting listed Belgian companies,* 2024, https://www.pwc.be/en/news-publications/2024/pwc-corporate-governance-and-executive-pay-report-2024.html?utm_source=linkedin&utm_medium=cpc&utm_campaign=tls_corporate_governance_report_2024&utm_term=lead_gen&utm_content=, date accessed February 10, 2024.

140 J. M. Berg, J. E. Dutton and A. Wrzesniewski, *What is Job Crafting and Why Does It Matter?,* 2007, Michigan Ross School of Business, https://positiveorgs.bus.umich.edu/wp-content/uploads/What-is-Job-Crafting-and-Why-Does-it-Matter1.pdf, date accessed February 5, 2024.

141 J. DeVaro, *Strategic Compensation and Talent Management,* 2020, Cambridge University Press.

142 C. Coton, *Pay structures and pay progression,* 2023, CIPD, https://www.cipd.org/en/knowledge/factsheets/pay-structures-factsheet/#issuespaystructures, date accessed February 5, 2024.

143 J. DeVaro, Strategic Compensation and Talent Management, 2020, Cambridge University Press.

144 idem

145 The Collection of Historical Scientific Instrument, *Frederick W. Taylor,* 2015, Harvard University, http://waywiser.fas.harvard.edu/people/7941/frederick-w-taylo, date accessed February 5, 2024.

146 J. F. Mee, *Frederick W. Taylor,* 1998, https://www.britannica.com/biography/Frederick-W-Taylor date accessed February 5, 2024.

147 A. Boyd, *Frank and Lillian Moller Gilberth,* University of Houston, https://engines.egr.uh.edu/episode/2686, date accessed February 5, 2024.0

148 A. Curcio and A. Woods, *Rethinking total reward strategies,* 2021, Strategy Business, https://www.strategy-business.com/article/Rethinking-total-reward-strategies, date accessed February 27, 2024.

149 European Commission, *Glossary: Minimum wage,* 2014, European Commission website, https://ec.europa.eu/eurostat/statistics-explained/index.php?title=Glossary:Minimum_wage, date accessed February 14, 2024.

150 European Commission, *Minimum wage statistics,* 2024, European Commission website, https://ec.europa.eu/eurostat/statistics-explained/index.php?title=Minimum_wage_statistics, date accessed February 12, 2024.

151 idem

152 Directive (EU) 2022/2041 of the European Parliament and of the Council of October 19, 2022 on adequate minimum wages in the European Union (consideration No. 19 and art. 1). *EUR-Lex,* 25 October 2022, L275/36 - L275/41, https://eur-lex.europa.eu/legal-content/EN/TXT/?uri=CELEX%3A32022L2041, date accessed February 27, 2024.

153 Directive (EU) 2022/2041 of the European Parliament and of the Council of October 19, 2022 on adequate minimum wages in the European Union (art. 4). *EUR-Lex,* 25 October 2022, L275/36 - L275/41, https://eur-lex.europa.eu/legal-content/EN/TXT/?uri=CELEX%3A32022L2041, date accessed February 27, 2024.

154 idem

155 PwC and WageIndictator, *Living wage: An emerging standard - Global research into the role of living wage in creating a sustainable business,* 2023, PwC, https://www.pwc.com/gx/en/services/tax/assets/global-living-wage-report.pdf, date accessed February 12, 2024.

156 Directive (EU) 2023/970 of the European Parliament and of the Council of 10 May 2023 to strengthen the application of the principle of equal pay for equal work or work of equal value between men and women through pay transparency and enforcement mechanisms.

157 D. Cafaro, *The World at Work handbook of total rewards, A comprehensive guide to compensation benefits, HR and employee engagement,* 2021, Ebooks.com, https://libro.eb20.net/Reader/rdr.aspx?b=210208782, date accessed February 12, 2024.

158 PwC, *Making executive pay work: the psychology of incentives,* 2012, PwC, www.pwc.com/gx/en/hr-management-services/publications/assets/making-executive-pay-work.pdf, date accessed February 5, 2024.

159 *Trends and Challenges in Long-Term Incentive Plans,* 2018, The Overture Group, www.theoverturegroup.com/resources/blog/trends-and-challenges-long-term-incentives-and-non-qualified-plans-privately-held-companies, date accessed February 5, 2024.

160 PwC, *Making executive pay work: the psychology of incentives,* 2012, PwC, www.pwc.com/gx/en/hr-management-services/publications/assets/making-executive-pay-work.pdf, date accessed February 5, 2024.

161 M. C. Jensen and W. H. Meckling, *Theory of the Firm: Managerial Behavior, Agency Costs and Ownership Structure,* 1976, Harvard University Press, Journal of Financial Economics (JFE), Vol. 3, No. 4, 1976, 305-360. Also available at www.sfu.ca/~wainwrig/Econ400/jensen-meckling.pdf, date accessed February 27, 2024.

162 *What Are Long-term Incentive Plans (LTIP) - Types & Working,* 2023, Comport, www.compport.com/blog/what-are-long-term-incentive-plans-ltip, date accessed February 8, 2024.

163 idem

164 B. Coburn and D. Liberson, *The Untapped Opportunity of Broad-Based Ownership,* 2022, Harvard Social Impact Review, www.sir.advancedleadership.harvard.edu/articles/the-untapped-opportunity-of-broad-based-ownership, date accessed February 8, 2024.

165 D. Jess, *The Untold Advantages of Your Employee Stock Purchase Plan (ESPP),* 2023, Plancorp, www.plancorp.com/blog/the-untold-advantages-of-your-employee-stock-purchase-plan-espp, date accessed February 8, 2024.

166 J. Blasi, D. Kruse, J. Sesil and M. Kroumova, *Broad-Based Stock Options and Company Performance: What the Research Tells US,* 2010, Rutgers University, https://smlr.rutgers.edu/sites/smlr/files/Documents/Faculty-Staff-Docs/broad%20based%20stock%20options%20and%20compan%20performance%20what%20the%20research%20tells%20US.pdf, date accessed February 8, 2024.
Is ESPP worth it?, 2023, Global Shares.from J.P.Morgan, www.globalshares.com/academy/espp-is-it-worth-it-pros-and-cons/#:~:text=An%20ESPP%20is%20a%20way,day%20of%20the%20offer%20period, date accessed February 8, 2024.

167 *Employee Stock Purchase Plan – ESPP (+ examples & timeline),* 2023, Global Shares.from J.P.Morgan, www.globalshares.com/academy/employee-stock-purchase-plan-espp/, date accessed February 8, 2024.

168 T. Kopelman, *A Millennial's Guide to Understanding Equity Compensation,* 2022, All Street Wealth, www.allstreetwealth.com/post/a-millennial-guide-to-understanding-equity-compensation, date accessed February 8, 2024.

169 IFRS 2, https://eur-lex.europa.eu/LexUriServ/LexUriServ.do?uri=CELEX:32005R0211:EN:HTML, date accessed February 8, 2024.

170 idem

171 idem

172 PwC Canada, *Guidance on Implementing IFRS 2 Share-based Payment,* 2020, https://viewpoint.pwc.com/dt/ca/en/iasb/standards/standards__1_INT/standards__1_INT/ifrs_2_sharebased_pa__2_INT/guidance_on_implemen__1_INT.html#pwc-topic.dita_0825052511080086, date accessed February 8, 2024.

173 IFRS 2, paragraph 7, https://eur-lex.europa.eu/LexUriServ/LexUriServ.do?uri=CELEX:32005R0211:EN:HTML, date accessed February 8, 2024.

174   IFRS, paragraphs 30 and 33, https://eur-lex.europa.eu/LexUriServ/
       LexUriServ.do?uri=CELEX:32005R0211:EN:HTML; date accessed
       February 8, 2024.
       PwC Canada, *Guidance on Implementing IFRS 2 Share-based Pay-
       ment*, 2020, https://viewpoint.pwc.com/dt/ca/en/iasb/standards/
       standards__1_INT/standards__1_INT/ifrs_2_sharebased_pa__2_
       INT/guidance_on_implemen__1_INT.html#pwc-topic.
       dita_0825052511080086, date accessed February 8, 2024.
175   B. Groysberg, S. Abbott, M.R. Marino and M. Aksoy, *Compensation
       Packages That Actually Drive Performance*, 2021, Harvard Business
       Review, https://hbr.org/2021/01/compensation-packages-that-
       actually-drive-performance, 102-111, date accessed February 8, 2024.
176   idem
177   idem
178   B. E. Becker, M. Huselid and D. Ulrich, *The HR Scorecard: Linking
       People, Strategy, and Performance*, 2001, Harvard Business School
       Press. Also available at https://read2book.com/pdf/The-HR-Score
       card-1626002126.pdf, date accessed February 8, 2024.
179   W. Kenton, *Mature Firm: Meaning, Characteristics, Examples*, 2023,
       Investopedia, https://www.investopedia.com/terms/m/mature-
       firm.asp#:~:text=Key%20Takeaways-,A%20mature%20firm%20
       is%20a%20company%20that%20is%20well%2Desta
       blished,cost%20cuts%20and%20efficiency%20improvements,
       date accessed February 8, 2024.
180   *What Is the Difference Between High Growth and Low Growth
       Startups*, 2023, Faster Capital, https://fastercapital.com/content/
       What-Is-The-Difference-Between-High-Growth-And-Low-Growth-
       Startups.html, date accessed February 8, 2024.
181   *PwC, Making executive pay work: the psychology of incentives*, 2012,
       PwC.com, www.pwc.com/gx/en/hr-management-services/publica
       tions/assets/making-executive-pay-work.pdf, date accessed
       February 8, 2024.
182   idem
183   idem
184   *Performance Rights vs Options: What should you choose when
       designing LTIs*, 2023, The Reward Practice, www.therewardpractice.
       com.au/rights-options-or-both-lti-design/, date accessed February
       8, 2024.
185   PwC, *Making executive pay work: the psychology of incentives*, 2012,
       PwC.com, www.pwc.com/gx/en/hr-management-services/publica
       tions/assets/making-executive-pay-work.pdf, date accessed
       February 8, 2024.
186   Pwc, *Transform to build trust: prioritising employees*, 2023, https://
       www.pwc.com/gx/en/services/family-business/family-business-
       survey/building-employee-trust.html#:~:text=In%20a%20recent
       %20PwC%20study,be%20aligned%20with%20their%20emplo
       yers', date accessed February 16, 2024.
187   A. P. Fiske, *The four elementary forms of sociality: Framework for a uni-
       fied theory of social relations*, 1992, Psychological Review, 99, 689–723.
188   J. Gallus, J. Reiff, E. Kamenica and A. P. Fiske, *Relational Incentives
       Theory*, 2021, Psychological Review, ISSN 1939-1471.
189   D. Johnson and A. Dickinson, *Employee-of-the-Month Programs:
       Do They Really Work?*, 2010, Journal of Organizational Behavior
       Management. 30. 308-324.
190   A.C. Daniels, *Bringing out the best in people: How to apply the astonis-
       hing power of positive reinforcement*, 2000, New York: McGraw-Hill.
       A.C. Daniels, *Oops! 13 management practices that waste time and
       money (and what to do instead)*, 2009, Atlanta, GA: Aubrey Daniels
       International.
       D. Johnson and A. Dickinson, *Employee-of-the-Month Programs:
       Do They Really Work?*, 2010, Journal of Organizational Behavior
       Management, 30, 308-324.
191   D. Sturt and T. Nordstrom, *Nails in the coffin: 6 examples of recogni-
       tion gone wrong*, 2014, https://www.forbes.com/sites/davidsturt/
       2014/03/19/nails-in-the-coffin-6-examples-of-recognition-gone-wr
       ong/, date accessed February 26, 2024.
192   S. O'Flaherty, M.T. Sanders and A. Whillans, *A little recognition can
       provide a big morale boost*, 2022, Harvard Business Review, https://
       hbr.org/2021/03/research-a-little-recognition-can-provide-a-big-
       morale-boost , date accessed February 8, 2024.
       H. Dai, K. L. Milkman and J. Riis, *The Fresh Start Effect: Temporal
       Landmarks Motivate Aspirational Behavior*, 2014, Management
       Science, vol. 60, No. 10, 2563-2582.
193   A. Cross, *26 employee recognition statistics you need to know in 2024*,
       2024, Nectar HR, https://nectarhr.com/blog/employee-recognition-
       statistics, date accessed February 26, 2024.
       E. Maese and C. Lloyd, *Is your employee recognition really authentic?*,
       2023, Gallup, https://www.gallup.com/workplace/508208/employee-
       recognition-really-authentic.aspx, date accessed February 26, 2024.
194   P. Bhatnagar, *Taylor Swift gives 'life-changing' $100,000 bonuses to
       Eras Tour truck drivers*, 2023, https://edition.cnn.com/2023/08/02/
       business/taylor-swift-100000-life-changing-bonus-truck-crew/ind
       ex.html, date accessed February 28, 2024.
195   *The importance of employee recognition: low cost, high impact*, 2024,
       Gallup, https://www.gallup.com/workplace/236441/employee-
       recognition-low-cost-high-impact.aspx, date accessed February
       26, 2024.
196   C. Littlefield, *A better way to recognize your employees*, 2022, Harvard
       Business review, https://hbr.org/2022/10/a-better-way-to-recognize-
       your-employees, date accessed February 8, 2024.
197   E. Greidanus, *Winning with a culture of recognition: rewards can be
       damaging*, 2022, https://arteel.com/news/winning-with-a-culture-
       of-recognition-rewards-can-be-damaging, date accessed February
       27, 2024.
198   J. Gallus and B. Frey, *Awards: a strategic management perspective*,
       2015, Strategic Management Journal, 37 vol. 8, 1699 - 1714.
199   PwC, *Episode 18: Rethinking Total Reward to deliver Total Wellness*,
       January 24, 2023, PwC's Workforce podcast, Apple Podcasts, Google
       Podcasts, Spotify, https://www.pwc.be/en/services/prs/reward/
       workforce-podcast-episode-18-rethinking-total-reward-to-deliver-
       total-wellness.html, date accessed: February 9, 2024.
200   PwC, *Employee Financial Wellness Survey*, 2023, PwC, https://www.
       pwc.com/us/en/services/consulting/business-transformation/
       library/employee-financial-wellness-survey.html, February 16, 2024.
201   D.L. Daum and J.A. Stoll, *Employee Preferences*, 2020, in W.H. Ma-
       cey & A.A. Fink (eds.), Employee Surveys and Sensing: Challenges
       and Opportunities, Oxford University Press, 153.
202   B.J. Pine, *Designing employee experiences to create customer expe-
       rience value*, 2020, Strategy & Leadership, 21-26.
203   T. Maylett and M. Wride, *The employee experience: How to attract ta-
       lent, retain top performers, and drive results*, 2017, John Wiley & Sons.
204   PwC Netherlands, *What does young talent want? - Workforce Prefe-
       rence Study 2023*, 2023, PwC, https://www.pwc.nl/nl/actueel-publi
       caties/assets/pdfs/workforce-preference-study-2023.pdf, date
       accessed February 12, 2024.
205   PwC Belgium, *PwC Workforce Preference Study 2020 - EMEA Focus*,
       2020, PwC, https://www.pwc.be/en/documents/PwC%20Work
       force%20Preference%20Study%202020.pdf, date accessed
       February 12, 2024.
206   PwC Belgium, *PwC Workforce Preference Study 2020*, 2020, PwC,
       https://www.pwc.be/en/FY21/documents/pwc-workforce-preferen
       ce-study-2020.pdf, date accessed February 12, 2024.
207   Willis Towers Watson, *The evolution of talent retention practices du-
       ring M&A - Findings from the 2020 M&A Retention Survey*, 2021, Willis
       Towers Watson, https://www.google.com/url?q=https://www.wtw
       co.com/-/media/wtw/insights/2021/04/the-evolution-of-talent-
       retention-practices-during-m-and-a.pdf&sa=D&source=docs&ust
       =1708962996678123&usg=AOvVaw3QP5rAtNfR795EXbJgiClp, date
       accessed February 26, 2024.
208   idem

209 Such a deal can also be a good occasion to dig deeper within the job architecture of the restructured organisation, in order to assess if the different job titles and the associated responsibilities and tasks are cohesive. For more information on this, see chapter 6 on job architecture.

210 For more information, see M. McAndrew and B. White, *What are Some Best Practices for Managing Long-Term Incentive Plans (LTIP) during M&A Activity and What Impact Do LTIPs Have On Employees?*, Cornell University, 11-2018, https://ecommons.cornell.edu/server/api/core/bitstreams/f92bbee3-0934-4878-b11c-a388b6979ea4/content, date accessed February 23, 2024.
See also W. Hafez, *Managing Long-Term Incentive Plans (LTIP) during M&A Activity*, August 25, 2020, LinkedIn, https://www.linkedin.com/pulse/managing-long-term-incentive-plans-ltip-during-ma-wael/, date accessed February 1, 2024.

211 For a specific case of a spin-off, see M. Gorski, *How to Deal with Equity Holdings During a Spin-Off*, 2016, WorldatWork, Workspan, Dec. 2016, https://semlerbrossy.com/wp-content/uploads/HowtodealwithEquity.pdf, Semler Brossy, date accessed February 23, 2024.

212 For example, *Service des Décisions Anticipées*, ruling n° 2016.754 of January 17, 2017, and ruling n° 2015.328 of July 14, 2015.

213 M. Engel, *Compensation Implications of Mergers and Acquisitions*, 2017, Compensation Advisory Partners, https://www.capartners.com/wp-content/uploads/2017/10/CAPintel-17-07-14-Compensation-Implications-of-Mergers-and-Acquisitions.pdf, date accessed February 23, 2024.

214 K. Gibson, *Why Every organisation Should Have a Long-Term Incentive Plan (LTIP)*, 18 Oct. 2016, VisionLink, https://visionlink.co/blog, date accessed January 9, 2024.

215 It is worth noting that some accounting and consulting firms are currently reconsidering the partnership organisation. The main drivers behind this change are taxation aspects, the need for external capital and the sometimes unwieldy decision-making process, especially in international partnerships.

216 A detailed analysis can be found in: T. Wiegmann, *Fairness, trust and motivation in Profit Sharing Systems within German law firms: a qualitative analysis of law firm partner needs in a peer-to-peer context (Doc Diss.)*, 2019, University of Bradford - Faculty of Management, Law & Social Sciences.
M.-L. Vandenhaute, K. Hardies and D. Breesch, *Professional and Commercial Incentives in Audit Firms: Evidence on Partner Compensation*, 2020, European Accounting Review, vol. 29(3), 521-554.

217 ecoDa, *Corporate Governance Guidance and Principles for Unlisted Companies in Europe*, 2021, https://ecoda.eu/wp-content/uploads/2019/08/ecoDa-Corporate-Governance-Guidance-and-Principles-for-unlisted-companies-in-Europe-1.pdf, date accessed February 9, 2024.
OECD, *G20/OECD Principles of Corporate Governance 2023*, 2023, OECD Publishing, Paris, https://doi.org/10.1787/ed750b30-en, date accessed February 12, 2024.

218 ecoDa, *Corporate Governance Guidance and Principles for Unlisted Companies in Europe*, 2021, https://ecoda.eu/wp-content/uploads/2019/08/ecoDa-Corporate-Governance-Guidance-and-Principles-for-unlisted-companies-in-Europe-1.pdf, date accessed February 9, 2024.

219 idem

220 Principle 14 (Phase II) of ecoDa, *Corporate Governance Guidance and Principles for Unlisted Companies in Europe*, 2021, https://ecoda.eu/wp-content/uploads/2019/08/ecoDa-Corporate-Governance-Guidance-and-Principles-for-unlisted-companies-in-Europe-1.pdf, date accessed February 9, 2024.

221 Art. 7:89 and 7:108 of the Belgian Code of Companies and Associations.

222 Art. 7:89/1, §1 of the Belgian Code of Companies and Associations.

223 Art. 7:89/1, §2 of the Belgian Code of Companies and Associations.

224 Art. 7:89/1, §§3-4 of the Belgian Code of Companies and Associations.

225 Art. 7:89/1, §5 of the Belgian Code of Companies and Associations.

226 Art. 7:91 of the Belgian Code of Companies and Associations.

227 Principle 7.11 of the 2020 Belgian Corporate Governance Code.

228 Art. 7:91 of the Belgian Code of Companies and Associations.

229 Art. 7:89/1, §2, 5° and 7:92 of the Belgian Code of Companies and Associations.

230 Principles 7.7-7.12 of the 2020 Belgian Corporate Governance Code.

231 Principles 7.4-7.6 of the 2020 Belgian Corporate Governance Code.

232 For more information, see PwC and the Diligent Institute, *PwC Corporate Governance and Executive Pay Report – Navigating uncertainty: ESG as a compass for success*, 2022, https://www.pwc.be/en/fy23/documents/corporate-governance-report-2022-executive-pay-report-navigatingnuncertainty-ESG-as-a-compas.pdf, date accessed February 10, 2024.

233 Principle 7.3 of the 2020 Belgian Corporate Governance Code.

234 Art. 7:89/1, §2, 7° of the Belgian Code on Companies and Associations.

235 Governance Insights Center, *Serving on - and chairing - the compensation committee*, 2023, https://www.pwc.com/us/en/services/governance-insights-center/library/assets/pwc-2023-trust-gic-compensation-committee.pdf, date accessed February 9, 2024.

236 ISS, *Continental Europe - Proxy Voting Guidelines - Benchmark Policy Recommendations, Effective for Meetings on or after February 1, 2024*, 2024, https://www.issgovernance.com/file/policy/active/emea/Europe-Voting-Guidelines.pdf?v=1, date accessed February 9, 2024.

237 See chapter 5 on narrow based strategies as part of reward scope for more information.

238 Communication from the commission to the European Parliament, the Council, the European Economic and Social Committee and the Committee of the Regions, *A Union of Equality: Gender Equality Strategy 2020-2025* (COM/2020/152 final).

239 This chapter is primarily dedicated to exploring the EU Pay Transparency Directive. Nonetheless, it is worth noting that certain interactions exist between the CSRD and GRI concerning pay gap reporting. All these initiatives align with UN Sustainable Development Goal 5 on gender equality.

240 Directive (EU) 2023/970 of the European Parliament and of the Council of 10 May 2023 to strengthen the application of the principle of equal pay for equal work or work of equal value between men and women through pay transparency and enforcement mechanisms.

241 Also see: A. Lettink, *Equal pay for equal work: A practical guide to implementing a successful pay transparency program*, 2023, Anita Lettink Publisher.

242 Directive (EU) 2022/2381 of the European Parliament and of the Council of 23 November 2022 on improving the gender balance among directors of quoted organisations and related measures.

243 OECD *OECD Corporate Governance Factbook 2023*, 2023, OECD Publishing, Paris, https://doi.org/10.1787/6d912314-en, date accessed February 9, 2024.

244 Governance Insights Center, *PwC's 2023 Annual Corporate Directors Survey. Today's boardroom: confronting the change imperative*, 2023, https://www.pwc.com/us/en/services/governance-insights-center/library/assets/pwc-gic-acds-2023.pdf, date accessed February 9, 2024.

245 PwC, *2024 Corporate Governance and Executive Pay Report - Trends and regulations impacting quoted Belgian companies*, 2024, https://www.pwc.be/en/news-publications/2024/pwc-corporate-governance-and-executive-pay-report-2024.html?utm_source=linkedin&utm_medium=cpc&utm_campaign=tls_corporate_governance_report_2024&utm_term=lead_gen&utm_content=, date accessed February 10, 2024.

246 For the requirements on the remuneration policy and the variable remuneration, see: art. 92-96 of the Directive 2013/36/EU of the European Parliament and of the Council of June 26, 2013 on access to the activity of credit institutions and the prudential supervision of credit institutions and investment firms, amending Directive 2002/87/EC and repealing Directives 2006/48/EC and 2006/49/EC (so-called CRD IV).

247 For the requirements on the remuneration policy and the variable remuneration, see: art. 1, (26)-(27) of the Directive (EU) 2019/878 of the European Parliament and of the Council of May 20, 2019 amending Directive 2013/36/EU as regards exempted entities, financial holding companies, mixed financial holding companies, remuneration, supervisory measures and powers and capital conservation measures (so-called CRD V).

248 Directive 2009/138/EC of the European Parliament and of the Council of November 25, 2009 on the taking-up and pursuit of the business of Insurance and Reinsurance (Solvency II).

249 For the requirements on the remuneration policy, see: art. 275 of the Commission Delegated Regulation (EU) 2015/35 of October 10, 2014 supplementing Directive 2009/138/EC of the European Parliament and of the Council on the taking-up and pursuit of the business of Insurance and Reinsurance (Solvency II) (so-called Solvency II Delegated Regulation).

250 For the requirements on the remuneration policy, see: art. 46 of the Belgian Solvency II Law.

251 Also in arts. 5, 12 and 13 of the Annex II of the Belgian Banking Law.

252 Art. 275 of the Commission Delegated Regulation 2015/35 of October 10, 2014 supplementing Directive 2009/138/EC (Delegated Regulation 2015/35); art. 67 of the Belgian Banking Law.
Art. 275 of the Delegated Regulation 2015/35, art. 67 of the Belgian Banking Law, Circular NBB_2016_44 / EBA Guidelines of 27 June 2016 on sound remuneration policies (EBA/GL/2015/22).

253 NBB, *Governance manual for the banking sector*, 2022, https://www.nbb.be/doc/cp/eng/2022/governancemanual.pdf, date accessed February 9, 2024.

254 Art. 68 and art. 1 of Annex II of the Belgian Banking Law.

255 idem

256 European Insurance and Occupational Pensions Authority (EIOPA), *Guidelines on the system of governance*, 2014, https://www.eiopa.europa.eu/system/files/2022-10/eiopa-bos-14-253_gl_on_system_of_governance.pdf, date accessed February 9, 2024.

257 Art. 7 of Annex II of the Belgian Banking Law; Circular NBB_2016_44 / EBA Guidelines of 27 June 2016 on sound remuneration policies (EBA/GL/2015/22).

258 Art. 6 of Annex II of the Belgian Banking Law.

259 European Insurance and Occupational Pensions Authority (EIOPA), *Guidelines on the system of governance*, 2014, https://www.eiopa.europa.eu/system/files/2022-10/eiopa-bos-14-253_gl_on_system_of_governance.pdf, date accessed February 9, 2024.

260 European Insurance and Occupational Pensions Authority (EIOPA), *Guidelines on the system of governance*, 2014, https://www.eiopa.europa.eu/system/files/2022-10/eiopa-bos-14-253_gl_on_system_of_governance.pdf, date accessed February 9, 2024.
Circular NBB_2016_44 / EBA Guidelines of 27 June 2016 on sound remuneration policies (EBA/GL/2015/22).

261 Art. 8 of Annex II of the Belgian Banking Law.
European Insurance and Occupational Pensions Authority (EIOPA), *Guidelines on the system of governance*, 2014, https://www.eiopa.europa.eu/system/files/2022-10/eiopa-bos-14-253_gl_on_system_of_governance.pdf, date accessed February 9, 2024.

262 European Insurance and Occupational Pensions Authority (EIOPA), *Guidelines on the system of governance*, 2014, https://www.eiopa.europa.eu/system/files/2022-10/eiopa-bos-14-253_gl_on_system_of_governance.pdf, date accessed February 9, 2024.

263 Arts. 10 and 11 of Annex II of the Belgian Banking Law.

264 Circular NBB_2016_44 / EBA Guidelines of June 27, 2016 on sound remuneration policies (EBA/GL/2015/22).